Argumentation as Communication: Reasoning with Receivers

Argumentation as Communication: Reasoning with Receivers

Richard E. Crable
Purdue University

Charles E. Merrill Publishing Company
A Bell & Howell Company
Columbus, Ohio

To Ann, Bryan, and Audrey—and Smoki

Published by
Charles E. Merrill Publishing Company
A Bell & Howell Company
Columbus, Ohio 43216

This book was set in Melior.
The Production Editor was Linda Hillis.
The cover was designed by Will Chenoweth.

International Standard Book Number: 0-675-08609-4
Library of Congress Catalog Card Number: 75-43299
1 2 3 4 5 6 7 — 82 81 80 79 78 77 76

Printed in the United States of America

Preface

To be human is to be involved in communication activities; and to engage in communication is to confront the process of argumentation: the presentation or examination of claims and reasons. I have attempted to treat argumentation as a process that is as relevant to a dinner table as it is to a speaker's table; as relevant to informal discussions as it is to discussion in the highest councils of government. The situations that I have focused upon, exemplified in the numerous case studies, are limited only by the number of settings in which people find themselves involved with other people.

I have viewed argumentation as a special sort of communication process rather than a kind of quasi-logical act. I do not mean to imply that argumentation is *illogical*, but rather that so much of the tradition of formal logic (or its interpretation) is less helpful in argumentation than one might at first suspect. As an alternative to the perspective of logic, I have attempted to view argumentation (at its best) as the sort of rational process described in the theorizing of Professor Stephen Toulmin of the University of Chicago.

One consequence of this particular perspective on argumentation is that I have attempted always to examine how the argumentative language *functions*, not what it looks like or what its *form* is. My concern is with the effect of argumentation upon the participants, and how that effect evolves as the process develops.

Relatedly, I have focused upon the receiver, rather than the individual who advances the claim and the supporting reasons. Although we cannot ignore the arguers in argumentation, we can acknowledge that the interpretation and response to argumentation is far more important than anything that an arguer "intended" but failed to do. Still, though I emphasize the importance of the receiver, chapters 7 and 8 make it clear that certain qualitative and ethical demands can be made of arguers and receivers alike to better insure productive participation in the argumentative process. I have abandoned the "rules" of logic and have sought to replace them with more realistic and practical guidelines.

Argumentation is difficult, uncertain, and often frustrating. To help with this problem, I have arranged the discussion of the material so that knowledge of the process is gained accumulatively: what is learned at a fundamental level in one chapter may become the entire focus for a later chapter. In addition, I have listed general and specific objectives at the beginning of each chapter; I have provided programmed questions, discussion questions relating to the numerous case studies in the Appendix, and supplemental information at the conclusion of the appropriate chapters.

In sum, I have developed certain beliefs about how we should conceive of argumentation. My claim is that we should view argumentation as a rational communication process; this book develops my support for that claim.

Professor Stephen Toulmin of the University of Chicago Committee on Social Thought has been the most profound influence on the development of this book. From our first meeting in 1972, until his comments on a draft of this text, he has been a source of challenge and insight. For his wise counsel and for his role as a colleague and friend, I am deeply grateful.

In addition, I wish to express gratitude to those colleagues and students who have contributed to the text with their questions, challenges, and probes about argumentation conceived as a rational communication process. In particular, I thank Professor Richard L. Johannesen of the University of Northern Illinois and Professor Douglas Ehninger of the University of Iowa for their close analyses of and valuable comments about the text as it was developed. The text is much stronger because of their attention to it.

Finally, I wish to express gratitude for the loving support I received from my family, especially Ann, Bryan, and Audrey.

Richard E. Crable

Contents

1

Argumentation as Communication: An Orientation

My *general objective* in this chapter is to provide a framework within which to understand argumentation as we shall discuss it in the chapters to follow.

My *specific objectives* are

to explain the importance of argumentation

to explain ambivalent attitudes toward argumentation; why it is both admired and avoided

to conceptualize argumentation as we shall use the term

to differentiate argumentation from such concepts as persuasion, quarreling, and communication in general

to discuss and justify various implications of studying argumentation as communication

The camera "pans in" on the tall, distinguished representative who, speaking through earphones and interpreters, is about to address the United Nations Assembly on the crisis facing all mankind. Her manuscript has been prepared with extreme care: her country's

1

foremost advisors have created the policy statement, the best writers have slaved over its expression, and her most intimate associates have worked with her on the "televisable" style of the delivery. The representative plans to contend that a recent truce has been violated by a neighboring force, and she has brought photographic materials to document the violation. She looks at the television camera as she begins to speak, and it becomes clear that her position is . . . never going to be heard. In this particular living room, her first word—and the rest—are drowned out by the shouting of a 4-year-old and his 4 1/2-year-old friend who are trying to decide who was "killed" first in the duel between the slightly broken, plastic pistol and the somewhat recognizable wooden rifle. As the UN representative gestures eloquently, shifts her gaze appropriately, and moves her lips slowly, all that can be heard is "I got you."

"How could you?"

"I saw you when you came out from behind the sofa. You were right there, so I fired—bam! I got you before you could see me."

"No, you didn't. I shot before you saw me . . . when I was behind the sofa . . . that's when I saw you."

"No, you didn't because I was behind the footstool. I got you first."

"No, you didn't . . . I got you first."

"You didn't come near me! I ducked! Mom, you saw it. Tell him I got him first."

The scene at the UN and the scene developing in the living room differ substantially from one another. The four-year-olds do not have the poise, the preparation, the knowledge, the forum, nor the permission to speak enjoyed by the UN speaker; on the other hand, the representative does not possess the vehemence, the directness, nor the ease of being heard that the children enjoy. At first observation, then, the simultaneous incidents seem to have little in common except their simultaneity. Yet, a more detailed analysis of the two situations will aid us in answering a series of crucial questions that can serve to introduce this study of argumentation. We shall seek to answer (1) How important is argumentation to the reader of this textbook?; (2) How favorably perceived is argumentation?; (3) How can we conceptualize argumentation to differentiate it from such terms as *communication* and *persuasion?*; and (4) What are the implications of studying argumentation as a kind of communication activity? The answers to these questions, it seems to me, will provide an overview of argumentation as communication.

The Importance of Argumentation

We must begin, though, by asking, *How important is argumentation?* In adopting a strategy that has become popular in texts on argumentation, I will stress the importance of argumentation in a free society where the necessity of stating and defending—or attacking—a claim or stand is essential to participatory democracy. One of the basic presuppositions of a representative democracy is that change does not have to come by revolution. Change occurs in the United States to the extent that bills, budgets, and policy guidelines are proposed, debated, refined, and passed by governmental powers that serve to balance one another and to protect the national interest. Argumentation, however, is not a process that is limited to the chief executive, Congress, legislatures, or courts. Traditionally, writers on argumentation demonstrate the need for Americans in general to be prepared to analyze the positions of the people who seek to hold those organized offices. When election day approaches, voters must be prepared to take stands on the people they feel are the most qualified candidates; such a prepared electorate, it is assumed, more easily will assure the election of competent candidates.

I agree with this traditional rationale for the study of argumentation, and I would also add the importance of the United Nations-type debate that, at least at times, seems to keep the world away from the edge of global conflict. Argumentation is certainly as important in international debate and decision making as it is in the legislative, executive, or town-hall offices of the United States. Thus, when the UN delegate represents her country in attempts to avoid further armed conflict with a neighbor, we are presented with one more example of the importance of argumentation in the affairs of mankind. In this respect, I concur with the traditional assessments of the importance of argumentation.

Yet few of us will ever be instrumental in UN debate, few of us will run for office, and few of us probably ever will be as well prepared to vote as we would like. We have other occupations, other commitments—indeed, some of us may be so disgruntled with politics, politicians, summit meetings, and conferences that the traditional rationale for the study of argumentation seems highly abstract, too idealistic, or generally irrelevant. For those few (or many) skeptics, I submit that an even better reason for the study of argumentation is suggested, not by the UN incident, but by the living room shoot-out.

In the living room incident, the children were involved in a contest where the winner was probably determined by the endurance and the volume of the respective shouters. Still, beneath the somewhat humorous (unless you were the mother) situation, the children were involved in the business of stating claims and trying to defend those claims in some way. Seen from this perspective, the UN argument and the living room dispute do not seem so dissimilar. That,

though, is my point: even if we are not concerned about the importance of argumentation as a cornerstone of the democratic tradition,
we ought to be concerned about it as an inescapable part of being
human. Whenever people are gathered together, whether in families,
in dorm rooms, or in highly structured organizations, situations
arise where we either must support our own positions or be prepared
to evaluate the support that someone else has offered. The situations
need not be crucial to the world or to the functioning of democracy;
they may be about a plan to go to a football game, a decision to begin
your weekend home on Thursday, or a judgment about when to offer
an engagement ring. Whatever your position in life, and regardless
of what academic goals you may have, argumentation will be among
the activities in which you must engage. In essence, argumentation
is not only important because of its potential in a free society but also
because it permeates so much of human activity. This universality of
relevance is, to me, the best rationale for the study of argumentation.

Perceptions of Argumentation

The living room shoot-out, however, does more than introduce the
idea of the universality of argumentation. The "gun" battle also
presents us with the question of the desirability of utilizing argumentation: *How favorably perceived is argumentation?* The question may seem trivial because we may normally think of argumentation in a UN-like context, and we surmise, no doubt accurately, that
argumentation is superior to force in settling disputes. When we take
argumentation out of the political or legal setting, though, we seem
to have a different feeling about it: we may shun argumentative
people, we end discussions because we don't want to argue, and we
urge friends not to antagonize old _____ _____ (the professor) by
arguing with him. In contrast to these admonishments and interpersonal guidelines, I am sure that I have never heard, "Let's argue,
because that is how democracy functions." My aim here is not to
scoff at the people who claim that argumentation is a crucial activity;
indeed, I have already agreed that it is. My point is that argumentation, regardless of how I might wish it to be, is not perceived as a
completely positive force in human activity. Frequently, we will
react to argumentation as an unwelcome attempt to influence, or we
will fear others will react negatively to our personal attempts to
influence. The result is a highly ambiguous situation where we may
perceive argumentation to be an important societal force—but a
force that we may hesitate to use.

The Nature of Argumentation

We best can explain the ambiguity between the answers to the first two questions about the importance of argumentation and its degree of perceived favorableness by answering a third question: *How can we conceptualize argumentation to differentiate it from terms such as communication or persuasion?*

The Process of Communication

Since this study is entitled "Argumentation as Communication," let us begin by describing communication and then by demonstrating the role of argumentation as a kind of communication activity.

Communication, I suggest, can be conceptualized as symbolic transaction aimed at the re-creation of similar meaning in receivers. This conceptualization involves several central ideas that are implied by the terms I have used. The term *transaction* normally implies the presence of two or more participants in the communication activity. Though I am aware of the current research and interest in human-animal communication and animal-animal research, I am inclined to see those activities as generally irrelevant to our twin concerns for argumentation and communication. Even if this research becomes highly successful in demonstrating the intricacies of such communication, I foresee no possibility that that kind of activity will be so crucial to argumentation as human-to-human communication. Similarly, I am aware of the arguments in favor of considering intrapersonal communication (speaking or thinking to yourself), and later, in fact, we shall investigate that idea. At this point, however, it is convenient to think of transaction as being between (or among) two (or more) people.

The concept of transaction also implies that both or all parties involved are *actively* engaged in the process of communication. Although one of the parties will initiate the activity, the other clearly does more than merely "soak up" the communication of the first. The receiver processes of perception, interpretation, and responding (which will be discussed in a later chapter) are inherently active instead of passive. Since the result of this activity is a constant change in the participants, their strategies, and their values and perceptions, we shall use the term *transaction* rather than the more static concept of *interaction*.[1]

[1]The term *interaction* is now commonly interpreted to mean an active process between or among people who have set positions, established values, and so forth. Since, as we shall see, argumentation is a process where such positions and values can change dramatically during the course of the process, the term *transaction* seems more appropriate to our concern for argumentation.

A second term in the conception of communication is *meaning*. Though entire books have been written about the term, our present need is served by suggesting that meaning implies that one of the participants has attached some importance to something in his environment. We sometimes see, feel, or hear something that has no meaning for us: we see an antique tool, we have no idea what it's for, and we ask, "What in the world *is* this?"; we read a textbook that is complicated and technical, and we ask, "What is this supposed to *say*?"; or a close friend makes a mysterious, (perhaps) insulting remark, and we ask, "What was *that* supposed to mean?" In contrast to these times when it seems that something has no meaning, we all have had experiences where the meaning of something is especially clear: upon entering a bar, we pass an elderly friend of our mother's, and we know what her expression means; we listen to a strangely worded television advertisement, and we say, "I see what it means"; or a date refuses to indulge in a good-night kiss, and we say, "Okay, I understand what she's trying to tell me." Thus, we are concerned with meaning in much of our everyday activity; what we may not realize is that meaning is at the heart of contemporary conceptions of communication. The transaction between or among the participants in the communication process is chiefly prompted by the meaning grasped by the communicator and that communicator's desire to share that meaning with someone else.

Meaning, of course, cannot be transmitted directly between people. The communication process and the communicator are dependent upon the use of certain types of symbols to send a message and thus establish meaning. The communicator attempts to put his thoughts into words or to express himself. In contrast to the earlier activity of understanding the meaning of something like language or facial expression, this process begins with some meaning that the communicator wishes to share, and he seeks to translate his meaning into words, expressions, or activities that will convey or send that message. It is in this sense that communication scholars make much out of the notion that meanings are not in words; meanings, rather, are in people.

When we agree that meanings are in people rather than in words or phrases, we have come far in our understanding of communication. We would no longer expect accurate communication to arise from the simple selection of the "right" words; instead, we would be concerned for how people interpret those words. Though that understanding is beneficial, it can lead to a total stress on the individual interpretations of words or the idiosyncrasies of the people involved. What we must realize is that when we say meanings are in people, we mean two things: first, some of the meaning in a situation will be created by an *individual interpretation* of the words, but that, second, some of the meaning of the language is created by the *collective significance* of the words in the situation in which we find ourselves.[2] All of us are, to a degree, the products of our training and culture. In that training and culture, we begin to realize that certain phrases, words, and ideas have an agreed-upon significance in particular situations. These collective interpretations, then, become important influences in how we interpret the meaning of language in communication settings. Thus, the attachment of meaning is partly the product of our individual and psychological role as a person and partly the product of our collective and sociological role as a person living amid other people: meanings are in people, both as individuals and as groups.

Whether we are discussing individuals or groups of people, however, we can classify the sorts of things that might be used to communicate meanings as symbols. Contemporary communication scholars normally categorize the kinds of symbolic transactions as either verbal (written or oral words) or nonverbal, which includes (but is not limited to) the study of gestures, facial expressions, the manipulations of time and space, touching, and eye contact. All these can be considered symbols because they stand for something other than themselves. We have societal or subgroup norms which "tell us" that a certain kind of touch means love or desire, while another kind may mean that we are in danger of being struck with a fist. Similarly, we try to use other sorts of words to threaten someone we dislike. In both cases—in fact, in all cases where we are attempting to convey meaning—we choose what we feel are suitable symbols: ones that will be seen as standing for what we mean.

Thus far we have explored ideas that are implied in the terms *meaning* and *symbolic transaction*. Equally important in the conception of communication are the last few terms in that definition; indeed, communication is more than meaning in a context of symbolic transaction. Communication, it seems to me, is an activity that aims at the re-creation of meaning. Two ideas are implied here: first, that communication involves intent (we aim to do something), and, secondly, that our purpose is to use symbols to re-create our meaning in others. In actuality, we have alluded to the second idea already. The purpose in trying to choose words that will mean what we mean is really to attempt to allow our receiver to create his own

---

[2]I am indebted to Professor Stephen Toulmin who continually has stressed the need for this psychological-sociological balance in his writings and in our conversations.

meaning in ways that we hope will be similar to ours. The process is one of trying to translate what we mean into some sort of symbolic message which, we hope, can be decoded so that others will know what we mean. If the process is successful, we can think of the receiver's meaning, not as an original meaning, but as a re-created meaning.

The phrase "aimed at the re-creation of meaning," moreover, implies that we as message senders are consciously attempting the re-creation process. Communication scholars, at times, debate whether accidental communication is still communication: Do we really communicate when someone finds meaning in our habitually sloppy dress? Does our choice of colleges communicate something to some people, even though we do not intend the choice to be anything beyond a personal one? The point of course can be argued, but I am inclined philosophically to call such accidental-meaning creations "mis-communications," primarily because they are not re-created messages. We can create some meaning by attaching significance to an interesting conglomerate, but I am not personally concerned about the communication potential of a rock.

In essence, then, I conceptualize communication as symbolic transaction aimed at the re-creation of meaning. Though the discussion of the various implications of this definition has taken considerable time, I have purposely taken that time. For students without background studies in communication, the discussion may be helpful in generating some idea about this business of communication. Yet, even for students with a background in communication studies, the foregoing discussion has been essential: we can now attempt to conceptualize argumentation as an aspect of communication activity in general, and then we can differentiate argumentation from such terms as persuasion.

Argumentation as a Communication Process

Let us think of *argumentation*, then, as communication where the symbolic transaction is aimed at presenting reasons for claims and/or examining reasons for claims. Thinking of argumentation as this special kind of communication allows us to assume certain ideas about it. Argumentation, as we will discuss it, generally involves two or more participants, one of whom initiates some sort of symbolic transaction aimed at re-creating a desired meaning. Our basic concerns in argumentation, therefore, will be with people; with their mutual activity, with their use of all sorts of symbols, and with their creation or re-creation of meaning. Clearly, argumentation must be considered first and most importantly as communication. Now we can explore the ways in which argumentation is a special kind of communication.

Though we will discuss the nature of claims in more detail in later chapters, we should note here the role of claims in differentiating argumentation from communication in general. We can think of *claims*, for the time being, as stands, positions, or statements that we are willing to defend and that we have been called upon to challenge or examine. Returning to the examples of the UN delegate and the children in the living room, the delegate was making the claim that a certain truce had been violated by a neighboring nation, and each of the children was making the claim that the other had been "killed" and, consequently, was unable to "kill" the other. Both of the statements were claims: contested positions that they were prepared to defend or to challenge (in the case of each child's perception of the other's claim). This concern for claims is simply not an inherent part of communication in general. In argumentation, meaning is still important, but it is important specifically because either we want someone else to understand the claim that we are making and defending, or we want someone to understand the challenge we are making to their claim. Communication, then, may involve the re-creation of meaning about ideas, attitudes, or simple bits of information; argumentation, on the other hand, will involve the re-creation of meaning about claims that people make.

The majority of communication activity in argumentation, however, will not be concerned with the claim itself but will center on the reasons that relate to the claim. We may either be presenting and defending those reasons, or (from the receiver's point of view) examining and challenging those reasons. Returning once more to the examples at the beginning of this chapter, the children realized as much as did the UN representative that their respective claims would not be accepted without some sort of reason why they should be accepted. The UN representative was prepared to give photographic reasons to believe that the truce had been violated by the other nation, and one of the children was prepared to submit an eyewitness to the "shooting" (his mother) as a reason why the other child should admit his own demise and respond accordingly. The need for such reason giving or reasoning is perhaps generally unrealized at the conscious level, but, it seems to me, it is a need that we respond to in everyday practice. When someone says that a certain test will be "hard," we press the person for a reason to believe that prediction. We treat the prediction as a claim, and we ask, "What makes you think so?" or "How do you know?" or "Why should I believe that?" Though the phrasing of the information seeking will vary, we must realize that what is being sought is not merely information; rather, what is being sought is a reason to accept or believe the claim.[3]

Argumentation, Persuasion, and Quarreling

The earlier discussion of communication, therefore, allows us to conceptualize argumentation as a specific sort of symbolic activity where the transaction is aimed at the presentation or examination of claims and the reasons for their acceptance. Consequently, we may now differentiate this conception of argumentation from certain other communication activities.

Persuasion, for example, is a sort of communication that is frequently confused with the concept of argumentation. Both persuasion and argumentation are methods by which human beings attempt to influence other human beings, and, indeed, both activities involve symbolic interaction that seeks to somehow affect the meaning of others. When we have persuaded someone, we assume that we have been instrumental in them doing, saying, feeling, or thinking something that otherwise they might not have done, said, felt, or thought. Yet, it seems to me that argumentation as conceptualized here differs substantially from persuasion in one crucial respect. Successful argumentation, unlike successful persuasion, requires that the receivers of our messages accept the justification of our claims.

An illustration of this difference occurs when a receiver says, "Well, I'll do it, but I don't think I should." Let us suppose that this receiver comment is the culmination of a communication act where you have presented the best reasons you could think of for your roommate to "cut" his ten o'clock class in order to give you a ride downtown. The roommate hasn't been overwhelmed with your argument that the class is unimportant anyway and that the trip will only take a portion of the class period. Despite his assessment that these are inadequate reasons for missing class, his friendship for you

---

[3]The nature of reasons, as we shall see in later chapters, can vary tremendously. As long as the statement or idea functions to say "why" the claim should be accepted—or why it *was* accepted (from the receiver's point of view)—we shall call it a reason. In viewing argumentation as a kind of communication, we must be prepared to find reasons that are based upon all sorts of communication symbols. A friend, for example, may argue that the local sewage-treatment plant should be modernized by challenging us to breathe deeply and using the odor we sense as the best reason for the change. Although the odor itself is not directly the reason, it clearly functions with the friend's statement to form what may be a sound reason. All kinds of nonverbal symbols can perform in much the same way in argumentation.

and the urgency in your voice make him decide to take you. We can analyze your level of success from two perspectives. From the standpoint of persuasion, your efforts have been highly successful: your roommate decides to take you. From the perspective of argumentation, your efforts have been utterly unsuccessful: your roommate has rejected both of your reasons why he should miss his class and decides to take you for reasons that are alien to your strategy. His concern for your welfare and your happiness are important and appropriate factors in the success of your persuasive efforts, but you should not fool yourself that you have succeeded at argumentation. My point is that argumentation and persuasion are closely related and generally (if not always) concurrent communication activities, although persuasion seems to be primarily a concern for whether an action was taken, and argumentation is concerned with the acceptance of the reasons that you advance for a claim. Consequently, we can label people as being really persuasive and at the same time deride them for their inability to support claims with sound reasons: success in getting what we want from someone may have little to do with our skill in argumentation.

Just as I think it is helpful to differentiate persuasion from argumentation, I think it is worthwhile to differentiate argumentation from quarreling. In fact, I attribute a great deal of the popular desire to avoid argumentation to the popular belief that arguing is equivalent to quarreling. If we were to listen to the two children arguing about the living room shoot-out, we would find that claims were being made. Two additional observations, though, ought to be made about this argumentative exchange. First, the latter part of the children's communication was almost exclusively comprised of claims: "I got you," "No, you didn't," "I got you first," "You didn't come near me," and "Mom, you saw it" all function as claims. One claim is met by another which is augmented by another which is met with a contrary claim, and so forth. Although the first part of the transaction involved reasons, the rest of the discussion is devoted to the statement of claims, and the attempt to submit the mother as an eyewitness and the idea that "I ducked" are the only efforts to provide *reasons* why a claim should be accepted. We can discuss the first part of the children's communication as argumentation, as I have done, but I am inclined to think that it deteriorated into something more properly classified as a quarrel, because the importance of the claims so completely overshadows the emphasis on reasons that are offered in support.

A second reason that would tempt me to classify the second part of the discussion as quarreling is that it became obvious that neither party was inclined to seriously examine the claims of the other. Consider the disagreement that so often happens when students miss class, get notes from a friend, and then find that the notes were of little value in a testing situation: "Your notes were rotten—they didn't help at all."

"Yeah, well, you should have been in class anyway."

"You should talk; Tuesday was one of the few days you were there."

"Look at the grades in the class; I'm doing a lot better than you are."

The disagreement is not much exaggeration beyond the sort of event that could accompany a low grade on an extremely important test. Here again, I would consider the discussion more a quarrel than an argument. First, the participants are much more concerned about making a whole series of claims, counterclaims, or accusations than they are about supplying support for any of the claims. My second point, though, is perhaps more important. Neither participant is willing to seriously examine the other's claim. *Were* the notes poorly taken? If so, what makes you think so? *Was* Tuesday one of the few days that the note-taker was in class? How do you know? *Is* the one student doing significantly better than the other? What reason do you have to believe that? None of these questions were explored by the person listening to the claim; both parties chose to ignore the claim of the other and chose to concentrate, instead, upon making a somewhat related counterclaim.

Finally, I feel that I must respond to something that you're probably already thinking: "Is not quarreling characterized by emotion, while argumentation is characterized by logic and unemotional thought?" We will discuss the issue later, but for the time being I will note two ways in which the presence or absence of something we call *emotion* is not a helpful distinction between argumentation and quarreling. First, it seems to me that much constructive, useful argumentation is highly emotional. Some of the great academic debates concerning the nature of man, the universe, or the presidency have been highly intense and strongly felt. Does that make them somehow less respectable? I think not. If by emotion, one means shouting and uncontrollable rage, then perhaps we ought to exclude that from the study of argumentation; however, I do not feel that that is the general conception of emotion, and I therefore would avoid using this term as a useful distinction between quarreling and argumentation.

My second response to the use of emotion as a distinction between argumentation and quarreling is that, as we will examine later, I am not certain that the term emotion is useful in discussions of argumentation. The term is, after all, merely a term that has been invented as a convenient way of describing certain happenings. We must never forget that it is a construct or category under which man puts part of his experience: emotion becomes emotion because we call it that. While this labeling is generally convenient, it becomes inconvenient when one is faced with only an emotional-unemotional set of choices. Some things do not fit well under either category (or they fit equally well under both), and I think that argumentation is one of those ill-fitting concepts. Because I do not feel that emotion is a consistently convenient way of describing human interaction, I would not use emotionality as a distinction between quarreling and argumentation.

Argumentation versus Logic: Argumentation as Communication

Thus far, we have attempted to distinguish argumentation from communication in general, from persuasion, and from quarreling. One more task of differentiation remains: *What is the difference between argumentation and logic?* The question is crucial, but it is not an issue dealt with in many studies of argumentation. I feel so strongly that there is a distinction between logic and argumentation that my students in argumentation often tell classroom passersby who stop to chat that logic is a word that they are not allowed to use in argumentation class. The comment (only a bit exaggerated) does not bother me as much as the incredulous looks from the passersby. "How," they seem to ask, "can you teach argumentation without teaching logic?" Though I think the distinction is important, I would like to approach that distinction positively, rather than negatively, by phrasing the question of distinction differently. Instead of assessing what I consider to be the weaknesses of the traditional study of formal logic, let us explore the strengths of contemporary communication studies, and how we may be able to build upon those strengths to make the study of argumentation more profitable and practical. In sum, we can begin this chapter's final task: an exploration of the implications of studying argumentation, not as logic, but as a kind of communication.

The first implication of this communication approach is that instead of being primarily concerned with the form of arguments or their parts, we shall be concerned mostly with their function. Though strides have been made by most logic and philosophy departments, logical argument is still popularly associated with the form of the parts of argument. Is it in deductive form? Does it have a major premise, minor premise, and the appropriate number of distributed terms? In general, the question can be summarized, "Does it *look* like it's supposed to?" or "Is it in the proper form?" In contrast, our communication perspective will ask: Did the statement or evidence (or whatever) *do* what it was supposed to do? Did it *answer* the appropriate question? In other words, did it *function to satisfy the demand* of the receiver? Clearly, we must also consider the shape or form of the argument, but our concern will always be primarily for the *transaction* in the argumentation and what *functioned* to help that transaction, rather than the *symbols* or the *form* of the symbolic transaction that we will call argumentation.

Secondly, in addition to emphasizing function rather than form, our consideration of argumentation as communication implies that we will not be as concerned with rules that should (or must) be followed as much as we will be interested in all the various ways in which people do argue. Phrased in simplistic (perhaps too simplistic) terms, our study will attempt to be as *descriptive* (of how people *do* argue) as possible in addition to recognizing the student need for the book to be *prescriptive* (of how people should argue in order to be most probably effective). Though the prescriptive-descriptive aspects of textbooks normally intertwine, texts in logic are generally much more concerned about prescription than they are description. The stress is upon the following of rules, and if the rules are followed, the argumentation is assumed to be valid: you have done with the argument what you were supposed to do. We shall attempt to improve your argumentative activity, but the absence of rules will be as noticeable as the existence of more complicated and less surefire suggestions.

My comment that the surefire rules will be absent in the present study introduces a third implication of considering argumentation as communication: instead of assuring students that argumentation can be easily mastered, we shall demonstrate the difficulty in achieving successful argumentation. Indeed, there have been times when teachers of oral communication assured students that if they did certain things in certain ways, they (automatically) would be successful orators, speakers, or salespeople. What students found, of course, was that they could follow the "Ten Easy Lessons in Effective Speech" (or whatever the program was called), and they still could be utter failures. The "easy" lessons could not make easy the difficult task of attempting to re-create meaning in communication situations. Similarly, student arguers have found that following the rules of argument, sometimes discussed as rules of formal validity (even if there were such things), will not guarantee effectiveness in argumentation. Just as successful communication is tremendously difficult to achieve, so is successful argumentation. The lessons learned from communication studies in general are clear: argumentation is apt to be troublesome, complicated, and absolutely frustrating, and it is anything but easy and automatic, as you will find out.

Much of the difficulty of achieving successful argumentation is related to the fourth implication of studying argumentation as communication: our focus will be upon the receiver of the original argumentation, rather than upon the sender of the argumentative message. Textbooks on argumentation and certainly ones on logic emphasize the activities of the source of the original argument: his strategies, his methods, and his materials. In what may be the single most important difference between this text and others in the area of argumentation, the critical role played by receivers in all phases of the argumentation will be emphasized: how the receiver's orientation determines the appropriate strategies and methods, how the receiver's perception determines the strength of the reasoning, and how the receiver's choice determines the direction and success of the argumentation. This emphasis upon the receiver is so integral to our approach that "Reasoning with Receivers" appears as the subtitle of the book.

A fifth and related idea that is implied in our approach to argumentation is that instead of highlighting argument as a prepared document or oral message, we shall focus upon argumentation as a process. In essence, it is possible to emphasize the argument of argumentation or the symbols in symbolic transaction. If such a course is followed the result is, it seems to me, an overconcern for argumentation as a thing, a set document, or an object. A communication orientation, however, implies that our concern will be for something else: we shall focus more upon the transaction than the symbols, written or oral; we shall emphasize argumentation as a process involving a multitude of complex and multidimensional variables in a communication setting. Such an orientation toward process makes our study more difficult, but the labor is worth the reward of a more practical and realistic view of argumentation.

The idea of practicability and realism, however, also serves to introduce a sixth and final implication of studying argumentation as a communication activity. Our study of argumentation will focus upon a wide variety of argumentative communication situations. Students who are interested in logic or intercollegiate debate should be aided by their study of the text, but the book has been created to meet a variety of demands to learn about argumentation. Consequently, examples and illustrations used in the text are concerned with argumentation in a multitude of communication situations.

Since most of our argumentation will occur in informal communication settings, the stress will be on such informal argumentative settings; that emphasis, however, will not hinder our examination of argumentation from formal courtroom debate to editorial argumentation to argumentation in professional journals. Since all these settings and forums are relevant to communication, they will all be within the focus of our study of argumentation as communication.

This final emphasis upon all the various communication situations represents an opportune place from which to look back at the first chapter. We began our orientation to argumentation as communication by assessing the importance of argumentation. Though the study of argumentation is most frequently justified by its importance to the democratic process and to rational and methodical decision making, I suggested an even stronger rationale is simply that we cannot avoid having to engage in argumentation. We do not have to be lawyers or legislators; all we have to be are human beings involved in communication. We went on to examine the ironic but seemingly widespread belief that this crucial process of argumentation was somehow distasteful and something to avoid. In reconciling the ambivalent attitudes toward argumentation, we spent considerable time conceptualizing communication, and then differentiating argumentation from communication in general, persuasion, quarreling, and logic. Our distinction between logic and argumentation, in actuality, was made by examining the implications of a contemporary view of communication studies. Such an approach completed our orientation into the study of argumentation as communication.

Programmed Questions

To test your understanding of the material presented in this chapter, you may wish to answer the following questions. In the multiple-choice questions, the answers may be all correct, all incorrect, or several may be correct. The suggested answers to the questions appear on the last page of this chapter. If you fail to answer the questions correctly, you may wish to review the material to increase your understanding and/or to discuss the items in class.

1. A rationale for studying argumentation is:
    a. the use of argumentation in prompting change in a democracy
    b. the need to have citizens be able to analyze the positions of election candidates and others
    c. the need for personal dominance

    d.   the benefits of international debate as a method of settling disputes

    e.   the notion that argumentation is an inescapable human activity

2.   A common perception of argumentation and arguers is that:

    a.   argumentation can be a highly desirable force in settling disputes

    b.   arguers are always straightforward and honest

    c.   arguers and arguments often are people and things to stay away from

    d.   argumentation may be an unwanted attempt to influence

3.   Communication, as conceived here, involves the idea of transaction; transaction implies that:

    a.   communication normally occurs within a legal setting

    b.   the message sender is actively involved

    c.   the receiver of messages is actively involved

    d.   nothing changes as the two parties interact

    e.   there is constant change as the parties interact

    f.   only two people can be involved

4.   The concept of communication, as we have conceived it, involves:

    a.   transaction

    b.   the creation and re-creation of meaning

    c.   verbal symbols only

    d.   accidental types of meaning creation

5.   Argumentation can be *contrasted* to communication because communication:

    a.   involves symbolic transaction

    b.   must involve intent

    c.   can be affected by or involve all sorts of symbols

    d.   is not involved exclusively with the presentation and examination of claims and reasons

6.   Successful argumentation, unlike successful persuasion, requires that:

    a.   we get someone to feel as we want them to feel

    b.   we get someone to engage in some desired activity

    c.   we get someone to accept *our* justification or reasons for our claim

    d.   we get someone to accept a claim, for whatever reason

7.   A quarrel can be best differentiated from argumentation by the idea that quarreling:

    a.   involves emotion

    b.   involves two or more parties who refuse to examine seriously the claim of any other party

    c.   involves a greater stress on claims and counterclaims, and a de-emphasis upon reason giving

8.   Argumentation, as we shall conceive it, will be more generally involved with:

    a.   prescription, rather than description

b. functions of language, rather than forms of language
c. difficulty and frustration, rather than ease and assured success
d. arguers, rather than receivers
e. argument as a prepared document, rather than argumentation as a process
f. widely diverse situations, rather than one or two structured and formal settings

Research Project for Advanced Students

I have attempted to make a distinction between argumentation and persuasion which undoubtedly is not accepted by every teacher, student, or writer on the subjects. Research other texts on argumentation (and debate, etc.) and persuasion to discover other conceptions of these activities and other interpretations of a distinction—if any—made between the terms.

SELECTED REFERENCES

Crable, Richard E. "What Can You Believe About Rhetoric?" In *Exploration in Speech Communication*, edited by John J. Makay. Columbus, Ohio: Charles E. Merrill, 1973.

Cronkhite, Gary. *Persuasion: Speech and Behavioral Change*. Indianapolis, Ind.: Bobbs-Merrill Co., 1969.

Eisenberg, Abne M., and Ilardo, Joseph A. *Argument: An Alternative to Violence*. Englewood Cliffs, N.J.: Prentice-Hall, 1972.

Fotheringham, Wallace C. *Perspectives on Persuasion*. Boston, Mass.: Allyn & Bacon, 1966.

Natanson, Maurice, and Johnstone, Henry W., Jr., eds. *Philosophy, Rhetoric, and Argumentation*. University Park, Pa.: The Pennsylvania State University Press, 1965.

Answers to Programmed Questions

1. a, b, d, e   2. a, c, d   3. b, c, e   4. a, b   5. d   6. c

7. b, c   8. b, c, f

2

Dimensions of Argumentation

My *general objective* in this chapter is to explore three particularly important dimensions or aspects of argumentation as a transaction.

My *specific objectives* are

to discuss various interpretations that can be made as to *why* someone is engaging in argumentation

to discuss the impact of these interpretations on how the transaction evolves

to explain how several of these factors may affect any one arguer or receiver

to differentiate two ways in which "winning" in argumentation can be interpreted

to discuss argumentation as an activity that occurs in a wide variety of communication situations

to differentiate among four different emphases that can be given to a discussion of argumentation

Chapter 1 was a general orientation to the present study of argumentation, which sought to provide answers to questions concerning the relationships among concepts such as communication, argumentation, persuasion, quarreling, and logic. With that chapter as a background, we are now prepared to examine more specific dimensions of argumentation; that is, having conceptualized argumentation as symbolic transaction aimed at presenting and/or examining reasons for claims, we can now ask: *Why* does argumentation occur?; *Where* does argumentation occur?; and *How* can the study of argumentation occur? Dealing successfully with these questions will take us far in understanding argumentation as communication.

Why Does Argumentation Occur?

None of the first chapter's discussion about the UN delegate and the children focused upon the motivation for the argumentation (or whatever) that occurred. We began a discussion of those events by analyzing *what* was going on, rather than *why* whatever-it-was was going on. Even so, everyone who read the chapter probably made certain assumptions about why it was that the participants became involved in argumentation; moreover, everyone who made such automatic assumptions was in equal jeopardy of being mistaken. Such mis-assumptions about motivation have grave consequences for argumentation because they may cause us, first, to perceive the entire communication situation incorrectly, and, second, they may lead us to respond to the attempted argumentation ineptly. Let us examine the related motivational problems of perception and response by analyzing the following case study.[1] This study, as others will later, will present a situation, include dialogue or narrative, pose certain fundamental questions for discussion, and then conclude with a discussion of the case study in relation to the point being made.

Case Study: The Proposal

Most organizations, whether business, governmental, educational, medical, or whatever, have some sort of system by which supervisory personnel periodically evaluate persons whom they supervise. The practice, however, is not normally reciprocal; most organiza-

---

[1] I am, of course, aware of the distinction between *motives* and *motivation* as terms used when we are trying to differentiate the *actual drives* (motivation) that psychologists or psychiatrists might discuss from the *socially exhibited or stated explanations* (motives) that sociologists might discuss. The discussion here will not explore that distinction, rather it will simply stress the participants' interpretation or perception of *why* someone is behaving as he is. Hence, I shall generally ignore the motive versus motivation question, and refer to these perceptions as *motivational interpretations*. Our major concern will be for how these perceptions and interpretations *affect* the argumentative transaction that occurs.

tions do not have a system whereby subordinate personnel evaluate their supervisors. My experience has been that supervisors usually think that their subordinates feel free to talk with them about anything, and so they view supervisory evaluation as being unnecessary: if the subordinate has a criticism, he can simply tell his supervisor.

Not all subordinates, of course, are satisfied with that arrangement. Some believe that subordinate employees do not feel free, in general, to talk about anything to the man or woman who will make recommendations about promotions, raises, or the lack of these. One employee who doubts the effectiveness of informal subordinate feedback is Joe Evans, a first-level supervisor with Miller and Company. In fact, today is the day when Joe is about to make a proposal before the company screening committee—a body that has the complete power to reject (or to sponsor) an employee suggestion. Joe has been toying for weeks with an idea for a system in which subordinates evaluate their supervisors.

In contrast to Joe, certain other employees on the company screening committee are charged with "weeding out" the worthless proposals from the promising before they get to top management. Adams, Baker, Clark, and Darby know Joe, at least to some extent, and they know that he is coming before the group to argue that the company should have a mandatory system of supervisor evaluation by subordinates. All of them know something about the proposal, and they are all against it, personally as well as collectively. The meeting is about to begin:

ADAMS: Come in, Joe.

EVANS: Thanks.

ADAMS: Joe, I think you've met everyone here . . . maybe not. Do you know Jim Darby?

EVANS: Yeah, I guess we've met a couple of times. Baker . . . hello, Ellen.

(All return greetings.)

ADAMS: Joe, why don't you capsulize your proposal for us. We already know something about it, but maybe you can put it in a nutshell for us.

EVANS: Well, okay. My point, I guess, is that the company would run more efficiently if we made sure that employees could make suggestions about the company or make criticisms of their supervisors. It's . . .

CLARK: Wait a minute. Do you feel, then, that subordinates can't communicate upward in the organization? Is that what you're saying?

BAKER: I don't buy that; my subordinates can come to me any time they want. I'm not going to rate them low on their evaluation just because they criticize me.

EVANS: Hold on. All I meant was that the kind of system I'm advocating would guarantee that feedback could occur in the organization.

ADAMS: Joe, I want you to know that we appreciate your concern for the company. If all our employees were so outspoken we wouldn't need your system. You've done a good service for the rest of the company.

BAKER: Yeah, everybody ought to be evaluated, even if the evaluation sometimes is mistaken. Even supervisors sometimes make mistakes in their evaluations . . . that's just part of the system.

EVANS: Well, we need to do more than just say it's a good idea.

CLARK: You're right, of course. How do you see this plan working? How would we do it?

EVANS: Well, the details are laid out for you—didn't you look at them?

CLARK: Yes, . . . but . . . I'd just like to hear them again.

ADAMS: Joe, no one in the company is better able to tell us the details of the plan. I don't think we can implement it soon, but certainly it is something that our people may want later.

BAKER: Later, yeah, later. It really is an interesting plan, but I'm not sure that . . .

EVANS: Later? You guys never had any inclination to consider this, did you? Did you?

CLARK: Well, I, for one, did. I appreciate the effort that you put into this, and I'm sure that if we really study this that . . .

EVANS: Why can't you look around you and see the benefits of this kind of thing? None of you had that slightest intention of really considering the proposal. This whole meeting has been just for the sake of form; you had to allow me to make the proposal, but you didn't have to take it seriously, did you?

ADAMS: That's not exactly the way it was . . .

CLARK: We just think that the proposal deserves more attention than we've been able to give it, and so . . .

DARBY: Actually, I'm not sure of that. The details of the plan are sketchy—I'm not sure that he put all that much work into it . . .

BAKER: Wait a minute . . .

DARBY: No, let me finish. Let's let Evans tell us what is so great about the proposal that hasn't been presented by someone else before.

EVANS: What are you trying . . . well, I'll tell you what is so unique about this. It gets over having to be afraid to tell someone like you what's really going on in the organization . . .

DARBY: Is that system necessary for that? You seem to be doing that right now, even without the sys . . .

EVANS: Well, obviously, you aren't going to consider this seriously. I've got better things to do than . . .

ADAMS: Wait, I don't think that anyone here is taking your proposal lightly.

EVANS: What about Darby?

BAKER: Not everyone is equally in favor of the proposal, but . . .

EVANS: I guess not. Well, who is favorable? . . . Just as I thought. Well, you can be sure that this is the last time I'll try to intelligently discuss this proposal. I'm sorry that I've taken so much time for something you consider to be so trivial.

Analysis of the Case Study

Evans leaves the room at this point, but the discussion of his proposal is hardly finished. Joe is obviously upset, his coworkers will undoubtedly hear about his meeting, and the members of the committee unquestionably will analyze what went on. If we probe the case in more detail than a casual reading will allow, we will find that what went on is more complicated than it might seem. Let's begin the analysis by asking some basic questions, which you should look at separately and pause to (at least mentally) answer.

1. Who "won" the argument? Joe? The company? The committee? No one?
2. What was Joe's motivation for entering the argumentative situation?
3. What were the committee members' perceptions of Joe's motivation? Did you even consider those perceptions and how they might influence the members' response to Joe?
4. Which member of the committee was the most constructive member in the process? Who was least constructive?

If you spent the time I suggested in formulating answers to the questions, then I suspect that you had no difficulty finding acceptable answers. If you are like most students who have grappled with the case study, you probably decided that the committee had won since they were opposed to the proposal prior to the meeting, and the meeting had ended with the proposal's rejection. You may be in that significant (and perhaps idealistic) minority who feel that since the company lost the benefit of a potentially good proposal, no one won. The answers to the motivations of Joe and the committee may have been less troubling to you: as you read the case originally, I'm sure that you assumed Joe's sole motivation during the argument was to win the assent of the committee, and you probably assumed that the committee's perception of Joe was the same. After all, why would anyone argue without being motivated by the desire to have the claim accepted? The final question, seen in this light, was probably also easy for you to answer: Darby was the least constructive member of the committee and could even be considered the force that finally caused the disruption and conclusion of the meeting. Your answers may have varied considerably in regard to who was the most constructive committee member. Still, however, your responses to the other questions are likely to have been of the nature that I've discussed.

Two problems arise that must be dealt with: first, I may be wrong in my predictions about how you answered; experiences in the past, as we shall see later, are not infallible grounds for claims, let alone predictions. The second problem is more serious: you have just answered certain questions about a fairly complex situation without having access to any "private" information. You did not know anything about the situation except the brief synopsis that I provided; when you needed more information than that (which you did), you acted upon assumption. The process of judgment based upon assumption is not an idiosyncrasy of case studies in argumentation books; it is, rather, an activity that we engage in daily. Let us now look more closely at the participants in the meeting and decide whether some earlier answers to questions should be revised. As he approaches the meeting:

Evans already "knows" (or thinks he knows) that his idea has almost no support within the company; he expects the proposal to be rejected and, in that context, doesn't really care all that much about it. After all, none of his proposals have been accepted in the past, so why should he become concerned now? On the other hand, his wife was grouchy that morning and snapped at him when he disciplined the kids. In the interest of harmony, he "bit his lip" and bottled up his aggression, he survived the late bus arrival and the old man who sat on his hat, but he has about had it. He sits smouldering at his desk and then suddenly remembers that he has this meeting to attend. That's all he needs . . . he has to go in there and face four committee members whose only reason for discussing the proposal is because it's part of their job. Oh well, he reasons, he might as well give it a try.

As they approach the meeting, each of the committee members has an earnest desire to hear what Joe has to say in support of the proposal; they are open to the possibility that he may present some better support for the proposal than he has presented in his statement of the proposal. Thus, each member is taking his or her responsibility to the company seriously. As they begin the discussion of the proposal, however, each member has certain other perceptions of Joe and the situation, which are going to affect how they react to the proposal and the reasons that Joe offers for the system of evaluation. Let's look "inside" each of the members to discover what sorts of perceptions controlled how they responded to the proposal and their task of examining it.

Adams, like the others, is initially against the proposal and feels that it has no chance of being accepted. He "knows" that Joe is only trying to play his favorite game: hero to the rescue of the employee. Consequently, even though he has to reject the proposal at this point, he tries not to hurt Joe's role playing and self-concept as a maverick.

Baker "knows" that Joe is simply upset about his last job evaluation and is trying to make himself look better by getting an opportunity to evaluate (unfavorably) his supervisors. He, therefore, tries not to hurt him more by attacking his proposal too hard—even though initially he must reject it.

Clark "knows" that Joe merely wants to have his idea examined carefully; he is a "team" player and is just trying to be helpful, even though Clark, herself, has chosen to reject Joe's proposal initially.

Darby "knows" that Joe is simply in a mood to blow off steam, and, after all, when is a better chance than right now? So, he encourages it: he confronts him, he baits and teases him a little about his proposal—knowing that such tactics will allow Joe to get angry enough to relieve his tension. He feels that the committee should give Joe a fair hearing.

Motivational Interpretations in Argumentation

The additional information about the committee members and Joe Evans will necessitate a reevaluation of the entire situation. Any such increase in our understanding of why something occurred will affect our prior interpretations of what, in fact, did occur. We can expedite the reconsideration at this point, however, by trying to differentiate (for the sake of convenience) among certain factors that may explain why argumentation occurs.[2]

---

[2]Some of the terms and parts of this analysis of motivation for argumentation and the nature of winning are suggested in Abne M. Eisenberg and Joseph A. Ilardo, *Argument: An Alternative to Violence* (Englewood Cliffs, N.J.: Prentice-Hall, 1972), chapters 2 and 5.

Argumentation may occur, first, because of the psychological needs of arguers or receivers. The phrase *psychological needs* is meant to encompass a wide variety of factors relating to the motivation to communicate and argue. We may engage in argumentation because we feel insecure, and we find in argumentation an opportunity to refute that insecurity: if we argue successfully, we may feel that we indeed have asserted ourselves over others. A second possibility is that we may simply be pugnacious: my sister-in-law, Bettye, frequently accused me (at the time of my intercollegiate debating experience) of being ready to argue about anything simply because I enjoyed it. A final explanation is that we may be somehow guarding a self-concept that we feel is threatened. This latter idea occurred to Baker in his perception of Joe's argumentation: Baker felt that Joe's ego had been bruised by the evaluation of his superior; consequently, Baker was prepared to believe that Joe primarily was interested in defending himself by attacking others through his plan to evaluate them. This perceived ego defense, then, is one of many diverse factors that we can place (for convenience of discussion) under the heading of psychological needs.

Although Baker's perception of Joe illustrates the motivating force of psychological needs, Clark's perception is an example of perceptions that assume the motivation for argumentation is the desire to try out an idea. This traditional notion of *idea testing*, then, is a second category by which we may seek to understand the motivation to argue. In the meeting, Clark was as much opposed to the proposal as the others, but she was convinced that all Joe wanted was a fair evaluation of his idea. Clark realized that people can engage in argumentation—even play devil's advocate—as a method of having a particular concept or notion tested. In everyday conversation, we may say to a friend, "What would you say if I told you I was going to drop out of school?" The friend may become vehement about the idea, or she may simply recognize your idea as a trial balloon or a scenario and simply present reasons against (or for) the decision that you mention. While her vehemence would indicate that she thinks you are serious, her calm discussion would demonstrate that she is aware that people sometimes argue simply to have an idea tested.

Adams's perception of Joe's motivation, however, illustrates a third category which can be convenient for describing the motivation for argumentation: *social needs*. Adams realized the motivating force of social needs when he attributed Joe Evans's proposal to his desire to play the social roles of hero to the rescue of the employee or organizational maverick. Adams knew that Joe had a history of making recommendations and proposals to the company, and that all the proposals shared a common regard for the subordinate's welfare. Consequently, when Joe formulated his latest proposal, Adams perceived it as another strategy in establishing his social role in the organization. Not all social roles, of course, are similar to Joe's. People may involve themselves in argumentation that they know they will lose as a way of solidifying their role of victim or martyr; they may reply later, "See, everybody is against me." Or, arguers may seem to be motivated by the desire to play the role of peacemaker; they will enter argumentation seemingly to help make a compromise or to urge modification of an extreme view. Further, they may engage in argumentation as proof of their espoused allegiance to the (say, for example) conservative cause. Clearly, these role types are related to ideas about psychological needs, but these social roles share a focus upon the part that the individual wishes to play in his social interaction.

For the sake of convenience, we may want to label *obligation* as a fourth term to describe the motivation for argumentation. Though, clearly, the obligation that we feel toward something will vary as our perception of it varies, we frequently contend that someone is doing something because he "has to." Joe Evans's perception of the motivation of the committee members was that they were engaging in the meeting—and the discussion of the proposal—because they had no option; their responsibility clearly involved the act of screening each proposal and making certain recommendations to upper-level management. The members, according to Joe's perception at least, were uninterested in examining the proposal fairly; they had already made decisions about his ideas. The same sort of motivational interpretation, it seems to me, is fairly common. We may receive a traffic citation in a small town, but elect to post bond and forfeit a hearing (scheduled next week); we say, in defense of our act, that the hearing would be *pro forma*: the judge is obligated to hear your story, and then he will fine you what he was going to fine you anyway. We may approach a professor about a grade that we just don't understand, knowing that he is obligated to listen to us, but knowing also that the chances of getting a grade that you do understand are slim indeed. Or, in occupational situations, we may argue with a personnel director who (we perceive) really agrees with us about a complaint, but who (we perceive) is obligated to defend company policy. In essence, times do exist when we, as Joe Evans, perceive that the argumentation in which we are involved is motivated by certain obligations.

In addition to factors that we can label psychological needs, idea testing, social needs, and obligations, a fifth factor that can be labeled as a potential motivating force is the need for *emotional release*, or the desire "to blow off steam." The description of Joe's disagreement with his wife, the late bus, and so forth, indicated that Joe was a human being suffering from contained aggression that could not be contained for long. Clearly, emotional release was a dominant need felt by Joe. His attachment to the proposal itself was certainly less than extreme, and he knew in advance that the committee was against the proposal. Still, tempers flared, and the meeting ended with several employees being unhappy with the discussion: one would have thought that Joe was highly ego involved in the defense of his idea. Interestingly, one of the committee members, Darby, accurately interpreted Joe's most apparent motivational force. Darby felt that Joe was up-tight, tense, and ready to vent his feelings—on someone. Darby perceived that Joe was not nearly so concerned about the proposal as he was eager for an opportunity to "blow off some steam." Consequently, Darby responded differently to Joe, not just because Darby was a different individual, but more specifically because he perceived Joe's motivation much differently from the others.

Thus far we have discussed a number of categories which can be convenient for the classification of the motivations that we perceive in ourselves and others. These categories, like any other classifications, are not intended to be real, perfect, or automatic. Our perceptions of motivations do not fall into one of these categories; rather, people who study argumentation and who are concerned with motivation can use them for convenience and comparison by labeling certain behaviors as being motivated in this way or that. Moreover, the list is not intended to be exhaustive; as you study argumentation in this book and elsewhere, you may find it helpful to add categories to the list for the sake of your own convenience. In fact, let us turn now to a final category of motivation for argumentation—a category that you probably expected me to turn to first: *the desire to actually have the claim we are advancing accepted or the desire to examine that claim.*

The case study of the proposal, with its limited initial information, is designed (ironically) to have the questions posed earlier answered incorrectly. Most of you, I suspect, assumed that Joe was motivated almost certainly by the desire to have the proposal adopted, and that the committee was motivated almost certainly by the desire to examine that claim fairly. The situation, explained by the additional information, was hardly this idealistic. Each of the committee members perceived Joe as being partly motivated by forces other than his desire to have his claim accepted: one thought he was responding to psychological needs, another that he was testing an idea, a third that he was playing a social role, a fourth that he was interested in achieving emotional release, but none felt that he was motivated by the desire to have the claim accepted. Similarly, the committee seemed not to be completely motivated by the desire to examine the claim seriously; individually and collectively, they had determined that the proposal probably would get no further than their committee. Even Joe perceived this, although he felt that their motivation was simply that of obligation: the discussion of his proposal was necessitated by the force of their job description. In short, none of the participants arguing about the proposal perceived the other "side" of the argumentation to be motivated by the straightforward desire to defend a claim or to examine the claim as presented. Clearly, times will exist when we perceive arguers or receivers to be engaging in argumentation primarily because of their interest in the claims or the reasons for claims, but it is also clear that times will exist when we perceive the motivation to be largely irrelevant to the actual outcome of the process.

In relation to the case study of the proposal, it is important to note that each participant seemed guided in the transaction *both* by his perception of the others' motivation *and* by a sincere desire to examine or present the claims and reasons. Since each participant was at least partially interested in the claims and reasons per se, the discussion falls neatly within the scope of argumentation. On the other hand, each member's participation in the discussion was the result of the combination of their desire to deal with claims and reasons and their motivational perceptions. Nor is this surprising. Since argumentation is a kind of communication, we should expect that most situations will involve a complex interaction of motivations where the transaction is conducted both in relation to the obvious goal or purpose and in relation to private expectations and perceptions of motivation. In all probability, argumentation will never occur without the intermixing of the aim to present or examine claims and other desires, goals, and motivational perceptions.

Winning in Argumentation

On the basis of this discussion and in light of the additional case study information, you now can answer more accurately the questions posed earlier about the motivations of Joe and the committee. Two other questions, though, need to be reevaluated: "Who won the argument?" and "Who was the most constructive person on the committee in terms of the argument?" Let us begin the reexamination by discussing, in general, what it means to win an argument.

Winning in argumentation, I suggest, can mean either (or both) of two things: either having the claim accepted (successfully examining the claim, from the receiver's point of view) or simply having your motivational needs met by the transaction. Thus, the idea of winning in argumentation is more complex than it might seem initially. If we assume, as we do in formal or collegiate debate, that your goal is to be awarded the judges' decision, then the matter of winning seems easily determined: you get the ballot or you do not. Tournaments, of course, are normally conducted and decided on the best win-loss record (or the best speaker points, etc., if there are ties). Winning, in this sense, is easy to conceptualize: your goal was to gain a decision from a judge, and if you did you were said to win the argument. Similarly, when attorneys try cases, the goal is clear-cut and obvious in most cases: they seek either guilty or not guilty verdicts, or some variation of these alternatives. Legal reputations can be made largely on the ratio of decisions won to those lost. Again, in the legal setting, the notion of winning is a fairly straightforward idea. Moreover, in certain less structured situations the idea of winning will be related directly to the question of whether a claim has been accepted, rejected, or at least examined thoroughly: when you want the car keys, you consider the argumentation "won" when you get the keys for the reasons you suggest; when you want someone to accept an engagement ring, you probably consider the argumentation successful when the offer is accepted. Indeed, frequently, the idea of winning in argumentation will relate directly to the claim in question.

When we consider argumentation as a kind of pervasive communication activity, however, it seems to me that we must be prepared to interpret winning also in a different sense. We should consider winning as being the time when your motivational needs were met in the transaction; whether your claim was accepted or not, or whether you were successful in examining the claim or not. The general statement that winning may merely mean that your motivational needs have been met can be related to two corollaries to this second interpretation of winning: first, because of the winning-motivation relationship, winning in the sense of having a claim accepted may be largely irrelevant if the argumentation has been motivated largely by factors other than the simple desire to have a claim accepted or to examine a claim. Second, again because of the winning-motivation relationship, winning can be experienced simultaneously by both (or all) of the participants in the argumentative situation. Let me illustrate these common, but not commonly discussed, possibilities.

We, for example, may want to play the social role of resident critic, a role that in social situations will necessitate our opposition to whatever is being discussed. At times we will be willing for our contrary claim to be rejected (and someone else's view adopted) if we have satisfied our need to play the role of critic. In this case, we have lost the argument (claim and reasons have been rejected) in one sense, but in another sense we have won in argumentation: our social goal was met. Similarly, if argumentation seems to have been motivated by the arguer's desire to fulfill some sort of psychological need, then the arguer will be more concerned about satisfying that need than she will be about having the claim accepted: she might, for example, rather rebuild her image of herself as being aggressive than actually have her idea accepted. If, on the other hand, the arguer is driven by an occupational obligation to engage in that argumentation, he may be satisfied with having fulfilled his duty— regardless of whether his reasoning was accepted. Finally, if a receiver is apparently motivated by a desire to examine seriously an arguer's claim and reasoning, then that receiver may win (i.e., have her goals met) by analyzing the arguer's position and accepting his claim. In all these situations, winning means having important goals met; it does not necessarily mean beating your opponent. Moreover, the situations illustrate consistently that both or all participants *simultaneously* can win in argumentation, assuming their different goals are met.

The final questions that I posed earlier can be reevaluated now that we have discussed various motivations for argumentation and the nature of winning in argumentation: Who, on the committee, was the most helpful or constructive? Who was the least constructive? I suspect that, originally, although there may have been disagreements about the most valuable participant, most probably labeled Darby as least helpful. You may still contend that his behavior was central to Joe's finally losing his temper and leaving, and I would agree with you. On the other hand, Darby was the member who most accurately perceived Joe's motivation, and he realized that Joe was more interested in emotional release than he was in having his idea accepted. Consequently, he baited Joe, teased him a little, and, yes, seemed to provide the stimulus which allowed Joe to lose his temper. In the context that the proposal had little chance of being accepted and that Joe was going to blow off steam to someone, Darby manipulated the argumentation to the point at which Joe got part of what he wanted: emotional release. True, there may have been a more tactful approach, but I will contend that Darby came as close as anyone in allowing the session to go the way that Joe desired. In that light I have argued in class (not always convincingly) that Darby was the most constructive member of the meeting. Joe was satisfied (or as satisfied as he could be), the committee had completed its task, and Joe received the release that was necessary for him.

Implications of Motivation in Argumentation

This highly nontraditional approach to motivation and winning in argumentation introduces several important and related implications for the remainder of our study of argumentation. First, the meaning of the argumentation we observe or engage in will be affected substantially by the motivation for that argumentation. The meeting about the proposal (before you had the additional information) is simply not the same meeting as the one after you were provided with the information. The initial description "set the stage" for a confrontation between opposing viewpoints about one claim. As you read the dialogue, you may not have been aware that the four committee members (except perhaps Darby) were acting at all independently. Various people, it seemed, made certain comments, and the argument degenerated rapidly into what we called (in chapter 1) a quarrel. You knew, however, that the proposal was not accepted. The additional information about the motivational perceptions, though, allowed you to see the confrontation, not between two opposing viewpoints, but among five individuals with varying perceptions of what the situation was and where it was likely to go. Rereading the dialogue (if you did that) demonstrated that the characters were engaging in the argumentation process in ways consistent with their perceptions of what Joe or the committee were trying to accomplish. You can understand, now, that the proposal was not only rejected; it really was never close to being accepted. The argumentation-turned-quarrel began as a serious attempt to present and examine claims; yet, as so often happens, those goals became lost. Motivation, then, affects substantially our whole understanding of the argumentation.

A second and related implication of our approach to motivation and argumentation is that, since motivational assessments so significantly affect the argumentation, the study of argumentation must reflect a concern for motivation. As receivers, we must be aware that argumentation will not always be initiated simply to have claims accepted; the motivation for argumentation can be perceived to arise from any number of personal factors. Similarly, arguers must recognize that not all receivers are listening or reading with the sole goal of seriously examining the claim at hand, nor are all receivers committed (as they are in debate) to arguing against the claim you advance. The arguer must realize that the motivation for his receivers can be as diverse as his own. Finally, of course, students of argumentation must apply a critical ear or eye to the argumentation in order to attempt some understanding of the motivation of all the participants in the process.

If we can accept the idea that motivational states (or at least the perception of them) can affect argumentation, and that this necessitates our paying more attention to motivation in argumentation, then a third and final implication follows: engaging in argumentation will require fewer automatic judgments and more understanding of communication in general. Our concern for this motivational dimension of argumentation impels us to think of argumentation as being between (or among) *people* with needs, drives, and goals rather than between (or among) *viewpoints* on a claim or proposition. Any automatic judgments about the goals or strategies of the participants (unless it is a formal debating situation) are likely to need modification as we progress. Any standard and stable "rules" that we attempt to employ are likely to need rethinking as we encounter nonstandardized individuals. Our approach throughout the book will be to discover how to deal with people, not with propositions; we will focus more on the human activity of argumentation, rather than on the immediate employments of logical strategies.

Our effort to answer the question, "Why does argumentation occur?" began with a trek through a fairly simple case study which quickly became more complicated with added information about the motivational perceptions of the participants who discussed the proposal to allow subordinate evaluation of superiors. We found that argumentation can be interpreted to arise from any one of a number of factors, only one of which is the desire to actually have the claim in question accepted. These various factors present a need to move beyond traditional conceptions of winning in argumentation to a view of winning as the achievement of goals (whatever they are) in the argumentation. Such a conception makes winning in the traditional sense less central and forces us to consider other factors when we judge who won the argument. This approach implies several ideas, all culminating in the belief that our study of argumentation will require fewer automatic judgments and more understanding of communication in general. Thus, though we shall devote most of our time to those situations where the goal is (ostensibly) to have a claim accepted or to examine a claim seriously, this discussion has provided a detailed look at human motivation as an important dimension of argumentation.

Where Does Argumentation Occur?

An equally important dimension in the study of argumentation is the factor of settings: Where does argumentation occur? To some students reading the text, the answer is simple. Argumentation occurs, in one of its most formalized states, in debate rounds across the country. From the time of Aristotle's concern for argument in the courts, in the assemblies, and in the public square, to our contemporary concern for collegiate debate, for Senate hearings, and for Supreme Court arguments, the importance of rule-enshrouded, formalized argumentation has seldom been doubted, even though attacks on specific aspects of all these have been launched. When we think of argumentation, then, the image of rules, of practice, and of formality is entirely appropriate. That image, however, should not be the exclusive one, and given the rarity of it occurring to most people, should not be the predominant one. As you recall, in chapter 1 I claimed that the strongest rationale for the study of argumentation was that it was an activity from which escape is not possible. Now, it is possible to avoid the rigors of collegiate debate, and certainly few people enter the legal profession or run for public office; still, no one can completely avoid various sorts of argumentation in diverse kinds of settings or situations. Let us, then, attempt to answer the question, "Where does argumentation occur?" by analyzing the case study of a day in the life of a young university student.

Case Study: A Day in the Life of Helen Wilson

Helen woke up for class as usual—a little later than she should have. She stumbled along a path that took her from her closet and dresser to the shower and back. As she was putting the finishing touches on her hair and face, she glanced down at the whistle sitting prominently on the dresser before her. She picked it up, headed toward her purse, but then returned to the dresser and left the whistle where it had been all night. The sight of the whistle, however, made her recall some of the details of the evening before that her drowsiness had kept her from remembering.

She had gone out with Tom, and, after dinner at "Vic's" they went to Tom's apartment to watch a little television and to be alone. In their attempt to escape from the world of textbooks, classes, and final papers, they had been willing to suffer the mediocrity of a made-for-television movie. Almost as disturbing as the seemingly endless bombardment of commercial announcements was the theme of the movie. The story involved a rape case, but the unsettling point that the movie made was that frequently, when someone has committed murder, the rape of the victim carries no additional penalty; conversely, when a victim is raped, the rapist might just as well murder the victim. Because of the statutes of many states, the movie "cops" contended, rape-murder penalties are levied *concurrently* rather than *consecutively* upon conviction: thus, in some rape-murder cases, one of the crimes is free.

Helen reacted to the movie as one might expect a young woman living alone. She had no desire to finish watching the movie, but she had to see if the movie was going to stir up anything more than public awareness: Was there a solution? Was the problem being alleviated? The movie, unfortunately, left Helen and all other potential victims without recourse. No strides toward correction were mentioned.

As the movie ended, Helen calmly and pessimistically suggested to Tom that the movie was probably just sensationalizing a situation that was not so severe. She said that this was the first time she had heard of the problem; that it was not even mentioned in her senior seminar on criminal law, even though a portion of the course had been devoted to "women and the law." She mentioned that she had not seen the issue discussed in *Cosmopolitan* or any other of the magazines that she read rather frequently. The movie must just be sensationalized, she concluded.

"I'm not so sure," Tom replied after hearing all this. "I think the network is careful not to present stuff that they haven't seen documented. In fact, they've been applauded for bringing some things like this to people's attention."

"All the same, I would surely have seen *something* about it before." Then she added, "Maybe that's just the situation in one or two states."

Tom retorted, "Yeah, but is this one of the states? It only takes one state to matter if you happen to be in it at the time."

"Oh, come on. You're making a joke out of this, but I think it's kind of scary."

"Okay, I was, but . . . wait a minute, I think that there was an article about this in *Time* . . . yeah, maybe a week ago."

Helen looked at him. "You don't read *Time*."

"Well, I did this one. Somebody left it in class, and I looked at it before the lecture started. Come on, let's forget about the stupid movie."

"Well, I don't like the whole thing . . . "

"Okay, if you're upset by it, I've got something that'll make you feel better. Stay here."

Tom left the sofa, and returned moments later with a distress whistle. "Here," he said, "wear this thing that people were distributing the other day. If anyone comes near you, you can blow the whistle, and it'll alert everyone that you're in trouble."

Helen had taken the whistle, and she remembered that the rest of the evening was more enjoyable than the movie had been.

But now she gazed at the whistle sitting on the dresser of her own apartment. She wanted to wear it, but she felt embarrassed at her fear. "I could just tuck it into my purse, rather than actually wear it," she thought. "On the other hand," she mused, "what good is it there? How would I ever find it if I ever was in trouble?" She tried to recall if any of her friends had been wearing one, but she could not remember any. "It would be easier," she thought, "if I wasn't the only one to wear the thing." She picked up the whistle, looked at it thoughtfully, then put it back down. "This is really silly. Besides, I'm late."

She collected her books, papers, and notebook, and darted toward the door on her way to class . . . stopping only momentarily to pick the whistle up and put it in her purse.

Her first class was her senior seminar in criminal law, and, as usual, she was late. Today, however, it was of little consequence because the instructor was going to arrive late also. That gave her time to catch her breath, retrieve her seminar notebook from the stack, and chat casually with some of her friends. She found that two of her classmates were discussing the same movie that she had seen with Tom the night before. Both were concerned about the issue raised by the movie, and both were wondering about the extent of the problem. Today was the day when the participants in the seminar were to decide what the next area of study was to be, and Dick (one of the ones discussing the movie) suggested that the issue introduced by the movie might be a good area of research and study.

When the instructor arrived, he explained the lateness of his arrival and asked if there were suggestions for the next unit of study. Dick responded by suggesting the rape-murder problem, and Helen also indicated her support for the topic. John Black, a student who was not noted for his enthusiasm for women's issues and problems, promptly replied that their earlier study of women and the law was enough, and he suggested that they study something in the area of plea bargaining.

"After all," John contended, "plea bargaining is a topic that might allow some people in here still to focus on the rape-murder issue."

"The point is," said Helen, "that the problem with plea bargaining is how all-inclusive it is. Sure, that would allow us to go off in different directions, but we wouldn't have enough time to study anything in any detail."

"Well," the instructor started, "I think . . . "

"Besides that," Dick interrupted, "the rape-murder issue is really a new topic and would be more exciting, I think, to investigate."

The instructor finally broke in. "Let's hear from you, Andrea. What do you think?"

"I didn't see the movie, but I did hear Dick and the others discussing it," Andrea responded. "The best reason I can think of for studying the murder-rape thing is that the university area is really not the safest place to be. I think we would be dealing with a more pressing and real problem—to us now—than if we studied plea bargaining . . . "

The instructor queried, "You mean the rape-murder issue is more pressing, right?"

"Yes."

The instructor looked around, and it seemed obvious that most of the seminar felt that the issue raised by the movie should provide them with an important area of study.

"Okay," John conceded, "I can go along with the murder-rape thing. I still think that plea bargaining may be important there, so, if no one objects, I'll work in that area."

The rest of the seminar was devoted to mapping out the initial responsibilities of the seminar participants: who would work with whom, who would look where for information, what sort of goals their investigation would have, and what would be the nature of the final projects in the unit. It was generally agreed that the university's pre-law student organization would be a likely forum to use to ask others for cooperation and advice about sources of information, methods of research, and potential problems in such an inquiry. For lack of a volunteer, Helen Wilson was selected as the spokesperson for the group to address the organization that afternoon.

Later during lunch, Helen pondered what she would say to the group. She decided that there was no way that she could prepare for the meeting with library research or anything (although that is what she would like to do), so she decided simply to use the movie and the class discussion as a way of introducing the idea: she hoped that would stimulate some thought, and that later some of the other members of the group might be able to contribute some information or advice. Maybe, she thought, the organization itself might be able to sponsor some guest speakers or something for the seminar's investigation. It was worth a try.

At the meeting, she introduced the idea and had generally good response until she concluded her remarks by summarizing that, in some cases, the rape "was free." Late afternoon on a college campus, she found, is not always the best time to use phrases that can be manipulated into jokes. Someone replied that that had always been the case: if you *did* pay, then it wouldn't . . . Helen, with the whistle in her purse, was really in no mood to see the humor in the situation.

"I think that we need to treat the problem more seriously," she scolded, "and I think that this is the appropriate group to sponsor some guest experts and perhaps even some small amount of money for the seminar's research, if it becomes necessary."

The advisor to the group, a professor in the university law school, agreed with Helen, but indicated that the group was not in a financial situation that would allow grants of this kind. Another member responded that the seminar was being premature in assuming that the topic would even require guest speakers or research funds.

Helen answered that she was aware of that, but that the seminar had wanted to test the organization's interest in the project—just in case financing was necessary.

The organization's advisor replied that he was sure the organization was interested, but that interest was probably all that they could contribute at the present time.

One of the other members of the pre-law group, however, had an intriguing suggestion. If Helen and the other members of the seminar were really interested in furthering discussion of the issue, perhaps they ought to use the movie and the current interest in the distress whistles to stimulate thought and activity on the campus as a whole: his suggestion was to use the student newspaper as a forum to begin the discussion (he happened to be on the newspaper staff). A letter-to-the-editor, he mused, might be the appropriate method with which to begin. Feature articles, he claimed, might follow from the initial discussion.

General discussion of this new proposal followed with (as usual) everyone thinking that it was a good idea, but with an absence of volunteers.

Later, back at her apartment, Helen tossed her books and purse on the desk. She thought about the whistle in her purse and again contemplated whether to wear it. She decided that the best solution was not to have to wear it, but until the campus and the nearby streets were safer, the whistle provided some security. She was tired, but she skipped dinner and sat down to write a letter-to-the-editor of the campus newspaper outlining the importance of the problem of coed safety, the already existent interest on campus, and the need for more people to become involved in the project.

She finished the letter, sealed the envelope, and put it with her purse so that she would remember to put it in the campus mail. She looked at her watch and it was 7:30: exactly the time, twenty-four hours ago, when she had been in Tom's apartment to suffer through a made-for-television movie. She left her apartment to get a snack.

The Settings for Argumentation

Helen's twenty-four hours were of course hypothetical, but the events are those that could have happened to a mature young student who cared about getting things done. The most artificial aspect of the case is not that all those events could have occurred, but that they all happened within a twenty-four-hour period. Similar situations might have evoked a response and activity that could have transpired over the course of days or weeks, rather than hours. Still, the case study can serve our purpose of examining the various situations or settings in which argumentation occurs. Clearly, Helen became involved in various efforts to assert claims or to examine claims; our task, then, is to retrace her steps as a way of understanding how these activities may be characterized as conveniently distinguishable settings for argumentation.

The Intrapersonal Setting.   The first argumentative situation in which Helen found herself was what we shall call the intrapersonal setting: Helen almost literally began debating with herself the reasons for wearing the whistle or not. Helen entertained several possible claims that occurred to her as potential solutions to her fear. First, of course, she could leave the whistle at home; the reasons for leaving it included her embarrassment at seeming afraid and the fact that she knew no one else who had one. In addition, Helen felt that a good reason for not leaving the whistle at home was the threat of rape and murder. Did the reasons for the claim (to leave it home) outweigh the reasons against it? Other claims, she realized, were apparent: for, secondly, she could wear the whistle. The claim that she should wear it was supported by the reason that she would be safest with that protection. Reasons against wearing the whistle included the embarrassment of revealing her fear and that she might be one of the few exhibiting the fear of rape so explicitly. A third claim was that she could keep the whistle in her purse, close enough to have it in an emergency, but not so close as to have her fear be obvious to everyone. The major reason against having it in her purse was the possibility that she might not be able to use it in time to be of help.

Her decision-making process, then, can be viewed as essentially intrapersonal argumentation, for it occurs solely with one person (or occurs in the person). Her options for the decision can be understood easily as claims: she should wear the whistle; she should leave the whistle home; or she should tuck the whistle in her purse. Having isolated the options (or, we might say, advanced the claims), Helen set about evaluating the solutions (or, we might say, examining the reasons for each claim). Finally, as she leaves for class, she accepts the reasoning that the presence of the whistle in her purse, even if it is difficult to get to, is the most acceptable solution.

Similarly, as we continue the study of argumentation, we will encounter more text examples of intrapersonal argumentation—when one person almost literally argues alternatives with himself. Moreover, in your everyday activity, I suspect that you will become increasingly aware of the many decisions you make during the day where your evaluation of the reasons for and against particular ideas are essential: Should you cut a class or not?; What are the reasons to do so?; The reasons against?; Should you go out on Friday with someone-or-other or not?; Why should or shouldn't you?; Is the philosophy of Wittgenstein a good topic for a paper or not?; Should you study for the test or should you do research for your paper first? All these are examples of the situation that we have labeled the intrapersonal setting in argumentation.

The Interpersonal Setting.   Helen's argumentation in that twenty-four-hour period, however, was not limited to *intra*personal decision making. Indeed, she had spent a significant amount of time the evening before arguing with Tom about the accuracy and extent of the issue raised by the movie. This second sort of argumentative setting, which we shall call the interpersonal situation, involves (at least) two people in the activity of presenting and/or examining reasons for claims. Helen had contended that the issue probably was sensationalized and exaggerated, and she offered as reasons for the claim that she had not heard the issue discussed elsewhere; that it had not been discussed in her senior seminar on criminal law; and that she had never seen discussion of the topic in *Cosmopolitan* or any other magazine that she read regularly. Based upon these reasons, she was confident that the issue must have been exaggerated.

As is typical in interpersonal argumentative situations, Tom responded immediately by challenging her reasons. He recalled that the network was usually careful in its documentation and, in fact, had been applauded for bringing to light issues just like this one. Helen chose to ignore his reasoning and tried to further her own position by suggesting that the problem may be one in only one or two states. So the argumentation progressed, through Tom's submission of the *Time* article, Helen's challenge that he never read *Time*, his explanation of it being left in class, and finally by his act of giving her the whistle.

Although we shall discuss later the specific strategies and choices made in such argumentation, the most important point is that the interpersonal setting is crucial to your understanding of argumentation. Not only are you continually involved in *intra*personal argumentation, but also much of your day is spent in interpersonal argumentation: you try to present reasons for an independent study to a faculty member, and she evaluates those reasons and maybe claims that another alternative is better; you attempt to demonstrate to your roommate that he should let you borrow his car by giving him the "one good reason" that he asks for; or you examine the reasons that your mother gives you to ask the-daughter-of-a-friend-of-hers for a date. Much of your argumentation, you will find, occurs in this second argumentative setting: the interpersonal.

The Small Group Setting. Helen's day, however, also included argumentation in a different and less frequent, but still important, third argumentative setting: the small group. Though there are numerous ways in which to conceptualize the small group, we shall consider the small group to be a gathering of (roughly) five to nine people who share a mutual goal, task, or responsibility. The sharing of a task is most important to this conception (since the numbers can vary), and so it is helpful to define the senior seminar in which Helen appeared in the morning to be a "small group": their common goal that morning was to determine the next area for group study. Thus, when the instructor arrived, and Dick suggested that the topic should be the rape-murder issue, the stage was prepared for the advancement of reasons for and against the claim that that was a suitable topic. The presentation of the reasons for the claim (that it was a new topic, that it would be exciting, that it was narrow enough to study adequately in the time allotted for the topic) was met by John who presented a counterclaim (that plea bargaining should be the area of study) and presented reasons for its acceptance: that it would allow diverse individual research, that they had already studied "women" issues, and so forth. In the end, of course, even John decided that the rape-murder was the better-supported proposal and agreed to pursue it—in terms of plea bargaining.

The sort of argumentation that occurred in the seminar is not atypical of that which occurs frequently in small groups. True, the commonsense advice to participants in small group situations is "don't argue," but that admonition must be refined. Whatever the small group's task, a need will exist for someone to claim that solution A ought to be adopted for reasons one, two, and three. That sort of process is essential to begin the evaluation of those reasons, and thus the solution. The process of defending a claim may give rise to a second suggested alternative, which is supported by other reasons, and a third solution for still other reasons. If the people making those suggestions insist upon defending the alternatives they have introduced, then the discussion obviously will end in a stalemate or, worse, a quarrel. On the other hand, if the participants introduce the claims with the goal of having them (and the reasons for them) fairly evaluated, and if they are willing to make the sort of compromise that John made, then argumentation in the small group becomes a valuable tool for the completion of the task at hand. Such a tool will be as relevant to a PTA meeting as it will in a senior seminar, a family decision-making meeting, or a task force in business and industry.

The One-to-Many Setting.   As a result of the seminar meeting, Helen was selected to enter into yet a fourth argumentative setting: one that we shall call the platform or one-to-many situation. Helen made a (rather unprepared) prepared statement to the university pre-law organization, where she argued that the organization ought to provide support for guest speakers or give research monies to finance the study of the seminar group. She cited the appropriateness of the pre-law organization as the primary reason in favor of the organization's lending its support and perhaps funds to the seminar activity. Helen's reason for contending that that was an appropriate body was not challenged; what was pointed out, however, was the crucial reason against the offering of aid: funds were not available. Consequently, Helen's claim was rejected without a great deal of discussion.

Similarly, nearly everyone will encounter instances where argumentation must be carried out on a platform or, at least, at the front of a room in a one-to-many situation. Frequently, business people must make formal presentations to a group of management personnel concerning a proposal that they think should be adopted by the company; such situations are clearly persuasive in nature, but the emphasis in the presentations probably will have to be on the reasons why the proposal should be adopted. Then, too, individuals at times must defend budget requests in business, professional, or charitable organizations: these will require the marshalling of the reasons for a proposed figure, and they can be expected to prompt a close examination of those reasons by organizational officers or supervisors. Indeed, the frequency of such one-to-many argumentative situations probably has been exaggerated in the past in the overconcern for formal public speaking, but occasions will arise when prepared, perhaps somewhat formal, platform argumentation will be an important human process.

The Mass Media Setting.   Helen's one-to-many or platform argumentation, though, was not the last argumentative activity in which she participated. She completed her evening with a letter-to-the-editor of the university newspaper, hoping to use the newspaper as a final forum in which to argue that the problem was potentially serious and highly relevant to the campus community, that support for more study and research had already begun, and that more students needed to be aware of the rape-murder issue. The letter reflected the personal suffering that can accompany crimes of violence and the urgent need introduced by the movie; indeed, she concluded, the campus community had every reason to become involved in and concerned about the study that the seminar was undertaking. Helen thus concluded her day by participating in a fifth argumentative situation: the mass media setting.

Helen's use of this fifth argumentative setting, of course, was not characterized by the glamour and force of a network news reporter, but it does illustrate perhaps the most common means by which nonprofessional people can use mass media for argumentative purposes. Their claims and reasoning can be transmitted by the letter-to-the-editor forum, but access to the mass media is not limited to newspapers. Magazines frequently will publish responses to their last issue (or at least an earlier issue); more and more radio "call-in" shows seem to be appearing; local television stations at times will ask for telephoned comments or responses from their viewers; and the spreading networks of cable television promise to provide (in some instances, they are required to provide) opportunities for more direct citizen access to the greater supply of channels. The average citizen's use of mass media as a forum for his argumentation appears to have even greater opportunity in the future. Although most of you will not have the opportunity to appear on *Meet the Press* or television commercials, your opportunity as receivers to examine the argumentation of others in the mass media remains as real as ever.

The Professional Setting.   Though Helen did not participate in such a situation, a sixth argumentative setting that I should mention is what I shall call professional argumentation. At times, claims are advanced and reasoning is explained by professional people who use professional media or gatherings to talk almost exclusively with other professionals. Medical doctors discuss professional topics, ideas, beliefs, and research at meetings of the American Medical Association. Engineers use engineering conventions to discuss and decide current approaches and future strategies in the study of engineering. Lawyers address other legal professionals in law journals and in courts of appeal where judges, not nonprofessional juries, are the receivers for their arguments. Communication scholars and professors use communication journals to argue for certain methods of research, certain future goals, or some new field of study. In all these instances, the argumentation is somewhat different from the sort of thing in which Helen was involved; here, the task of argumentation is to aid in the advancement of knowledge or understanding in the profession. Assumptions are made by contributors to these scholarly journals, conventions, and sessions that the receivers have a background in the field, that they are equipped to analyze the reasoning presented, and that they may have something to say, not only about whether the claims are accepted, but more importantly whether the claims become accepted as a part of the "knowledge of the field." Before Einstein was credited with all the accomplishments that we (nonprofessional receivers) gave him, he spent years researching, writing in professional journals, and speaking at professional gatherings. True, Einstein and his colleagues eventually succeeded in altering much of what was known about physics, but that advance did not come automatically or easily. It was accomplished by the process of argumentation in professional settings with professionals in physics: and yet today some of the claims of Einstein and others are no longer accepted, since they, too, have been successfully argued against in professional settings. What is known in physics, psychology, history, anthropology, and communication has been the product of ongoing professional argumentation.

Our study of the settings of argumentation, then, began with the acknowledgement that argumentation does occur in formalized settings such as debate or legal argument. Most argumentation in which you will participate, however, will be in different settings: intrapersonal, interpersonal, small group, one-to-many, and mass media situations. Some of you may even become involved as arguers or receivers in professional argumentation in your career field. This section on settings, therefore, has introduced convenient categories for the argumentation that occurs in human communication. The settings introduced here will be analyzed again as we examine various case studies, in which you will be able to appreciate fully the demands and opportunities inherent in each of these situations. But we have accomplished the primary goal: we have considered a second dimension of argumentation by looking at the question "Where does argumentation occur?" and we have answered it briefly by investigating the various settings of argumentation.

How Can the Study of Argumentation Occur?

Having looked at the questions "Why does argumentation occur?" and "Where does argumentation occur?" we can now approach a third dimension of argumentation asking, "How can the study of argumentation occur?" The question is important because argumentation can be treated very differently by various texts; individual instructors will supplement, delete from, or modify the concerns for such texts and courses; and students will approach a course in argumentation with vastly different views as to what they shall study in argumentation classes. Though it would be impossible here to attempt a delineation of all the various emphases that could exist in a study of argumentation, let me at least suggest a basic way of differentiating facets of the study of argumentation. We can differentiate, for the sake of convenience, four of these major emphases, including the *practice*, the *critical study*, the *theory* (or theories) and the *philosophy* (or philosophies) of argumentation.[3]

The *practice* of argumentation is, perhaps, the most commonly conceptualized focus for the study of argumentation. Since students enter classes in mathematics in order to learn certain mathematical skills, and since students enroll in technical theatre courses to learn the techniques of staging dramatic productions, it is reasonable for students to study argumentation in order to improve their actual ability to argue. This desire is particularly understandable for students who are majoring in communication, pre-law studies, and theology; the desire, however, is equally understandable among students of other majors who realize that much of their time in the future will be spent in advancing claims and the reasons for them and in examining the claims and reasoning of others. This kind of practical need—the need to learn the actual practice of argumentation—has been recognized for years, and numerous textbooks have been written expressly to fill this demand. Some of these texts are termed handbooks, since they almost literally can be referred to as the argumentation progresses; they discuss strategies, methods, and specific approaches to argumentation that can help

[3]A similar differentiation concerning the term *rhetoric* appears in Richard E. Crable, "What Can You Believe About Rhetoric?" in *Exploration in Speech Communication*, ed. John J. Makay (Columbus, Ohio: Charles E. Merrill, 1973), pp. 299-314. Parts of that differentiation were suggested by Maurice Natanson, "The Limits of Rhetoric," in *Philosophy, Rhetoric, and Argumentation*, ed. Maurice Natanson and Henry W. Johnstone, Jr. (University Park, Pa.: The Pennsylvania State University Press, 1965), p. 101.

people involved in the day-to-day practice of dealing with claims and reasons.[4] Other texts treat the practice of argumentation in more general terms; that is, the concern is not exclusively for the technicalities of argumentation. Most texts, it seems to me, can be placed into this category: they treat the practice of argumentation, but they also deal with other matters.[5]

Some of these other matters that texts can approach can be labeled as the second basic sort of emphasis: the *critical study* of argumentation. The criticism of argumentation, to me, connotes the analysis and evaluation of the argumentation as practiced by arguers and receivers. When a news commentator, for example, "breaks down" the reasoning of the President and Congress into the major reasons advanced for a presidential budget proposal and the congressional challenges to that budgetary claim, he is not simply commenting; instead, he is analyzing (breaking down the argumenation into its basic parts). Further, when that commentator begins to assess the degree of truth in or strength of the reasoning, he is doing more than merely commenting; in addition, he is evaluating (judging the merits of the reasoning by using certain standards, such as truth or effectiveness). Seen in this context, criticism is not merely the process of finding fault with something or tearing something apart, but is a conscious and systematic analysis and evaluation of the argumentation that occurs between arguers and receivers.

Criticism, though, cannot be conducted without a third emphasis for argumentation studies: the *theory* or *theories* of argumentation. It seems to me that it is not possible to analyze and evaluate (criticize) the practice of argumentation without some prior conception of the nature of argumentation. Indeed, much of chapter 1 was devoted to a conceptualization of what argumentation was and how it differed from communication in general, persuasion, quarreling, and logic. That conceptualization was not submitted as a definitive definition of what argumentation was; rather, it explained for you the kind of thing that I would consider to be argumentation (even though such conceptions vary among writers and teachers of argumentation). The conceptualization was generally what we would call theoretical: it attempted to relate who might be involved in argumentation, what sorts of symbols they might use, what their argumentative goals might be, and what their responsibilities might be as arguers and receivers. That information allows you to begin "breaking down" or

[4]See, for example, Austin J. Freeley, *Argumentation and Debate*, 3rd. ed. (Belmont, Calif.: Wadsworth Publishing Co., 1971)

[5]See, for example, Douglas Ehninger and Wayne Brockriede, *Decision by Debate* (New York: Dodd, Mead and Co., 1963).

analyzing the argumentative practice that you engage in or witness; it tells you the important parts of the process of argumentation and the relationship among those parts; and thus it allows you to perform the critical function of evaluating the argumentation. Not everyone who engages in argumentation, of course, would be able to explain the theory that they utilize, but everyone will be making (conscious or unconscious) assumptions about what argumentation is, what it's for, and what occurs as it progresses. A theoretical understanding of argumentation, then, is a crucial, potential focus for the study of argumentation; indeed, it seems to me that the most concise way to envision the relationship among the practice, criticism, and theory of argumentation is to understand that criticism, most basically, is the application of a theory of argumentation to argumentative practice. Thus, while your chief goal in reading this book may be to enhance your argumentative practice and to evaluate the argumentation of others, a concern for argumentative theory is an absolutely essential aspect of the study of argumentation.

As I mentioned earlier, my conceptualization of argumentation in chapter 1 is clearly not the only one available to the teacher or student of argumentation. The important point, for us here, is not that different theories or approaches exist, but that the differences largely can be explained as products of varying philosophical viewpoints. These various *philosophies* of argumentation, in fact, constitute a fourth and final focus for the study of argumentation. Although the nature of a philosophy is difficult to grasp or explain, our purposes can be served by thinking of philosophies as basic and fundamental views and assumptions about such ideas as the human race, reality, existence, knowledge, truth, and so forth. These views may not be explicitly stated, nor even consciously recognized, but they will form the basis for many of the theoretical conceptions that we believe. For example, if philosophically we are convinced that humans are molded and formed by their environments, we are likely to believe in Skinnerianism as a psychological theory and programmed learning and behavioral objectives as the "right" approaches to education. Moreover, we may believe that successful argumentation can occur only when the reasons for a claim are sufficiently rewarding to receivers. If, on the other hand, we believe philosophically in the primary importance of the media of messages (a la McLuhan), then we are likely to reject certain educational methods as being irrelevant to the electronic era. Similarly, we would probably pay much attention to whether argumentation was initiated through the effective use of film, television, unconventional printing formats, and so forth. Finally, if we were to believe philosophically (as I do) that humans create their world with language and thought and communication activities, then we are likely to believe that most educational approaches are useful as convenient ways to allow us to discuss education. These approaches are not how education occurs; rather, they are mankind's various ways to explain a great part of his activity. Consequently, we likely would view argumentation as a process where we emphasize, not environment or media, but people who create claims, support them with reasons, and, in the end, say whether any of that was in any way important. Regardless of what sort of philosophical assumptions about the human race, reality, existence, and truth that we believe, the important point is that we will make these kinds of assumptions (even the assumption that we don't make such assumptions, is an assumption), and these philosophical statements will affect our acceptance of relevant theories, critical methods, and thus our perception of the practice of argumentation.

In essence, then, the question "How can the study of argumentation occur?" can lead us to a staggering multitude of diverse approaches, or, as we have done here, it can focus upon some general sorts of emphases for the study of argumentation. We can focus upon the *practice* of argumentation, looking at the strategies and procedures for presenting and examining claims and reasons for claims. Second, we can highlight the *critical study* of argumentation, where we analyze and evaluate the argumentative practices of others. Third, of course, we can emphasize the *theoretical aspects* of argumentation, by explaining one theoretical approach or comparing a number of them. Finally, we could treat the *philosophical facets* of argumentation: Is argumentation purely persuasion? (We disagreed in chapter 1.) Is argumentation always manipulative and questionable? (We shall disagree with that in chapter 8.) Is argumentation a *method* of inquiry and research rather than a *process* of influence? (As we shall see in certain case studies, it can be either.) My point is that our present study of argumentation encompasses all of the emphases discussed here: we shall be concerned about the practice of argumentation, but we must also critically approach such argumentation on the basis of some of the theoretical and philosophical ideas discussed. Your goal may be to study exclusively argumentative practice, but you will find that that study alone is narrow and unhelpful in studying argumentation as communication.

Summary

We began our investigation of dimensions of argumentation by posing and then attempting to answer three essential questions: Why does argumentation occur?; Where does argumentation occur?; How can the study of argumentation occur? In terms of the first question, we found that such argumentative communication can be motivated by numerous factors other than the sole desire to have a claim accepted. People argue in part for what we can call psychological factors, social needs, obligations, emotional release, and idea testing (and we must always add that other categories of motivation for argumentation are possible). The perceived motivation for argumentation has implications for what the meaning of winning in argumentation is; we should define winning in terms of goals met or needs fulfilled, as well as in terms of simply having a claim accepted. Moreover, the study of argumentation must take these relevant motivations into account, forcing us to approach argumentation with fewer automatic judgments of strategies, procedures, and guides for effectiveness.

Secondly, we turned to a description of various settings in which argumentation occurs. Though we may envision formal debate when someone speaks of argumentation, most will occur in other settings. We discussed a particularly hectic day in the life of a university student to illustrate argumentation that occurs in intrapersonal and interpersonal situations, small group occasions, platform occurrences, and mass media usage. To these potential argumentative situations, I added a concern for argumentation that occurs in professional settings, such as conventions or journals, that have something to do with the advancement of knowledge in that professional field. An exploration of these situations, then, provided an answer to the question "Where does argumentation occur?" Argumentation is a potential occurrence in any communication setting.

Our final question in this chapter was one aimed at trying to make more sense of a possibly confusing situation: "How can the study of argumentation occur?" Our answer was that argumentation can be studied any number of ways, but that it was perhaps helpful to say that when someone says she is studying argumentation, she may either be highlighting the practice, the critical study, the theory or theories, or the philosophy or philosophies of argumentation. Although all these dimensions of the study of argumentation probably will be present in any lengthy treatment of argumentation, one or another of them most likely will be highlighted. Our present study is concerned more with the practice and critical study of argumentation, though we shall also develop theoretical perspectives and delve into philosophical questions. Indeed, such attention to theory and philosophy is both the basis for the rest of our study and the central thrust of the next chapter.

Programmed Questions

To test your understanding of the material presented in this chapter, you may wish to answer the following questions. In the multiple-choice questions, the answers may be all correct, all incorrect, or several may be correct. The suggested answers to the questions appear on the last page of this chapter. If you fail to answer the questions correctly, you may wish to review the material to increase your understanding and/or discuss the items in class.

1. Argumentation may be interpreted to be "motivated" by:
   a. psychological needs of arguers
   b. psychological needs of receivers
   c. a desire to test an idea
   d. some sort of obligation
   e. social needs
   f. the need for emotional release
   g. the desire to have a claim accepted

2. Normally, we would expect argumentation to arise:
   a. from one and only one "motivation"
   b. from an intermixing of motivational forces
   c. for no reason at all

3. Winning in argumentation can be interpreted as occurring:
   a. only when the individual has a claim accepted
   b. when a claim is accepted or when our motivational forces have been satisfied
   c. only when our motivational forces have been satisfied
   d. only when one individual clearly defeats his opponent and keeps the opponent from winning
   e. when a receiver successfully examines a claim and comes to accept it

4. Our perspective on motivation and argumentation clearly indicates that:
   a. we shall need to make more immediate and automatic judgments of argumentation
   b. as receivers and arguers, we must reflect a concern for motivation
   c. the "meaning" of the argumentation will be affected substantially by motivational perceptions

5. Argumentation, as we shall conceive it, can occur:
   a. in small group settings
   b. in intrapersonal settings
   c. in interpersonal settings
   d. between animals and humans
   e. in the one-to-many or platform setting

    f.   in the mass media setting

    g.   between professionals in professional settings

    h.   between machines and humans

6.   In studying argumentation, we may emphasize four somewhat distinct aspects of argumentation, including:

    a.   simple quarreling in argumentation

    b.   the theory of argumentation

    c.   the philosophy of argumentation

    d.   the refutation of argumentation

    e.   the perception of argumentation

    f.   the practice of argumentation

    g.   the debate of issues in argumentation

    h.   the criticism of argumentation

Discussion Questions for Appendix Case Studies

To test your understanding of the material in this chapter, you may wish to answer the following questions that refer to the case studies in the Appendix of this book. You may wish to (a) work on the questions individually; (b) work on the questions in pairs or in groups in or before class; (c) develop written answers to the questions; (d) have class discussion based upon the questions; (e) prepare an extended paper on several related questions; or (f) develop a major paper about one case study (using the questions related to it that appear in the various chapters).

1. Study "Address to the Catholic Lawyers' Guild" by Senator Dick Clark of Iowa beginning on page 259. Recalling our discussion of various motivational perceptions of *why* an individual engages in argumentation, what are several factors that might have affected Senator Clark's decision to address the group as he did? Your attention should be drawn to *all* the potential factors that might have motivated him. Which of these factors do you think were most influential in his message to the group? Defend your choice.

2. Study "A 2 or a 4?" beginning on page 266. Why is this instance of argumentation a *special* interpersonal setting? What factors make it different from the casual discussion you might have with a friend? How might certain other motivational factors have affected Stoner's desire to examine Alice's claim that she deserved a 4? How might certain other motivational factors have affected Alice's desire to examine Stoner's claim that she deserved a 2?

3. Study "The Success of the Program" beginning on page 264. Consider the social needs and roles played by the Head Administrator and by Professor Wallace. How might these have affected the exchange about the program's

success? In what ways may the individuals have seen each other as a threat to their social roles?

4. Study "Satisfaction (Almost) Assured" beginning on page 258. In what ways does the telephone situation make this a special sort of interpersonal setting? Can the situation also be viewed as something of a "negotiation" between two parties? If so, how? If John Deal accepts the manager's offer, who "won" in the argumentation? Did *both* parties "win?"

5. Study "How Free is Free Will?" beginning on page 254. Ellen, in some ways, is going through the same process that Helen Wilson did when she was deciding whether to wear the whistle. In what sort of argumentative setting, then, does Ellen find herself? There are differences, however, since Helen was attempting to decide between several courses of action. In contrast to action, what does Ellen's decision involve?

6. Consider the several emphases by which the study of argumentation can be characterized: argumentative practice, the criticism and evaluation of argumentation, the theory of argumentation, and the philosophy of argumentation. Which of these emphases is most prominent in the chapter? In the case studies alluded to? In your answering of the questions above?

Research Project for Advanced Students

The complexity of "motives" or "motivation" in relation to human behavior has perhaps been illustrated best by the American literary theorist and critic, Kenneth Burke. Research Burke's approach to motives and human action as a way of understanding more clearly this chapter's treatment of the perception of motive. An introduction to the concept and an extensive Burkeian bibliography can be found in Richard E. Crable and John J. Makay, "Kenneth Burke's Concept of Motives in Rhetorical Theory," *Today's Speech* (Winter 1972), pp. 11-18.

SELECTED REFERENCES

Burke, Kenneth. *A Grammar of Motives.* Berkeley: University of California Press, 1969.

———. *A Rhetoric of Motives.* Berkeley: University of California Press, 1969.

Crable, Richard E., and Makay, John J. "Kenneth Burke's Concept of Motive in Rhetorical Theory." *Today's Speech* 20 (1972): 11-18.

Eisenberg, Abne M., and Ilardo, Joseph A. *Argument: An Alternative to Violence.* Englewood Cliffs, N.J.: Prentice-Hall, 1972.

Pace, R. Wayne, and Boren, Robert R. *The Human Transaction: Facets, Functions, and Forms of Interpersonal Communication.* Glenview, Ill.: Scott Foresman, 1973.

Scheidel, Thomas M. *Speech Communication and Human Transaction.* Glenview, Ill.: Scott Foresman, 1972.

Answers to Programmed Questions

1. a, b, c, d, e, f, g   2. b   3. b, e   4. b, c   5. a, b, c, e, f, g

6. b, c, f, h

3

Communicative Functions in Argumentation

My *general objective* in this chapter is to discuss the various ways in which language can be said *to function* in argumentation.

My *specific objectives* are

to explain the common and, at times, justifiable concern for argumentation as a prepared document

to explain and illustrate the commonly accepted forms of argumentation such as deduction and induction

to explain certain problems that arise from focusing upon the forms of argumentation—what it looks like

to explain and justify my emphasis upon how argumentation functions rather than what its form is

to introduce the ideas of claim, evidence, warrants, backing, qualifier, and reservation as terms for how language functions

Our attempt in chapter 1 to conceptualize argumentation and our effort in chapter 2 to examine certain general dimensions of argumentation allow us now to begin an examination of argumentation in more specific detail. In this chapter, we shall examine the common and practical desire that students have to put an argument together. While we will admit that the desire is understandable and valuable at times, we will see that the wish to construct an argument has led to an overemphasis on a set form of argument—on what the argument looks like. We will attempt to get away from the problems involved with the forms of argument by borrowing and adapting some of the theorizing of Professor Stephen Toulmin[1] on the importance of how parts of the language of argumentation serve individual-collective functions for receivers. This concern for function, we will find, is essential to a receiver-oriented view of argumentation as communication. In this chapter we shall first look at the traditional concern for argument as a prepared message; second. at the traditional concern for the form of the argument; and, finally, at the importance of function in the process of argumentation.

Argument as a Prepared Statement

My experience in teaching argumentation has been that most students who enroll in classes such as argumentation, reasoning, or debate do so with the expectation that they will learn to construct a good argument. As I indicated in chapter 2, it seems to me that a concern for the practice of argumentation is certainly an acceptable goal for the study of argumentation. The concern for the ability to construct an argument, however, is even more specific than the concern for practice: the construction of an argument implies a purely source-oriented or arguer-oriented goal. The concern is not for practice in *engaging* in argumentation, but rather for *initiating* it; the concern is not for *analyzing* argumentation, but rather for *creating* it. Thus, the goal of learning to construct an argument is a highly specific aspect of the study of argumentation.

I have no objection to the student's desire to put an argument together except that it is such a narrow and limited desire. The narrowness of that point of view, it seems to me, is partly the result of the human inclination to emphasize the phrase "construct an argument" in practical affairs. Attorneys who are about to represent clients in appeals to higher courts, for example, prepare their arguments. Political parties, similarly, prepare their arguments (or party platforms) prior to the initiation of major national or state elections. Moreover, you yourself may have prepared arguments for your parents when you were notified that a particular course (or term) was

---

[1]This approach to the analysis of argumentation was introduced by Professor Toulmin in his *The Uses of Argument*, 2nd ed. (Cambridge: Cambridge University Press, 1969). His approach has been adapted by numerous teachers and writers on argumentation. I owe parts of this interpretation to personal discussions with Professor Toulmin.

not going your way. Indeed, many times when we use the admonition "Prepare yourself," we mean more precisely "Prepare your arguments." In all these instances of argumentation in practical human affairs, we understand the construction of arguments as an inherently important aspect of argumentation.

One of the implications of the concern for preparing arguments is that we may tend to think of argumentation almost exclusively as a prepared document that presents reasons for the acceptance of claims. The attorney's brief, the party's platform, and your "Well, the grade was low because . . . " are all examples of how the concern for constructing an argument seems to include an emphasis upon the message or argument as a created document. Textbooks on logic, debate, and argumentation generally reflect this concern and contain extended strategies to follow, rules to abide by, or points to check as students develop their own argumentative messages—as they construct their arguments. The use of these lists, guidelines, or rules, it is assumed, will result in the construction of a suitable and effective argumentative message.

Conversely, from the perspective of the receiver, the traditional emphasis upon the construction of arguments results in a strong emphasis upon the argument (the prepared document) that we hear. If the message is prepared in light of the rules and guidelines that we have come to value, then we as receivers may be overwhelmed by the arguer. If, on the other hand, we perceive the original argument to have been prepared weakly, then we are likely to attack the arguer's position by citing those weaknesses. In debate rounds, the first negative speaker generally has the responsibility to expose the faults of the initial affirmative position, and, in informal argumentation, we may deride an arguer who has violated one of the rules of logic in which we believe. From the point of view of both arguer and receiver, there is a traditional, and a highly comfortable, concern for the worth of the argument as a prepared document. Although I will admit the relevance of this concern, the emphasis upon argumentation as a prepared message has resulted in certain less desirable emphases.

Forms of Argument

The desire to learn to construct an effective argument has led to the emphasis upon certain forms of argumentation. I think it was sixth grade (at least, it was long ago) when I was first told that there were two basic ways to argue: one was called deduction and the other induction. Though these terms were introduced to explain something called the scientific method (which I also was uncertain about), I was told the terms could be used to explain much more than the development of science. It seems that deduction was when someone argued from the general to the specific, and induction was when someone argued from the specific to the general, or something like that. The difficulty I had with grasping the idea—beyond the fact that I had no notion of general or specific—was that I could never recall which way of arguing was which.

Deductive Reasoning: The Syllogism

Later, of course, that confusion was clarified for me. I learned that the most commonly discussed (if not commonly occurring) sort of deductive argument was the syllogism. Moreover, I discovered that the reason the syllogism was so frequently used as an example was that it was so easy to see the movement of thought from general statements to specific conclusions. If we know, for example, that "All men are mortal" (a very general statement) and that "George is a man" (a very specific observation), then we also know something else about George: we know he is mortal (a conclusion). That whole process may be difficult to grasp unless you understand deductive reasoning to be modeled after geometry; indeed, there is as much concern about shapes and boundary lines in deductive logic as there is in geometrical mathematics.[2] Consider figures 1 and 2.

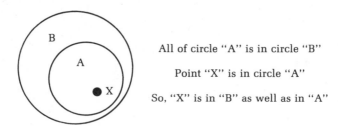

All of circle "A" is in circle "B"

Point "X" is in circle "A"

So, "X" is in "B" as well as in "A"

FIGURE 1

The classification of all *men* is completely within the boundary of the category *mortal*, which means, of course, that every man is indeed mortal. The circle of mortal, however, includes more than men since lower forms of animals are also within the group called mortals. Phrased differently, if you are a man, then you are mortal; you are within that circle. Now, since we know that George is a man, we know that he also has to be mortal; he will die like the rest of us.

---

[2]I was first made aware of the significance of the relationship between deductive logic and geometry in discussions with Professor Stephen Toulmin of the University of Chicago.

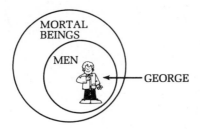

FIGURE 2

Again, phrased differently, since we know that George falls inside the circle of men, we know that he also falls within the boundaries of the category called mortal. In this instance of logic, we have moved from general statements about the mortality of all men to the conclusion that George also is mortal; to use the confusing cliché, we have moved from the general principle to the specific statement.

The concern for boundary lines, for points within those lines, and for the spatial relationships among things is a concern shared by geometry and the deductive logic which grew from it. Implied in this concern is the strict following of rules, axioms, and principles which are at the heart of geometry. Textbooks emphasizing deductive logic as a model of argument, in fact, attend seriously to the rules of (especially) the syllogism: there must be three statements, including a major premise, a minor premise, and a conclusion; there must be three and only three terms; no term may be distributed in the conclusion if it is not distributed in one of the premises, and so forth. Though we shall not go into any of these concepts in more detail, I introduce some of these various rules because of what they imply for deductive argument: that you can tell what sort of argumentation it is and how strong it is by looking at it and discovering whether it has the appropriate parts in the correct places in the right numbers; the concern, in other words, is whether it has the proper geometric form. At first, the rules may be somewhat difficult to master, but, once they are, argumentation becomes relatively easy, and the deductive form of argument becomes comfortable indeed.

Deductive Reasoning: The Enthymeme

A major departure from the syllogism that was still within the realm of deductive logic was the enthymeme, introduced by Aristotle.[3] The

---

[3]For a discussion, see Lane Cooper, trans., *The Rhetoric of Aristotle* (New York: Appleton-Century Crofts, 1960), pp. 154-81.

enthymeme is distinguishable from the syllogism in two ways: first, one of the three statements of the traditional syllogism will not be mentioned by the arguer, but instead will be supplied mentally by the audience. The audience already believes that all men are mortal, so all the arguer must do is supply the "George is a man," and "So, George is mortal.[4] The other distinguishing characteristic is that Aristotle assumed that the enthymeme would deal with probable matters, while the syllogism would continue to deal with matters of certainty (after all, man is either in the circle or he is not; probability, in syllogisms, seemed irrelevant). In the context of these differences between the syllogism and the enthymeme as representatives of deductive logic, it is clear that the enthymeme retained a concern for the *form* of argument. If one could take an enthymemic argument, put it into the form of a syllogism, and apply the rules, then argumentation could be examined easily once again.

Inductive Reasoning

In contrast to the deductive form of argument, the other way of arguing traditionally has been explained as the inductive method, or, again in terms of cliché, argument from the specific to the general. In its simplest and perhaps rarest form, inductive reasoning seeks to examine *each* specific instance of something-or-other and then to generalize about that whole group. For example, we may investigate everyone in the room who has red hair to discover the relationship between red hair and the sex of the individual. As we survey the room, we discover that three people have red hair: Jill, a girl, has red hair; Audrey, another girl, has red hair; and Jackie, a third girl, has red hair. After citing these *specific* instances of the existence of red hair among girls, we create the *generalization* that all red-haired people in the room are girls. In doing so, we have moved from the specific to the general, or, more precisely, we have created a generalized conclusion from the examination of specific instances. Seen in this light, inductive logic closely resembles, not geometry, but *arithmetic*.[5] Consider figure 3.

The fact that induction in this simplified form is so much like arithmetic enables this sort of argumentation, also, to reflect a concern for form. We ask certain questions of such arithmetic procedures: Have you examined *all three* of the cases? Is there any *one* of

[4]Either of the premises or the conclusion may be implied in the argument or assumed to be supplied by the audience.

[5]Again, I am indebted to Professor Toulmin for insight about the relationship between induction and arithmetic.

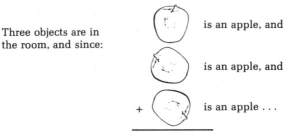

Three objects are in the room, and since:

is an apple, and

is an apple, and

+ is an apple . . .

. . . then all the objects in the room are apples.

FIGURE 3

the three who does not have red hair? Have you *counted* all the examples correctly? By following these rules about the proper form and procedure, inductive argumentation, like arithmetic, can be conducted easily and flawlessly. You can know if the argument is a good one simply by looking at it and making sure that it follows the rules of (primarily) addition.

Inductive Reasoning: The Sample

In most instances, of course, an examination of all the objects we wish to generalize about is not possible. Our concern may be for the number of monarch butterflies in a particular country or for the public's response to an action by an American president. In both situations, the actual counting and addition of all the members of the group about which we wish to know something is not possible. Our strategy, then, is likely to be to find a representative sample of either monarch butterflies or American citizens and to examine it as a way of generalizing about the whole group—even those which we have failed to analyze. The sample, of course, is just a small group of a larger whole, but all samples are not representative. If we choose to study the monarch butterflies in one acre of clover, for instance, we cannot generalize about the number found in the countless number of acres of land in the United States: the clover bed is a highly specialized acre of land, rather than an average or representative acre. Similarly, if we are interested in the public view of a presidential action involving retirement pensions, we should not merely question those people already on a retirement income: their special interest in the proposal clearly will not represent accurately what "Americans as a whole" think about the plan. On the other hand, if we can show that our sample *is* a fair and representative group from among the larger group, then we can proceed essentially with the same sort of arithmetic rules as we used when we examined the whole group: we add, we count, we see if we must subtract some from the total (find exceptions to the generalization).

Inductive Reasoning: The Example

An even more frequent variation of inductive reasoning than the use of a sample is the use of what Aristotle called the example: the use of one specific instance to illustrate a general point.[6] I already have used the example as a method of arguing the accuracy of a claim when I utilized (among other ideas) the case study of *The Proposal* in chapter 2 to illustrate varying motivations or perceptions of motivation for argumentation. If you will recall, I claimed that argumentation often can be seen as motivated by psychological needs, and I used one of the committee members' perception of Evans as an example of that sort of perception. In other contexts, we may argue that Michael is highly intelligent and base our claim upon one instance in which his intellectual ability seemed impressive; we may cite a particularly bad or ambiguous item on a test and use that one example as indicating that the test was a poor one; or, we may submit the evidence that one politician was proved to be corrupt as a first step in demonstrating that all politicians are dishonest. In all these examples of the use of examples, we use an arithmetic model to say that one (specific case) equals all (the cases). Instead of examining all the cases (as we would if the process were perfectly inductive) or a sample of the cases (as we would if we were able to find what was representative), we simply take one case and argue that all of whatever we are discussing are like our one example.

Moreover, as it was with deductive approaches to logic, all these variations of induction have led to a concern for the form of the argument. If we claim to be dealing with induction (in its pure form), we are likely to be asked whether these are, in fact, all the available cases and whether our addition of these cases is accurate and verifiable. If we have utilized a sample, we are likely to be asked whether the sample truly represents (is really like, or really looks like) the whole of the group; we probably will be asked if the numbers are sufficient and selected in the proper manner; and we may even be asked if our sample has been secured with the appropriate sampling model in mind. Finally, of course, if we use an example, we almost certainly will be queried as to how closely the example resembles a

---

[6]Other kinds of induction, such as *argument from sign* (smoke is a sign that fire exists) also rely upon the process of assuming that one instance represents a whole group of things.

representative group or the whole of the cases that are being discussed. The concern quickly will be for the similarities and differences between the example and the whole of things that it is supposed to represent. In essence, the inductive concern is for whether the arguments look as they are supposed to look; the concern is for form and composition.

Problems with Argumentative Forms

Thus, it seems to me that the traditional concern for argumentation as a constructed message has influenced the traditional approaches to inductive and deductive argumentation. Both approaches normally focus upon the forms, the rules, and the procedures of argumentation that can be taught, learned, and utilized. It seems to me, however, that such a focus tends to lead students of argumentation to two misleading beliefs: first, that the understanding and analysis of argumentation will be comfortably automatic and conducted similarly by everyone; and, secondly, that the following of the forms and rules virtually will guarantee the success of argumentation.

You will find, first, that in contrast to how comfortable automatic knowledge of argumentative forms can make you feel, you invariably will have difficulty with the application of the forms to actual argumentation. The concern for forms of argumentation seems to be especially comfortable for the student who wishes to construct an argument: you simply follow the procedures. Yet, in actual argumentative situations, you will find that it is not always easy to construct a "good" inductive argument or a "valid" deductive argument. You will find that the models or forms of argumentation must be interpreted, modified somewhat, or supplemented somehow to make them reflect the intended argument. Similarly, the analysis of other people's arguments is even more difficult: Was the argument deductive or inductive, or (as arguments frequently are) both? If it is inductive, what sort of inductive argument is it? (We have not discussed any except argument by sample or example, but there are others.) Once we know what sort of argumentation it is (if we decide), how strong is it? The discouraging aspect of these questions is that normally the answers vary among students attempting to follow a seemingly easy form for argumentation. When you begin dealing with actual argumentation, you will find that one argument tends to look like another, that real arguments are not as easy to decipher as textbook models, and that the form of argument is not the ideal path for learning about argumentation.

A second adjustment that you will have to make in thinking about the forms of argument is that, in contrast to the belief that the following of rules will guarantee argumentative success, you will find that there is not always a relationship between the successful creation of (the form of) an argument and successful argumentation. You will encounter situations in which you have followed the procedures implied in deductive argument but have been utterly unsuccessful in having a claim accepted. Conversely, you will perceive instances where arguers have abandoned the guidelines for effective inductive argument but have been successful in supporting a claim. In both circumstances, you are likely to feel the frustration of learning material that somehow does not apply to the "real world." The situations become analogous to times when you might learn the intricacies of Newtonian physics only to discover that physical phenomena are no longer explained that way; or, to times when you learn the complexities of Freudian psychology only to be confronted with the information that Freudian psychology has been largely abandoned by many practicing psychiatrists and psychotherapists. Such is the frustration when you have mastered the technicalities of the forms of argumentation only to find that the following of such procedures may be irrelevant to the ultimate fate of the argumentative claim. In the end, the mastering of argumentative forms as the easily successful and comfortable method of approaching argumentation is neither very comfortable nor very successful.

An Approach to Function in Argumentation

With the goal of overcoming these limitations inherent in the quest to "have arguments look like they are supposed to look," let me reiterate three points that I made earlier in discussing the implications of treating argumentation as a communication activity. First, instead of assuring you that argumentation can be mastered easily, I must indicate that successful argumentation is difficult. Taking cues from the contemporary communication belief that communication is apt to be frustrating, regardless of the application of easy lessons, we must give up the quest to find the easy method of argumentation and admit, instead, that argumentation is likely to be troublesome, complicated, and absolutely frustrating. We shall not find any strategies that can guarantee success, and we certainly will spend much of our argumentative activity being frustrated at our failures. Argumentation simply is not easily conducted, nor effortlessly successful. In studying practical argumentation, you will be much less certain of what you are doing than you probably would wish; you will find that the examination of argumentation will be more complicated than you had anticipated; and you will discover that the chances of success in argumentation are less than you thought; but these discoveries should not discourage you.

Related to the idea that we must accept argumentation as a difficult enterprise, however, is a second implication of approaching argumentation as communication: we will benefit more by examining how people do argue than by stressing how they should argue. Discussed earlier as the difference between *prescribing* the correct manner of argument and *describing* the manner of argument actually used, the distinction is obviously not absolute. The concern for how people should argue is legitimate, and the forms of argument can help you construct an argument and examine argumentation according to the rules and procedures. Unfortunately, however, the prescriptive emphasis may blind you to argumentation that flaunts the accepted concerns for form. Although some argumentation will reflect a stress upon the following of rules and the validity of the resultant argument, much argumentation is conducted by people who neither know about nor follow such procedures. We, therefore, must temper our emphasis upon the forms that should be followed, with the recognition that much argumentation in which we will be involved will violate those forms and prescriptions.

These two ideas implied in studying argumentation as communication—that we must accept the difficulty of argumentation, and that we ought to emphasize the ways that people do argue—introduce a third and even more important implication of studying argumentation as communication. In essence, we need to abandon much of our zeal for learning the *forms* of argument, and concentrate, instead, upon *functions* in argumentation. Instead of asking, What does the argument *look* like (and getting disturbingly different answers), we should ask: Did the statement function to answer whatever doubts the individual had, based upon his individualistic and culture-bound interpretations of the argumentation? Did it answer the challenge? Clearly, we must at times examine the apparent form of the argument, but our chief concern will be for how the symbols functioned and whether they functioned to satisfy the demands of receivers. Let me illustrate this analysis of function by describing an approach to argumentation introduced by Professor Stephen Toulmin and adapted in several ways by many of his readers.[7]

[7]The following emphasis on these terms as labels for functions in language is based, in part, on discussions with Professor Toulmin.

Terms for Argumentative Functions

This approach to argumentation utilizes six terms as labels for crucial functions that language (in various forms) can perform in argumentation: *claim, evidence,, warrant, backing, qualifier,* and *reservation.*[8] Though the rest of this chapter will be devoted to increasing your understanding of what these are, let me briefly introduce how language would function in argumentation in order for us to label it with one of these terms.

First, when language functions for us to express a statement that we wish to have accepted by a receiver, but which we find is somehow challenged, we will call that unit of language a *claim.*[9] A claim might be virtually any number of linguistic expressions, such as "You should eat more vegetables," "The President is a great leader," "Budweiser is the king of beers," or "Ohio State will beat Southern California in the Rose Bowl." Regardless of what composition of language we create or what ideas we include, if the language unit reveals a statement that we wish to have accepted but that is actually challenged, we can call the phrase a claim.

Second, when such language functions to express an idea that is already acceptable or evident to our receiver(s), we will call that language unit *evidence.* In a useful play on words, anything can function as evidence in the argumentation so long as the statement is already evident or obvious to the people we are addressing. Since it is generally recognized that Ohio State does indeed have a pair of great running backs, the expression that "Ohio State has a great running attack" would be a reasonably safe statement of evidence for the claim that OSU will defeat USC. If it were generally known that the President had just completed a successful trip to China, the idea that "The President has just completed a major trade agreement with China" could be submitted as evidence that "The President is a great leader." Again, the language can be infinitely variable, but if it serves to express an idea that is already acceptable, or evident, to the receiver, we shall call the statement evidence.

When we have engaged in argumentation to this point, however, we have only a statement that has been challenged and a statement that seems acceptable to our receiver. The question, of course, becomes, "What does the one have to do with the other?" Or, more precisely, "How does the acceptance of the evidence make the claim

---

[8]See Toulmin, *The Uses of Argument,* especially chapter 3.

[9]Since, as we shall find in chapter 6, virtually *any* statement is challengeable, we shall consider as claims those statements actually challenged. We shall return to the point in chapter 5.

more palatable?" In essence, we need some sort of language unit that functions as a bridge between the claim and the evidence; a bridge that leads us—or authorizes the move—from the evidence to the claim. When language functions in this third manner to demonstrate how our thinking moved or should move from evidence to the acceptance of the claim, we call the language unit a *warrant*. The warrant, then, shows how something that is already evident (evidence) helps make a less acceptable idea (claim) more acceptable. In the cases above, we may have a claim that Ohio State will defeat Southern California, and we may have submitted the evidence that Ohio State has a great running attack. When (or if) we are asked what the running attack has to do with our prediction of victory, we may say, "A great running game assures Rose Bowl victory." Since that statement would describe *how* we moved from the statement of evidence to a claim (because it would demonstrate the relationship between the claim and our evidence), we would refer to it as a warrant. Similarly, if we know that the President has completed the trade agreement (evidence function), we may ask whether that evidence authorizes the claim that the President is indeed a great leader; that is, we may ask about the relationship between the evidence and the claim. Our answer would function as a bridge between the evidence and the claim; it would function as a warrant to authorize the movement to accept the claim: "Presidents must be great leaders in order to negotiate major trade agreements with formerly hostile nations."

Clearly, however, we may feel that our warrant needs some support or further explication. The warrant has been a *general* statement containing a normative conclusion about the relationship between the claim and the evidence. We may be required, then, to supply *details* of that general statement: What kinds of events have been responsible for that normative relationship existing? Language that expresses this sort of support for the warrant would function as *backing*, our fourth term for how language functions in argumentation. Thus, a listing of all the Rose Bowl victories that have been based on superior running attacks would serve as backing for the warrant in the Rose Bowl prediction. In the same way, if we were to list the instances in which only superior Presidents have been able to negotiate treaties in contrast to a listing of examples where (apparently) weaker Presidents have failed, we would be supplying backing for the warrant. By doing so, we would assume that the warrant would be stronger, the movement from the evidence to the claim clearer, and thus the claim itself more acceptable.

To be reasonable, however, we must admit that no bit of evidence can guarantee the accuracy of our claim beyond all doubt. When we use language that functions to reveal how confident we are in the claim and how confident our receiver should be in the claim, we shall call that language by a fifth term, *qualifier.* The qualifier can be expressed in statistical terms, such as when we say, "The chance of rain today is 70 percent," or "The odds are two-to-one against Great Sprinter winning the fourth race." Although the statistical expression of a qualifier may lend an aura of exactness to it, the most common qualifiers are such expressions as probably, in all probability, it seems likely, it is unlikely that, or possibly. Hence, based upon the evidence, "Ohio State has a great running attack," we can claim at best that "OSU probably will defeat USC in the Rose Bowl"; we must qualify that original claim for we cannot be certain based upon limited amounts of evidence. Similarly, the evidence of a major trade agreement does not guarantee that the President is great, but perhaps only that he probably is a great President. Language that functions to qualify a claim merely reflects that, to be realistic, we probably cannot be certain of anything.

Finally, we may add a sixth term, *reservation,* when language functions to demonstrate what circumstances may make us want to retract our claim altogether. I may take note of the possibility that, although OSU has a great running attack, USC may have an even greater one. If they do, then I probably would want to abandon my claim. Reservations frequently are begun with such expressions as unless or until. Thus, I may say that "Unless USC has an even greater running attack (reservation), then OSU probably will win the Rose Bowl." Correspondingly, I may contend that "Until we find that the trade agreement is detrimental, it seems that the President is indeed a great executive." In both cases, certain language units function to reveal what doubts we might have about a claim we advance.

Graphic Views of Argumentative Functions

In essence, then, we can utilize the terms claim, evidence (often called data, as Toulmin actually does), warrant, backing (sometimes called support-for-the-warrant), qualifier, and reservation (called rebuttal by Toulmin himself) in order to describe the primary functions that language can serve in argumentation. You may see more easily the relationships among these functions by examining the following diagrams, based in large part on Toulmin's own model.[10]

---

[10]The diagrams here are based primarily upon those found in *The Uses of Argument* and upon discussions with Professor Toulmin.

Figure 4, then, is an attempt to provide you with a visual representation of the functioning of the terms. Note, as you study the model,
that the focus of the terms is on how they lead, support, or explain
one another.

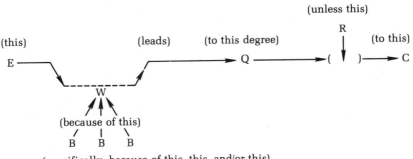

FIGURE 4

The argument now reads: this evidence, because of this warrant and
specifically because of this detailed backing, leads to this degree of
confidence in this claim unless this reservation is in effect.
Note that:
1. We are concerned, in general, about the evidence *leading* to an
    acceptance of the claim (this leads to this).
2. There is no *direct* connection between the evidence and the
    claim; the warrant supplies the connection.
3. The evidence leads to the claim with varying degrees of confi-
    dence (Q or qualifier).
4. The warrant may need further support (B or backing).
5. The reservation (R) is a situation that can enter the argumenta-
    tion as a variable that changes the effect of everything else in
    relation to the claim: the claim may be abandoned in this situa-
    tion.
Figure 5 shows how the situation becomes more complex if there
are two statements of evidence with the same warrant, and figure 6
demonstrates the situation when two statements of evidence function with different warrants to support the same claim. These two
figures are simply indicative of the way the model can be altered to
demonstrate any sort of argumentative transaction.
If we visualize the functions of argumentative language in this
way, we should always be conscious of the dynamism of the language we are using: the warrant authorizes our movement from the

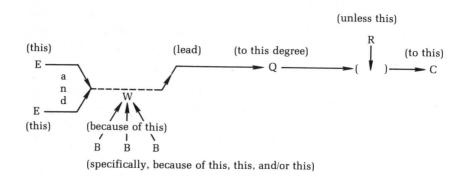

FIGURE 5

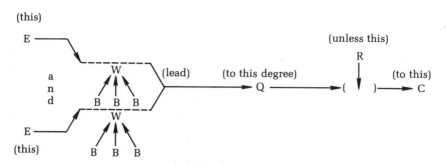

FIGURE 6

acceptance of evidence to the acceptance of the claim; the backing fills in the details of the warrant by citing the specific dimensions, facets, or elements of the general statement we call the warrant; the qualifier places our claim squarely in the realm of the realistic, by noting the complexity and uncertainty of the ideas with which we are dealing; and the reservation attempts to reveal those situations that might arise or that have arisen and might begin to affect our confidence in the claim. Language functioning in argumentation, then, can be seen as a dynamic, changeable, and complex system, rather than a series of timeless and certain propositions. Indeed, the system is such that some specific and special situations must be discussed.

First, we have assumed here that the language offered as evidence will be acceptable to the receiver, and, clearly, this is not always the case. Frequently, the evidence offered will be questioned. In such a situation, what we intended to have judged as acceptable so that it could serve as evidence begins to function as a claim itself: our intended evidence, in fact, is not acceptable. When that occurs, we may have to introduce new argumentation to settle the matter of the (questioned) evidence before we can proceed. The new claim must be supported with additional evidence of its own, and conceivably we might need a warrant authorizing the movement from the additional evidence to the new claim (originally intended as evidence). We may, for example, claim that a certain politician embezzled funds and support that claim with what we intend to have function as evidence: columnist Jack Anderson said so. To our surprise, our receiver denies that intended evidence by questioning whether Anderson really said so. Our intended evidence functions instead as a claim, and we shall have to present evidence that Anderson made such a statement. If that intended evidence is accepted, the Anderson quote can now function as evidence in the manner originally wished. In essence, a whole other argumentative process may be required if the evidence we present is challenged by the receiver.

A second interesting aspect of how the argumentation may proceed is the situation where the warrant is challenged, and when we present backing to give the specific nature of the warrant, that too is challenged. We may say, "Jones is experienced, so vote for him." As warrant and backing, we may say, "He has the experience needed: four years school board; three years city council. . . . " A receiver may examine the specifics of the backing and reply, "Well, I don't think that seven years of public service is enough." Our first reaction might be that since the warrant has been challenged, it too becomes a claim, and the backing merely serves as evidence: then the challenge might seem to be demanding a warrant to relate the backing to the warrant-turned-claim. Toulmin, however, does not agree. The question of whether seven years experience is enough is a highly general question; one involving all candidates and the general concept of experience. That is, really, an entirely new argument that takes us ever farther from the original claim. If we begin accepting all such challenges, we shall never get back to the claim: this literally can go on as long as anyone cares to keep answering. In general, then, we should answer a challenge to the warrant and backing by suggesting the discussion be held some other time and by inviting our receiver to allow us to get back to the major claim under consideration.

Though these brief descriptions may have given you some insight into how we can visualize language (in all sorts of forms) functioning in argumentation, these concepts are so important that we will need to spend more time with them. Let me, then, further illustrate our concern for the functions of language in argumentation by creating an argumentative message (the traditional idea of constructing an argument) and then analyzing it in terms of how certain parts of it function.

Case Study: Smoking and Self-Image

For a number of years, I have observed the "don't smoke" mass media messages of groups such as the American Cancer Society and the American Heart Association in the antismoking campaign, and it seems to me that the managers of these campaigns have seriously misperceived the relationship between American smokers and the motivation for smoking. Indeed, as I look at full-color magazine advertisements for cigarettes, I am struck that a product can still be sold when the ad is forced to contain words of warning that the product has been determined to be dangerous to human health. I am amazed that cigarette smokers will pay fairly large sums of money for a pack of cigarettes, when each pack clearly warns the buyer that the product may bring respiratory disease along with the pleasures of the smoke itself.

In the context of continued high cigarette sales, I fear that the problem with the smoking and health campaigns by the heart, cancer, and respiratory associations is that, although dying of cigarette-related diseases is not glorious, it is also not stigmatized. Indeed, there may be those who think smoking in the face of the dangers of disease is equivalent to laughing in the face of danger as you are about to jump ten Mack trucks with a motorcycle; neither activity, it seems, is for the squeamish. In answer to these advertised antismoking advertisements, it is socially acceptable to say, "Yeah, I know smoking is dangerous, but . . . I just like to." Or, "Well, I'll quit later when I'm not under so much pressure . . . like when I'm twenty-five." We need, then, to find a different argument against smoking—one which is more basic and less easily "handled" than health-related issues. In contrast to these arguments that give the prospect of disease and death as the predominant reasons to quit smoking, I would suggest a campaign where the claim "you should quit smoking" is supported to a greater extent by the reason that smoking is a habit that taints the social image of the smoker. Let me illustrate how I would construct this argumentative message, stressing the function of certain language rather than its form—by stressing what I would hope the language would do, rather than what it would look like.

If my medium were television, for example, I might picture an attractive young woman being approached by a desirable looking and seemingly available young man at a party. Without any dialogue being heard, I would show the young woman exhaling smoke to form a delicate wreath around her head, I would focus upon the smile they exchange, and then I would close-in on the disappointed young lady as she watches the young man, repulsed, make excuses and leave her presence. As the camera focused on her face, I would have a calm, gentle, and sophisticated voice relate: "If you are uninterested in your social life, then ignore our message. But if you are interested in the relationships you have with others, then you should know the simple fact that smoking is completely distasteful: it darkens or yellows your teeth and makes your breath stale and unpleasant. Americans spend millions of dollars for ways to improve their appearance because they know that problems like unattractive teeth and breath greatly affect the success they have relating to others. You already try to help yourself to be more socially desirable, but you can help more: you probably ought to quit smoking cigarettes."

Analysis of the Case Study

If you were to attempt to analyze my argument with an eye to the forms, you might be successful, but you also might find that one statement looks very much like another. Instead of focusing upon the forms of argumentation, then, let us review those labels for how language functions and then analyze my argument in terms of what I wanted certain of those statements *to do* for the receivers of the argument.

The Function of Claim. Phrased in terms that we discussed earlier, I included something that functions as a claim: the idea that "you ought to stop smoking cigarettes" is the disputed stand or position or proposition that I was prepared to defend. That idea could be rephrased into any number of different versions of the original, such as everyone should stop smoking, or the smoking of cigarettes ought to be stopped. Regardless of the change in the structure or form of the statement, we understand the argument to be presenting the same sort of idea. Any similar form of the argument, that is, will serve the same function; it will present the basic thrust or position of the argument.

The Function of Evidence. In presenting the basic reason for accepting the claim, I rejected the surgeon general's warning on cigarette packages and presented instead the idea that cigarette smoking makes the teeth yellow and the breath stale. This idea serves a second function in argumentation: evidence, the supporting material that the receiver takes to be evident or obvious. Instead of more traditional definitions of evidence, I like the (unfortunately punlike) view that evidence is what is taken as evident. The surgeon general's report, for example, is *supposed* to function as an obvious indication that smoking is extremely dangerous, but it simply does not. Even though the report sounds and looks like a piece of evidence, the point is that it *seems* largely impotent in making the dangers of smoking seem evident or obvious to a smoking public. Put in terms of our form-function distinction, we need something that does more than look like what evidence is supposed to look like: we need something that functions as evidence.

Based upon the earlier analysis of the self-image and danger relationship, I submit that something that *would* function as a way of deterring smokers would be the evidence that smoking causes yellow teeth and stale breath. The notion that smoking causes these two (socially unacceptable) states looks virtually the same as "smoking causes lung disease and heart ailments," but our concern for function in argumentation must always include a regard for the receivers of our argumentation. Not all those receivers (the smokers of cigarettes), in general, have concluded that the health threat to them is so evident that they should quit smoking. Smoking in the face of danger, in fact, may be perceived as an actual enhancement of self-image. Smoking may still be grown-up, cool, where it's at, or otherwise acceptable; in contrast, yellow teeth and stale breath, to a nation that spends millions of dollars for dental care, breath mints, mouthwashes, and toothpaste, might seem more evident and much less socially acceptable. If so, the phrase "smoking causes yellow teeth and stale breath" may have the same form as "smoking causes health dangers," but this new strategy might function much differently—and much better— as evidence, our second crucial term in the process of argumentation.

The Function of Warrant. A third essential function in the process of argumentation, you will recall, is that which is performed by the warrant: some stated or unstated idea which authorizes the movement to the claim from the evidence. Reviewing my antismoking argument, we now have the notion that "you ought to quit smoking cigarettes" (the claim) and the belief that "smoking yellows the teeth and makes the breath stale" (the evidence). What is at times necessary is to answer the question, "What does the evidence have to do with the claim?" or "How are the claim and evidence related?" Translated to our example, the question becomes, "Okay, given that smoking causes yellow teeth and stale breath, why should that make me want to quit smoking?" The answer that functions as a warrant would be something like "stale breath and yellow teeth are highly undesirable in a society concerned about cosmetic freshness and should be avoided." Phrased altogether, our argument now is "Since smoking causes yellow teeth and stale breath (evidence), and since these things are socially stigmatizing and undesirable (warrant), then it seems that you really ought to quit smoking (claim)."

We do not need to be concerned about what a warrant looks like. Indeed, any phrase that shows how the evidence relates to the claim being advanced should be considered a warrant: just as a legal warrant allows the search of a home or a person, an argumentative warrant permits the evidence to function in support of the claim. Often the warrant will be expressed as a written or spoken phrase showing why the evidence relates to the claim. On the other hand, often the connecting bridge between evidence and claim will be unspoken or unwritten and assumed to be already understood by the receiver. In the case of the antismoking argument I created, the idea that functioned as a warrant was the "stale breath and yellow teeth are socially unacceptable" (or some approximation of that idea), yet that phrase would not have to appear in the text of any argument I would construct; I could assume that it is already known and believed by my American receivers. To a less odor-conscious receiver, I might have had to supply this phrase that functioned as a warrant; the function of a warrant here could have been performed by beliefs acknowledged by the American audience. Again, our concern with constructing an argumentative message is for the function, not the form, of parts of the argumentation.

The Function of Backing.   If I, as the creator of argumentation, had felt that the receivers for my message were generally naive, then I might not have sensed the need to include any other argumentative elements in my message. On the other hand, since my concern was for all those people who smoke, I assumed that at least some of them would be highly discriminating in their consideration of argumentative claims. I felt the need, for example, for something that functioned to support or confirm the warrant; my concern was for backing, the fourth functional aspect of this view of argumentation. Some smokers, even those who may agree that yellow teeth and stale breath are socially unacceptable, may still believe that the image of aloofness, independence, or sophistication offsets the other social drawbacks. For the benefit of those individuals, I introduced some backing for my warrant that yellow teeth and stale breath are undesirable. I might have chosen to cite the comment of a voluptuous young girl who recently said that she would much rather date a "mousy" fellow who has fresh breath and white teeth, than date a ruggedly handsome guy with less attractive teeth and breath. I would predict, if my backing for the warrant were believed, that the rugged guy might reconsider his condition as he left his room for an evening out. In contrast, what I chose to function as backing for the warrant was that virtually millions of American dollars are spent for teeth whiteners and capping of unsightly teeth, mouthwashes, and breath mints; thus, the warrant obviously should be believed—not rationalized away. My goal with either choice of backing would have been to find something (whatever its form) that would serve the function of supporting or backing my warrant. My discovery of something that would perform that function, in turn, would allow my warrant to function as a bridge to indicate how my evidence supported the claim. In short, my discovery of effective backing would put me well on my way to creating a potential antismoking argument.

The Function of Qualifier. Since I knew my receivers might be discriminating evaluators of argumentation, however, I sensed the need for something that admitted that I was not absolutely certain that they should stop smoking. Any evidence, even that smoking causes yellow teeth and stale breath, will not prove my point beyond the shadow of a doubt. Instead, evidence simply provides us with varying degrees of certainty that lie somewhere between the absolutely not true and the absolutely certain. In other words, I may feel a need to supply what we called earlier a qualifier, a fifth term that will demonstrate the degree of confidence that I have in my claim. Phrases such as probably, possibly, in all probability, almost sure, and near certainty are expressions showing that we are not absolutely certain of what it is we are claiming. Though we frequently will omit any such expression, we probably should be prepared to add that qualification if someone confronts us. When someone asks, "Hey, how sure are you that I really ought to quit?" we are likely to say, "I'm *almost positive* that you should, based upon the available evidence." Clearly, we may feel so strongly that what we claim *is* the case is true that we hesitate to qualify our claim at all, yet even this belief is the product of fallible human perception, observation, and reasoning; consequently, we really must be prepared to consider our claim as likely and contingent, rather than absolute and certain. If we do so, we will find the numerous instances where we ought to provide some expression that qualifies the claim we advance. That qualifier may exist as a "maybe," an "I'm not certain, but . . . ," an "in all likelihood," a "probably," or any number of other forms.[11] Regardless of the form such qualifiers take, they will function to express or relate the degree of confidence that the arguer says can be placed in the claim.

The Function of Reservations. Related to the concern that I felt to qualify my antismoking argument was a need I sensed to indicate the instances in which my claim might not be acceptable. Language structures that function to show circumstances in which I might retract my claim can be termed reservations, a sixth and final basic concept in the analysis of argumentative functions. I prefer the term reservation (rather than rebuttal as it is also called) because of its commonsense relationship to the idea of having doubts about something. If we are asked to comment upon something, we may say, "Well, I have some reservations about it, but I think that. . . . " What that sort of communication reveals is that we are prepared to make some sort of claim, but we realize that situations or events may arise that will prompt us to retract our claim or to claim something counter to our original claim. In my creation of the antismoking argument, I began by saying essentially that "Unless you are a social nonconformist, you probably ought to quit smoking since smoking yellows the teeth and makes the breath stale and unpleasant." My reservation (unless you are uninterested in your social life) demonstrates that I recognize that certain circumstances will make my claim inoperative. If, that is, you are unconcerned about social advantages and stigmas, then you probably will be unimpressed with my argumentation. I might even go so far as to believe that, if you are totally committed to flaunting social pressures and expectations, you may find yellow teeth and stale breath to be rewarding. If I found that to be so, I would alter the nature of my claim or say that it was irrelevant to you personally.

Just as the qualifier is not always an aspect of argumentation that is included in the original argument, the reservation may be something we express only if we fear someone may respond, "But does your

---

[11] In addition to such standard language forms for qualifiers, again it is also the case that qualifiers can be expressed in percentage terms. Hence, the local office of a weather service may report that "There is a 20 percent chance of showers," meaning that they are only 20 percent confident of the claim that it will rain. Conversely, of course, they would be saying that they are 80 percent confident that it will not rain. In other situations, probability theory may be used to express the chances of an event occurring, or geneticists may use a similar method in calculating the degree of confidence of any particular characteristic occurring in a litter of kittens. Both probability and genetic theory present a qualifier in statistical rather than verbal terms.

claim apply to all situations?" In such cases, we will indicate any reservations we have at the outset of the argumentation. The advantage of the early inclusion of the reservation is, of course, that we make allowances for events or situations which we do not foresee or cannot predict. Careful politicians, for example, will contend that "As of now (meaning events could change), I think that. . . . "; parents will promise to take their children to the zoo unless . . . ; and professors will commit themselves to reading and returning class papers, "Providing that. . . . " In all those instances, the argumentative claim is not weakened; rather, the arguer is perceptive enough to realize that his argument may have to be abandoned or altered as the immediate situation evolves into a different set of circumstances. Regardless of the manner in which arguers phrase their acknowledgement that things may change, the phrase can be considered the reservation of the argument.

In sum, then, I constructed my antismoking argument by acknowledging certain basic functions that needed to be performed by my constructed message. I included, of course, my claim that you should quit cigarette smoking, and I submitted the (image-related and health-unrelated) evidence that smoking yellows the teeth and makes the breath stale. Further, I submitted that my claim was not one that I was willing to defend as being certainly true or absolute; instead, I explained that my claim seems *probably* the best alternative for most people, *unless* individuals were prepared to flaunt the social consequences of unattractive teeth and breath. Having presented language that acts (I hope) as qualifier and reservation, I presented backing for my warrant (that something that taints the teeth and breath is something to be avoided) by alluding to the millions of dollars spent annually by Americans on products to clean their breath and teeth. My hope was that the backing would be perceived as supporting my warrant; that the warrant would be deemed effective in showing how the evidence bears upon the claim; that the evidence would be seen as evident; and that my reservation and qualifier would be accepted as honest and reasonable statements reflecting my degree of certainty and the situations that might make my claim no longer something I would defend. If, in fact, all these aspects of my message *functioned for the receiver* in the manner in which I planned, then my argument had every chance of being successful, and the claim had every chance of being accepted. Again, my concern throughout has been with the function that certain phrases might have performed rather than with the form of the phrases (what they have looked like or what they have contained).

Exercises in the Functions of Language in Argumentation

Since the six terms that I have discussed will be such crucial concepts to the rest of the book, let us leave the example of the antismoking argument and discuss several other argumentative positions in terms of how certain aspects of the argument may be said to function for the receiver. We shall discuss two of these argumentative case studies in detail, we shall discuss one case in somewhat less detail, and we shall leave two cases for you to analyze individually or in class. Consider the following arguments.

Example One

(A portion of a legislator's remarks in introducing a bill for consideration by the state legislature)

"and so, ladies and gentlemen, I submit to you that we all-too-frequently have situations where incumbent candidates for office refuse to debate their opponents, even though debate, as Jefferson suggested, is essential to the better conduct of elections. Right now, and until we get officials of higher integrity and courage—by that I mean people who *will* risk debate—it seems to me that perhaps we ought to pass legislation that requires candidates to debate their opponents in order to run for reelection. All of the more progressive state legislatures are considering such legislation. . . . "

In analyzing such argumentation, I urge a basic approach that will be followed throughout the book: first, find the major claim being advanced; then, seek the major ideas (evidence) supporting the claim; then, find the connecting ideas between the claim and the evidence (warrants); and, finally, try to discover the language functioning as backing, reservations, and qualifiers which may be present. The most fundamental and frequent mistake that students make, I think, is to examine each phrase as it occurs, hoping that real argumentation will be expressed in an appropriate sequence. As we shall see, such is not the case.

Our first task, thus, is to find the language functioning as the major claim. As you examine the argument, you will find that much of it looks like much of the rest of the argument. Seldom is the desire to discover the form of the claim going to lead you to the claim. Think, instead, "What is the main position or point that the arguer wants to defend?" I predict that you will agree with me that the major claim is that "we ought to pass legislation that requires candidates to debate their opponents in order to run for reelection." Everything else in the argument really supports that point in some way; and, from an opposite point of view, the claim does not support anything else. That is the key, it seems to me, in finding the claim: it will be supported by all the other relevant material, but it will not, by itself, support anything else.

In our quest to find the evidence that supports the claim, you probably will agree that "we all-too-frequently have situations where incumbent candidates for office refuse to debate their opponents" functions as evidence; it attempts to support an unacceptable idea by being something that is evident or obvious to the receivers. Phrased as a question-answer formula, you ask, "Why should we have the legislation?" and you should answer, "Because at times there is no debate between incumbents and challengers." This answer is phrased in the argument as the most basic reason to accept the claim; it attempts to support the claim by being something already acceptable.

Instead of agreeing that the evidence automatically makes the claim obviously acceptable, you may ask, "Well, what does the evidence have to do with the claim; how does it really relate?" The answer to that question will require the discovery of a warrant, and here, it seems to me, the warrant is clear. The evidence (no debate now) relates to the claim (we need legislation) because "debate is essential to the better conduct of elections" (warrant). That idea of the crucial role of debate in good elections, then, provides the bridge between the claim and answers the reasonable question, "Does the evidence really make the claim evident?" The answer: "Sure, we don't have debate, and since we need it, we ought to make it occur by legislation."

Parts of the rest of the argumentation function significantly also. The legislator realizes, for example, that the claim is not obviously certain. She does not contend that the legislation simply must be passed; instead, she qualifies her claim by suggesting that legislation perhaps ought to be adopted. The qualifier does not weaken her argumentative position; instead, it implies that the legislator knows that she deals with less-than-absolute ideas. Similarly, her argumentation reveals certain reservations that she has about the claim. She is aware that circumstances could change, but she says that "right now, and until we get officials of higher integrity and courage" the claim should be adopted. Finally, of course, she cites Jefferson's comment. How does that function? I think you will find that it supports the warrant by saying why we might want to believe that debate is essential to better elections; we should believe that warrant because the highly respected Jefferson said so.

In sum, we can see the argumentation in better light now as communication in which certain language elements function in certain ways (hopefully) for the receivers of the message. Oh, and what about the idea that all the more progressive state legislatures were considering such action? I think that you can consider that as another piece of evidence functioning to support the same claim. Moreover, though no warrant is expressed for this idea, you simply have to ask what sort of notion would show the relationship between the claim and the warrant: the unstated warrant probably would be something like, "We should do what other progressive state legislatures have done," or "What is good for other progressive state legislatures is good for us." That last argumentative appeal is a statement that is wholly consistent with the rest of the argumentative strategy.

Example Two

(A discussion between two friends)

GAIL: Hey, I'm getting ready to register for classes. What do you think about Crable's class in argumentation and reasoning?

JOHN: Whatever you do, don't take it. I wish I hadn't taken it.

GAIL: That bad, huh?

JOHN: Well, if you want to work your tail off, go ahead and take it.

Clearly, we can understand this brief exchange as a hypothetical (and, of course, somewhat exaggerated) critique of a particular class and instructor, but we can understand it better in terms of interpersonal argumentation between friends. Again, we ask, what is the major point that John is trying to make? What is it that he is prepared to defend? The answer, I think, is the idea that Gail should not register for a class. As evidence, John cites his own unfortunate experience in the course, summarized aptly by the testimony "I wish I hadn't taken it." What Gail might have asked, but failed to do so, was "What does that evidence (your experience and perception) have to do with my avoiding the course?" John might have thought that a strange question, since he assumed (as the unstated warrant) that whatever he disliked is something that no one else should take. We may assume that Gail believed that warrant to be acceptable, or she might have asked for the warrant to be stated explicitly. Her acceptance of the warrant obviously precluded her need to have backing for the warrant: Why is it that whatever John disliked should be avoided by others? Gail, of course, did not seek either the warrant or backing for the warrant, but she did ask a question that prompted John to add a reservation. Under what circumstances *should* someone register for the course? Only if he wanted to "work his tail off." But she did not have to ask about the qualification of the claim; even with the reservation, John claimed that "Whatever you do . . . " the course should not be selected: no qualification was made.

Example Three

(An intrapersonal decision)

"I wonder if I ought to go to the game this weekend? No, I guess not. Wait, I really should attend anything that Julie does, so that I have the chance to see and talk to her more. I wonder if she'll go? I forgot! She told me that she was going. Well, maybe I shouldn't keep appearing where she is—maybe she'll start thinking that I plan to always be there. Well, I guess I do plan like that; besides, if she thinks I'm concerned about being where she is, maybe she'll be flattered and like me more. I guess, all in all, I probably ought to go."

In this instance, a student is arguing the merits of a particular course of action. What is the major claim? What is the evidence he remembers? What does he believe is the idea that relates the evidence to the claim or serves as the principle of behavior in which he believes? The idea that "maybe she'll be flattered" functions, it seems to me, as backing. Do you agree? Are there phrases that express any reservations? How qualified is the claim?

Example Four

(An extended comment at a social gathering)

"You think that it will snow, huh? Well, I think that if the weather bureau says that it's going to snow, you can put your snow shovels away. In all the months I've lived in Des Moines, they have hardly ever been accurate. Going to snow? I don't think so: they have predicted snow for tonight and that's all I need to know. Ten-to-one, it won't snow tonight, unless they've hired new predictors."

What is the major claim that the arguer is advancing? What does he cite as support or evidence? Be careful, because what you label evidence might be the backing for the warrant that he uses to bridge the gap between the claim and the evidence. Is the argument qualified? What is the reservation that the arguer cites as the only way in which he will retract his claim?

Example Five

(An interpersonal argument)

RALPH:　　I can't decide if I want to go to law school or graduate school. Maybe I shouldn't . . . I just don't know.

SCOTT: I don't think that's a hard decision. I think that you probably ought to go to law school; after all, lawyers normally make more money than Ph.D.'s.

RALPH: They do, huh?

SCOTT: Yeah, and, let's face it, although money shouldn't be the only thing in life, it helps.

RALPH: I guess so.

SCOTT: If you marry a rich girl, I guess it doesn't matter, but otherwise, I'd suggest law school.

RALPH: Do you think that money is that important?

SCOTT: Listen, my father is always saying, "Son, be whatever you want to be, but you ought to make enough money to get along better than I have all these years."

RALPH: I guess he's right.

Analyze the argument, keeping in mind that since much of the argumentation will look much like all the rest of the communication, you will need to assess argumentative function instead of form. Focus upon the claim first, and then how all else functions to provide reasoning for the claim.

Summary

Having examined various arguments in detail, we are now in a position to review the chapter as a whole. We began, you will recall, by discussing the tendency to think of argumentation, not as a process, but as a prepared document. That concern for the creation of a prepared document explains the desire for certain traditional forms of argument, including the syllogism, the enthymeme, the pure form of induction, and the example. Although any of these can be utilized effectively in creating and analyzing argumentation, I suggested that a more fruitful method of approaching argumentation was to concentrate upon the function and not the form of argumentative language. This departure allows us to analyze argumentation even though evidence *looks* very much like claims, and major premises (if you call them that) *look* very much like other premises and even conclusions. Using the terms claim, warrant, evidence, reservation, backing, and qualifier, I then created an antismoking argument, showing how different parts of my argument were meant to function in various ways for the receiver. We then examined various other arguments, focusing in various ways upon the function for the receiver. We then examined various other arguments, focusing upon the function of the expressions. From examples where we discussed the functioning of argumentation in great detail, we progressed to where the student was primarily responsible for the analysis. With some understanding of the importance of the function of argumentation, we now are prepared to study, in the next chapter, how this concern for function is crucial when we study argumentation as a process.

Programmed Questions

To test your understanding of the material presented in this chapter, you may wish to answer the following questions. In the multiple-choice questions, the answers may be all correct, all incorrect, or several may be correct. The suggested answers to the questions appear on the last page of this chapter. If you fail to answer the questions correctly, you may wish to review the material to increase your understanding and/or to discuss the items in class.

1. Studying argumentation as a prepared document is:
    a. always unjustifiable
    b. indicative of a concern for initiating or creating argumentation
    c. related to the emphasis upon the form of the argument
    d. too narrow, if our concern is for argumentation as a kind of communication activity
    e. extremely important in certain situations

2. The concern for the deductive and inductive form of argumentation is:
    a. related, respectively, to the models of geometry and arithmetic
    b. indicative of a concern for rule-following behavior
    c. indicative of a quest for certainty
    d. related, respectively, to Aristotle's concern for the enthymeme and the example

3. A major problem in studying argumentation from the standpoint of forms is that:
    a. the forms, generally, are extremely difficult to master
    b. difficulty often arises from the attempt to put actual argumentation into these forms or molds
    c. not everyone knows the appropriate rules for following the forms
    d. following the rules and forms may have little effect on successful argumentation

Match the terms in the left-hand column with the description of how language functions in the right-hand column.

4. _____ evidence   a. language that serves to disclose how confident we are of the claim

5. _____ claim

    b.   language that serves to state the idea that we wish to have accepted, but which has been challenged

6. _____ warrant

    c.   language that serves to give the details of the warrant

7. _____ backing

    d.   language that states the conditions or situations under which we could no longer defend a claim

8. _____ reservation

    e.   language that tells why the movement to the claim is justified

9. _____ qualifier

    f.   language that serves to express an idea that is already acceptable to the receiver

10. In order for something to function as a claim, it must:
    a. look like a claim
    b. begin with "I claim that. . . . "
    c. be presently unacceptable to the receiver
    d. only be potentially challengeable

11. In order for something to function as evidence, it must:
    a. be presently acceptable to the receiver
    b. look like evidence
    c. be truthful
    d. be either testimony or a statistical finding

Consider the following argumentative message and answer questions 12 through 17. Match the phrase at the right with the term that describes its function.

"Unless the present economic situation changes, there is no doubt but that we should begin government price-controls. Prices are soaring to unprecedented levels—levels that clearly indicate the need for immediate control: the price of sugar demonstrates the need for control; the price of gasoline demonstrates the need for control; the cost of food supports the need for controls. . . . "

"Wait a minute, friend, I don't agree. . . . "

12. _____ claim

    a.   there is no doubt but that

13. _____ evidence

    b.   unless the present economic situation changes

14. _____ warrant

    c.   prices are soaring to unprecedented levels

15. _____ backing

    d.   levels that clearly indicate the need for immediate control

16. _____ reservation

    e.   the price of sugar demonstrates the need for control; the price of . . .

17. _____ qualifier

    f.   we should begin government price-controls

Discussion Questions for Appendix Case Studies

To test your understanding of the material in this chapter, you may wish to answer the following questions that refer to the case studies in the Appendix of this book. You may wish to (a) work on the questions individually; (b) work on the questions in pairs or in groups in or before class; (c) develop written answers to the questions; (d) have class discussion based upon the questions; (e) prepare an extended paper on several related questions; or (f) develop a major paper about one case study (using the questions related to it that appear in various chapters).

1. Study "Address to the Catholic Lawyers' Guild" by Senator Clark beginning on page 259. Senator Clark knew certain things about the specific audience he was addressing. How might this knowledge of his audience have allowed him to choose certain kinds of things as appropriate claims? As acceptable evidence? The Senator clearly was in a one-to-many argumentative situation. If he had been able to have more direct contact with his audience, might he have had an even better idea of how his language was functioning? Why? How might that have affected his message?

2. Study "You Find Good Assets in Des Moines and Iowa" by John R. Fitzgibbon beginning on page 256. What is Mr. Fitzgibbon's major *claim*? What sorts of factors does he offer as *evidence*? How does he use the unparalleled success of the bank as *evidence* to support his claim?

3. Study "Letter-to-the-Editor" beginning on page 254. What was the major *claim* that Elbarc was advancing? What were the three major "reasons" or supports for his claim? If Elbarc had had a more specific audience than newspaper readers, would he have been able to make his argumentation more detailed and adapted to his audience? The "dots" indicate that the editor "cut" certain parts of the letter out. What influence might such cuts make on the specificity of the argumentation?

4. Study "Satisfaction (Almost) Assured" beginning on page 258. John Deal indicates that when he bought his first sweeper, the store claimed that it was the most powerful one available. How has that *claim* been altered now that Deal has had a problem with his sweeper? What do you think of the evidence that the manager gives Deal about why this second sweeper is more powerful? The manager claimed that both sweepers are good ones— what *same* bit of evidence does he give to support his claim? Do you think that Deal will find such evidence really evident based upon his experience? Why or why not?

5. Study "How Free is Free Will?" beginning on page 254. Ellen now looks at the Skinnerian perspective on free will as a claim to be evaluated. If she decides to accept that claim and integrate it into her personal beliefs, how might the statement function for her later in regard to some other claim?

Research Project for Advanced Students

Toulmin's six-term "model" of argumentation has sometimes been labeled merely a "syllogism on its side." Research the nature of the syllogism and Toulmin's critique of the syllogism to discover the distinctions that do exist between the two approaches. I suggest you begin with Toulmin's discussion in *The Uses of Argument*, 2nd ed. (Cambridge: Cambridge University Press, 1969), especially chapter 3.

SELECTED REFERENCES

Beardsley, Monroe C. *Thinking Straight.* 3rd ed. Englewood Cliffs, N.J.: Prentice-Hall, 1966.

Ehninger, Douglas. *Influence, Belief, and Argument.* Glenview, Ill.: Scott Foresman, 1974.

Ehninger, Douglas, and Brockriede, Wayne. *Decision by Debate.* New York: Dodd, Mead and Co., 1963.

Freeley, Austin J. *Argumentation and Debate.* 3rd ed. Belmont, Calif.: Wadsworth Publishing Co., 1971.

Smith, Craig R., and Hunsaker, David. *The Bases of Argument: Ideas in Conflict.* Indianapolis, Ind.: Bobbs-Merrill Co., 1972.

Toulmin, Stephen. *The Uses of Argument.* 2nd ed. Cambridge: Cambridge University Press, 1969.

Answers to Programmed Questions

1. b, c, d, e   2. a, b, c, d   3. b, c, d   4. f   5. b   6. e
7. c   8. d   9. a   10. c   11. a   12. f   13. c
14. d   15. e   16. b   17. a

4

The Process of Argumentation

My *general objective* in this chapter is to describe the important aspects of argumentation conceived as a kind of communication process.

My *specific objectives* are

to describe a basic model of argumentation that is fashioned after a basic communication model

to explain argumentation as a part of an entire system of human communication

to explain the specific aspects of a detailed model of the argumentative process

to discuss the relationships between argumentative choices and argumentative functions

In chapter 3, we dealt with three basic topics. We looked first at the traditional and common desire that students have to put an argument together or to construct an argument. I contended that, although the desire was common and highly appropriate for certain occasions, it was a narrow goal indeed; the desire to learn to construct an argument is usually source-oriented and aimed specifically at the ability to initiate an argument, rather than at the abilities to initiate and to analyze argumentation. Moreover, I claimed that one of the unfortunate results of the desire to put an argument together was the reliance upon certain forms of argumentation. An analysis of various traditional forms of argument, then, became the second topic of the preceding chapter. The final emphasis in the chapter was an introduction into how you as a student might better understand argumentation by thinking of the functions, rather than the forms, of argumentative language.

Initially in this chapter, we shall return to the first topic of chapter 3: the desire to put an argument together. Although I disclosed some of my reservations about that desire, our later discussion of the functions of argumentation still assumed that our chief concern in the study of argumentation should be the construction of arguments. In fact, I constructed an argument to illustrate argumentative functions. Now, however, we need to reexamine that concern. My basic point in this chapter will be that armed as we are with an awareness of how language can function in argumentation, we should emphasize these functions as they relate to the process of argumentation, rather than to argument as a constructed message.

To begin our understanding of the importance of argumentation conceived as a process rather than a constructed message, we need only recall the argumentative situations in chapter 2 in which our hypothetical friend Helen Wilson found herself. Recall that the issue of rape-murder prompted her to engage in argumentation that we considered intrapersonal, interpersonal, small group, platform, and mass (media) argumentation. Helen was interested in the prior construction of the argument in only two of those situations: the platform presentation (to the pre-law organization) and the mass media message (to the newspaper editor). In those situations, Helen responded to the need to provide some sort of fairly formalized and prepared argument, even though she had little time to devote to either of those arguments. In contrast, she failed to present a constructed message for her intrapersonal decision about the whistle, her interpersonal argumentation with Tom about the merits of the network movie, or her defense of the class research project in the small group setting. Moreover, Helen was entirely justified in approaching those three situations as settings in which prepared argument (argument as a prepared document) was generally irrelevant.

Helen responded (admittedly unconsciously) to the idea that most human argumentation will involve our skill, not as the creators of an argumentative message, but as the participants in the process of argumentation. Just as it is fair to conclude that most of your communication activity is informal and unstructured, it is also fair to claim that most of your argumentative activity will be likewise. Most of your need to engage in argumentation will emerge as you sit informally with friends at lunch, as you walk to class with an acquaintance, as you weigh the merits of certain alternatives you are faced with, or in some similar intrapersonal, interpersonal, or small group setting. Thus, although in some situations it is important for you to know something about the construction of an argument or the evaluation of someone else's constructed argument, those situations, in comparison, will be rare. Consequently, while you will benefit (as discussed in the previous chapter) from your focus upon the function rather than the form of constructed arguments, you will benefit even more from understanding how those argumentative functions relate to argumentation that develops and progresses without anyone ever constructing an argument beforehand. To aid your understanding of argumentation conceived as a developing and progressing process, this chapter will focus, first, upon a basic model of argumentation viewed as a communication activity; second, we shall discuss this activity as argumentation in an entire system of communication; third, we shall explore a more detailed model of argumentation; and, finally, we shall focus upon the relationship between argumentative choices and argumentative functions. Such investigations should result in a clear grasp of the process of argumentation.

A Basic Model of Argumentation

Let us, then, look first at how we might conceive argumentation as a process that is much like any other type of communication process. We can assume, first, that someone that we shall call an *arguer* initiates the argumentation. In oral situations, we might call that person a speaker or a communicator; in written situations, we might call the person an author, a writer, a commentator, or any one of a variety of titles. The point is that regardless of the commonsense labels attached to such a person in various situations, we can think of the person as an *arguer* when the message involved specifically advances claims and reasons for claims.

Secondly, a communication perspective on argumentation requires that the arguer present his claims and reasons to someone. Certainly, it is possible for someone to advance a claim on paper and then to destroy the document; it is possible to present a claim in the middle of a forest where no other human being is present and where we do not listen or heed our own message. The problem is that neither of those possible (but unlikely) situations creates any opportunity for the re-creation of a corresponding meaning in anyone. Hence, I would exclude those possibilities from the realm of communication, and I would refrain from calling them argumentative situations where the goal is the re-creation of meaning aimed at the presentation and advancement of claims and reasons. Based upon those judgments, I conclude that the second crucial element in the process of argumentation is the *receiver,* someone who will receive, interpret, and examine the argumentation of the arguer.

The *argumentative message* itself, obviously, is a third basic aspect of the argumentation process. The communication initiated by the arguer includes symbols that are meant to function as either evidence, warrant, claim, reservation, qualifier, or backing. In contrast to our earlier discussion about constructing arguments, not all of these language functions need be performed in the same initial communication. Most argumentation will involve somewhat extended transaction between arguer and receiver, and thus some of the argumentative message will be communicated after the initial contact and as the argumentation develops and evolves. Indeed, the initiation of the argumentative message may include only language that functions (for example) to express the claim; all else in the argument may depend upon the response that the receiver has to the initial message.

This response that the arguer expects from the receiver, which we shall call *feedback,* is a fourth elementary aspect of the process of argumentation. Though the concept of feedback seems originally to have been borrowed from the study of electrical and electronic systems, the term is now widely and popularly used in the way it is meant here: the verbal or nonverbal response that a receiver has to the message of the communicator or arguer. We shall note the variety of feedback responses later in the chapter, but for now it is important for you to understand that in the argumentation that develops and evolves informally and in unstructured situations, the message of the arguer and the feedback response (also a message) will become *continuing* stimuli for the participants. A claim may be advanced that will elicit some sort of response; that response (feedback) will prompt the arguer to (let us say) present evidence that, again, stimulates feedback from the receiver; the feedback from the evidence, then, may motivate the arguer to advance a warrant; and so argumentation continues as a dynamic and ongoing transactional process of messages and feedback between or among the participants.

Neither the argumentative message nor the feedback response, however, can be communicated to the other participant without some sort of *channel*, a fifth concept that describes how the transmission of the communication is possible. Just as a river channel allows the flow of water from source to mouth, a communication channel permits the flow of messages from arguer to receiver and from receiver to arguer. If you are engaged in face-to-face oral argumentation, then the space between you and the other person would be considered the channel: without the air molecules between you in that space, no argumentation or other communication would be possible. If, on the other hand, your argumentation is conducted by mail in ongoing correspondence, then both your stationery and the postal service would represent the channels for the argumentation: both, though in different ways, allow the messages to flow. Finally, if your argumentation is conducted by telephone, then the space between you and the telephone (as well as the whole telephone system) would fit appropriately under the heading of channels. Frequently the argumentative message and the feedback, in contrast to these examples, will utilize different sorts of communication channels. You may hear a certain claim being made by your minister, and you may decide to respond to it by letter; you may be offered something by a friend that functions as evidence for you, and you may wait to respond to it by telephone later in the evening; or you may read a statement in your school newspaper and respond to the claim in person when you see the author of the article. Whatever facility allows the flow of argumentative messages or feedback, then, can be conveniently called the channel for the argumentation.

Thus far, we can envision the process of argumentation, most basically, as an ongoing activity where argumentative messages and feedback flow through channels between transacting arguers and receivers. It seems to me that what must be added to this basic model is an understanding of a sixth element: the *conceptual screens* of the participants in the process. Though basic conceptions of a process, by their nature, oversimplify the process under investigation, our purpose here would be hindered if you failed to realize from the start that participants in the argumentation process were people with highly complicated and potentially vastly different feelings, attitudes, experiences, values, biases, and levels of knowledge. Any of these factors can screen a received message and affect how the participants conceptualize what it is they are arguing about. Receivers do not simply listen to an arguer and respond solely on the basis of that argumentative message, nor do arguers advance arguments that just occur to them. Although I am not prepared to adopt the belief that all human action is conditioned,[1] I think it is helpful to note that what we argue about, how we argue about it, and when we are satisfied with argumentation will be influenced significantly by past and present factors that screen (let in, keep out, or distort) ideas. Such conceptual screens would include the influence of religion, the direction of our education, our political biases, our value systems, our intellectual ability, and numerous other influences.[2] We, then, need to think of arguers and receivers, not in terms of "symbols on a model" or "people, just people," but rather as highly varied and complicated individuals transacting in a complex situation on the basis of multi-faceted conceptual screens.

Perhaps even more significant to our study of argumentation, we need to perceive that the products or results of the conceptual screens of arguers and receivers will overlap in some areas. In the (impossible) situation that the participants would share identical (screened) experiences, beliefs, and values, no argumentation would be necessary: there would be nothing about which to disagree. On the other hand, if the participants shared no (screened) commonality in such areas (an equally impossible-sounding situation), no argumentation would be possible: there would be nothing with which to communicate, understand or argue.[3] In contrast to these implausible situations of complete similarity or dissimilarity, the probable situation in argumentation is for the participants to share certain experiences or beliefs that allow significant (but not complete) similarity in what is screened. This overlap of conceptual environments allows some communication and argument to occur and guarantees at least potential disagreement.

With the addition of the concern for the kinds of conceptual screens that influence participants in argumentation, we have completed a survey of what seem to me to be the basic elements in the process of argumentation. The arguer and the receiver, affected by their respective conceptual screens, transact with argumentative messages and feedback through a variety of communication channels in a continuing, developing, and evolving process that we can

[1] I, of course, refer to the philosophical and theoretical thinking usually identified with B.F. Skinner.

[2] Indeed, a discussion of the whole range of these potentially important experiences—and an analysis of their possible effects—would require explanation beyond the scope of this book. These are merely examples.

[3] Theorist Kenneth Burke, for example, is noted for his development of the important construct "identification" where we "commune" with others to the extent that we can point out those areas of overlap. Without such overlap, he implies, communication is not possible.

call argumentation. Consider the following model (figure 7) which, while it cannot show the actual transaction among the various factors involved, can demonstrate how that transaction might be visualized.

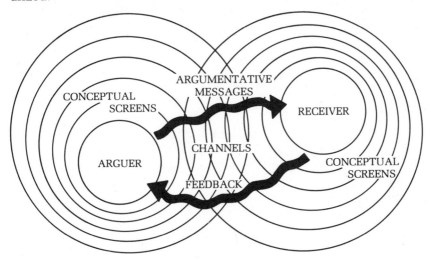

FIGURE 7

In essence, your grasp of the importance of considering argumentation as a process that people engage in, rather than a document that is developed fully ahead of time, will take you far in understanding a highly practical view of argumentation. You have begun to understand argumentation as a common communication activity.

Argumentation in a Communication System

The model of argumentation described and illustrated above is an adaptation of a fairly typical approach to diagramming the process of communication. The model, then, is advantageous as a method of further visualizing argumentation as a kind of communication process. On the other hand, the model suffers from the same sort of weakness inherent in many communication models: you may interpret the model as reflecting the idea that a specific instance of argumentation takes place as an isolated and separate human activity. Indeed, our basic model suggests that, beyond their established screens of political beliefs, education, values, and so forth, the receiver and the arguer are the only influences upon one another. You can interpret the model as illustrating that the receiver is affected only by the arguer and his message, and that his feedback is a response to those factors alone. Similarly, the model seems to indicate that the arguer's only concern is for the receiver, and that he continues the argumentative process solely in response to the feedback from the receiver. All of these conclusions are possible by examining the basic model, but none of the conclusions are appropriate and helpful when viewing argumentation. We, therefore, must refine our basic model so that you understand argumentation as a process, but as a process that occurs in the midst of an entire communication system. Consider figure 8.

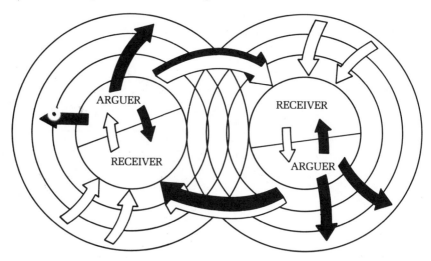

FIGURE 8

To me, figure 8 represents some of the complexity in both communication and argumentation and helps explain why both processes are likely to be difficult, complex, and frustrating. Though we can look at the model and see the major argumentative message of the arguer and the feedback messages of the receiver, we also begin to realize the diversity and the magnitude of all the other forces that affect the progress and completion of the argumentation.

You as an arguer, for example, will never be in the position where you will be influenced only by the primary receiver: you will function as your own receiver to an extent, and, as the argumentation evolves, you probably will provide yourself with ongoing feedback about your own interpretation of how things are going. Moreover, this second model illustrates that other people, messages, and events will become influences upon you as you engage in the argumentation. Finally, of course, it is rare that your argumentative message will be received only by the primary receiver: other receivers will hear or see the original message, or the primary receiver will tell or write others about the message. In one way or another, you as arguer probably will influence several or many people. Seen in that perspective, argumentative communication must be viewed as a part of a whole system of transaction. What you do as an arguer will affect (possibly a great many) other members of the social system in which you find yourself; and you as an arguer *will be affected* by an equally great number of other influences other than the primary receiver. When you initiate argumentation, then, you make a decision that can affect a surprisingly wide range of human activity.

Similarly, when you participate in argumentation as a primary receiver, you become a part of a correspondingly complex human system. Contrary to the basic model, you will be influenced by a multitude of other factors as the argument progresses. You probably will provide some of the input into the system yourself. As figure 8 indicates, there is no reason why the receiver cannot act as an (intrapersonal) arguer of sorts. You will receive and process the argumentative message of the arguer, but, no doubt, you will provide some input, some critique, and some analysis yourself. Hence, as you attend to the primary arguer, it probably is helpful to think of yourself as an extremely active participant in the process of argumentation. Then, too, as the figure also illustrates, you likely will be influenced by other arguers or at least other communicators who have said something that will influence how you perceive and react to the primary arguer. In the age of mass media and ease in communication and transportation, it is difficult for me to imagine that you will hear or read anything about which you have no information. The information or prior arguments may be less than clear to you or less than recent, but they probably will be influences upon how you engage in the process of argumentation. Finally, of course, your feedback response, in all likelihood, will not be received exclusively by the primary arguer. You will tell a friend what it is you are thinking, and he may feed back a response that also becomes a part of the input into your reception; you may simply be in the presence of another person who overhears your feedback response; or you may respond to the arguer, who passes your response on to another person. In one or all of these ways, your feedback probably will not be received exclusively by the arguer: instead, your response can affect, again, a whole human system.

When you begin to view the roles of arguer and receiver as being influenced by and as influencing a whole range and series of human relationships, then you have begun to understand the argumentation process in all its complexity. The argumentation process is a dynamic and ongoing activity. It takes place in a larger, more complex, and more involved human context where the influences are diverse and continually interacting. In such a situation, a point I made earlier may be more clear: there are no easy rules to follow that will control all the variables or guarantee success in argumentation; argumentation is complicated, troublesome, and likely to be difficult and frustrating. Such a point is not extremely comfortable for students or teachers, but it is a necessary one to be made if we are to view argumentation realistically as a complex process that occurs in a still more complex human system of communication.

A More Detailed Model of Argumentation

At this point in the chapter, we have looked at the process of argumentation and visualized it as a kind of communication activity involving arguers, receivers, argumentative messages, feedback, channels, and conceptual screens of various types. Then we found it desirable to conceptualize this process as occurring within a vastly more complicated system of human communication. From that basic view of argumentation and the extremely general view of argumentation as part of a system, we shall now proceed to examine the process of argumentation in more detail. Our primary questions will be: Given the idea that argumentation is more commonly a process rather than a prepared document, what is it that occurs between arguers and receivers during that process? What constitutes the argumentative message that we have discussed? What sorts of activity create the feedback from receiver to arguer? Answers to these questions will occupy us for the duration of the chapter.

Let us begin by creating a conception of the processes involved when a receiver receives an argumentative message and then responds somehow to the arguer. Earlier in our discussion of argumentation in a communication system, we noted that the response probably would not be based exclusively upon the arguer: other arguers, prior beliefs, earlier information, and similar factors inevitably would influence the whole process. Yet we did not explore that process in specific detail. Now, however, let us think of the receiver, not as a circle in a model surrounded by conceptual screens and interacting with all sorts of other people, but as a human processing system.

Reception in Argumentation

Seen as such a system, the receiver becomes (unfortunately and again) more complex. The first subprocess in this system is the activity that we can term *reception*: the basic physical process that includes the activities of seeing, hearing, touching, and so forth. All these sensory activities are important since our concern for argumentation as a communication activity implies that the message symbols (as discussed in chapter 1) can be verbal (oral or written) or nonverbal (touching, facial expression, etc.).[4] Since human arguers utilize a variety of symbols to attempt to re-create similar meanings in their receivers, the reception of those messages will require equally diverse receiving activities. Our way of noting that messages can be received by seeing, feeling, hearing, or even (more rarely) by tasting or smelling will be to refer to all these activities as major facets of the basic activity of reception.

Interpretation in Argumentation

Though the subprocess of reception seems simplistic enough, it is complicated tremendously by its relationship to a second subprocess of the receiver: *interpretation*. We will consider interpretation to be the attaching of some sort of meaning to the received message, and that attachment of meaning seems to be an almost inseparable activity from the subprocess of reception. For example, we normally do not merely receive the oral-verbal symbol *fire* without attaching a certain significance and meaning to it. We consider where we are, what we are doing, whom we are with, what the context of the communication is, and what the person uttering the symbol is doing after saying the word. In various situations, we may interpret the word *fire* to refer to the great Chicago fire, the great fire in the fireplace last evening, how the coach tried to fire-up the team, the fact that the boss tried to fire a friend, that the store owner fired his shotgun, that fire was considered one of the basic elements in early chemistry, that a friend's stomach was on fire from too much spicy food, that there was a devilish fire in someone's eyes, or that your classroom was on fire. Normally, the reception and interpretation subprocesses are going to occur simultaneously: we will not merely (and physically) receive the symbol, but, instead, we will assign some sort of meaning to that symbol.

At times when the reception and interpretation subprocesses cannot occur simultaneously, you as a receiver of symbols probably will seek help with what sort of interpretation to give to a particular symbol usage. I may say, for example, that the writing of this text has required many hours of lucubration. I am fairly confident that you have received the proper symbol, but I am also fairly confident that

---

[4]As I mentioned earlier, our primary concern for symbols and the reception of symbols will be for *verbal* symbols. On the other hand, since arguers and receivers will frequently allude to certain sense impressions such as a sour taste, a particular gesture, or an unfamiliar odor, it would be unfortunate if we ignored the reception of nonverbal stimuli and sense data in our study of argumentation.

you are uncertain about what interpretation to give to my statement. In contrast to the illustration of the variety of interpretations of fire where you realize numerous interpretations of the word, the problem here is that you probably have no familiar interpretations. If my assumptions are correct, then you have a number of options in trying to interpret what it is that the writing of this book required: you could simply ignore the interpretation, hoping to impress me with your vocabulary; you could consult a dictionary, seeking the denotation of the word; or you could say, "Hey, what does lucubration mean?" These alternative approaches to the process of interpretation are similar to the obvious options when an acquaintance says to you, "Well, I'll never forget you." Undoubtedly, you have received a symbolic message, but the reception alone probably does not satisfy you. Did the person mean that she likes you extremely well and will never get over knowing you? That she is trying to tell you the relationship is over? That she is impressed with how distasteful you are? Your problem is with the interpretation of the symbols. Should you ignore the problem and assume it was a compliment? Should you ask another acquaintance what the young lady meant? Or should you ask her yourself? You probably will not be satisfied until you find out what meaning such a cryptic message was supposed to relay.

Choice in Argumentation

The subprocesses of the receiver, however, are not completed with the establishment of a (hopefully) accurate or approximate interpretation of the meaning of the received message. A related receiver activity involves choice: the decision about what sort of response that you will make to the message as you have received and interpreted it. Though later in this chapter we shall discuss some fundamental choices in argumentation, it is obvious that the response that you have to the message will vary tremendously according to your interpretation of the symbols involved. If you thought that the word *fire* meant that there was a fire in the building, your response most likely would be one of alarm, fear, panic, or something of the sort. If, on the other hand, you interpreted the meaning of fire to be that a person no longer had a job, that someone's stomach burned, or that a fireplace was particularly attractive, your response undoubtedly would be different. The response, though, would be a matter of choice: not all individuals respond to the same meaning stimuli in the same manner, nor will the same individual respond identically in all similar situations. The choice will be either highly conscious or primarily below the level of consciousness; it will be either well-reasoned or primarily a reflexive response; and it will be either simple or complex, but the process of choice is an inevitable activity among receivers.

Symbolization in Argumentation

Just as the receiver, then, engages in the subprocesses of reception, interpretation, and choice, receivers also become involved in the activity that we shall call *symbolization*: the subprocess whereby receivers attempt somehow to translate their choice of response into a meaningful message or action. Obviously, the receiver subprocesses are not completed when a response is formulated by the receiver. In terms of a communication perspective, the receiver will symbolize that response (say of fear of a fire) into a meaningful response, such as a verbal command that "everyone should follow the exit lights until . . . ," a cry of panic, or an attempt at quieting those people seated nearby. While such a response may be strictly behavioral (such as jumping across seats to get to the exit first),[5] our particular concern will be for when the response is symbolized as a more traditional verbal message. Seen from that perspective, the subprocess of symbolization is the counterpart of interpretation: while the receiver attempts to decode the meaning of a received message in interpretation, he tries to encode some sort of message for others to receive in symbolization. Instead of our receiver trying to discover the meaning of a message, when he engages in symbolization he attempts to make his own response meaningful for others. You as a receiver will interpret a received message, choose some sort of response to that meaning, and then formulate your own meaningful message as a symbolized response.

Transmission in Argumentation

A related and final subprocess of the receiver is *transmission*: the subprocess whereby the symbolized message is fed back to the original sender of the message. Just as interpretation and symbolization are related and opposing subprocesses, reception and transmission are also related and opposing subprocesses. The symbolized response must be transmitted in some manner so that it functions as a feedback message. The receiver can transmit such messages by the same modes available for the original sender of messages. The transmitted feedback could be facial expression, bodily movements,

[5]Obviously, even the behavioral activity of jumping might be seen as meaningful nonverbal activity and hence a sort of message.

a written memo, a series of oral symbols, or a variety of other methods of communication, employing any one of a number of communication channels.

At the point that we discuss the transmitted feedback to the original communicator, we must begin thinking (as in figure 8 in this chapter) that the receiver also functions as a communicator and arguer as the process of argumentation occurs. Not only will you as a receiver receive and interpret messages, but you will also symbolize and transmit responses. From the other point of view, of course, the original arguer (also as depicted in figure 8) will function as receiver to the extent that she must receive, interpret, and make choices about feedback messages. The implication of this similarity between the original arguer and receiver is that all the discussion about the subprocesses of the receiver also applies to the arguer. Thus, while it is obvious that the arguer will symbolize and transmit argumentative messages, it is apparent that an equally important part of the arguer's task will be to act as receiver for messages that are relevant to the argument in progress. Figure 9 illustrates these ideas by presenting a more complete view of the process of argumentation. The model includes the concepts of arguer, receiver, argumentative message, channels, and feedback, and it expands the idea of argumentation to include the subprocesses of argumentation that are common to both arguer and receiver.

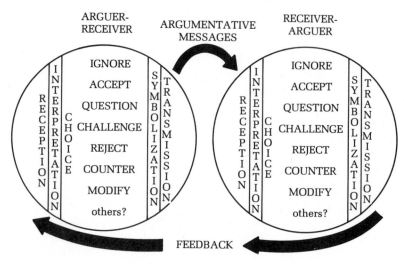

FIGURE 9

Argumentative Choices and Argumentative Functions

Figure 9, however, does more than illustrate the subprocesses of argumentation that we have just discussed. In addition, this more detailed model refines the concept of argumentative choice into what seem to me to be basic options available to the participants engaged in argumentative communication. Indeed, it is not the case that receivers of argumentation normally listen to a constructed message and then respond with a general yes or no to the entire argument; instead, receivers make (or at least *can* make) a number of more specific judgments as the argumentation develops. Similarly, it is not the case that receivers are the only parties who make argumentative choices; instead, arguers normally are compelled to make a number of choices about their response to the feedback from the receiver or other sources. Since such argumentative choices are crucial to both arguer and receiver, let us examine and illustrate each choice individually, including the options to accept, to reject, to ignore, to question, to challenge, to modify, and to counter.[6]

Argumentative Choices about Claims

Obviously, when you as a receiver or an arguer of argumentative communication are confronted with a claim or a response to a claim, you can opt *to accept* it. A friend may say, for example, that you should go to see a particular movie, and you can choose to accept the claim by saying, "You're right, I think I should." From the point of view of your friend (the arguer), she easily could have exercised the same option: to accept your response, regardless of what response you chose to make. While this choice to accept is clear, it is no more self-evident than a second choice, the option *to reject*. In response to the claim that going to the movie is desirable, you could have chosen to reject the idea and replied simply, "No, thank you. I don't think I should." Your choice to reject the claim, however, has created a different situation for the arguer, for if the arguer is really convinced that the movie is a good one, then she may (in kind) reject your rejection of her claim. She may then begin to create a more detailed set of reasons why you should go to the movie. On the other hand, she may choose simply to accept your rejection and forget about the matter completely. Thus, in regard to our first two choices, a number of possibilities exist as to the combination of argumentative choices made by the arguers.

In contrast to merely accepting or rejecting the claim to go to the movie, you, as a receiver, might have chosen simply *to ignore* the claim as advanced. In doing so, you might have interpreted the recommendation about the movie to be mere conversation, rather than a seriously considered belief. In response to your ignoring of

---

[6]Though these options are available to both receiver and arguer, I will illustrate the process first from the receiver's viewpoint. I owe the idea of the modification response to Professor Richard L. Johannesen.

the claim, then, your friend could have exercised any one of the options that we have discussed: she could accept your choice to ignore her claim (in which case she could change topics altogether), she could reject your ignoring of the claim (in which case she probably would have reasserted her claim by developing support for the claim), or, finally, she could choose to ignore your ignoring of the claim. In this latter instance, she would neither end her advancement of the claim (acceptance of response), nor would she develop it further (rejection of response). Instead, she simply would reiterate her claim, perhaps even with the same words. Her assumption would be that you either had not heard her, that you were not paying attention, or that you needed the claim repeated for emphasis.

Another argumentative option that you would have available in response to your friend's review of the movie would be to question the claim. Since you might feel that you do not have enough information about the movie to make a fair decision, you could have asked, "Why is it so good?" or "Why is it that I should go?" Your choice in this case is to get more information, reasoning, and feelings from your friend so that you can make a decision later about whether (ultimately) to accept or reject your friend's claim. In response to your questioning of the claim and your call for reasons, your friend herself might have responded by questioning. She might have asked, "Hey, don't you trust my critique of movies?" or "Well, what do you want to know about the movie?" or some other such question. Thus, she might either question your motives in asking for more information, or she might simply ask what it is she can tell you that you want to know. Moreover, of course, she could accept your question and immediately provide some sort of reason (rather than asking her own questions), she could reject your questioning and become upset that you would have the gall to question her taste, or she could ignore your question altogether and repeat her claim or move to another topic. But clearly, just as you had the option to question her claim, she was able to question your response.

If you had information about the movie from another acquaintance or from a published review, and if that information was not favorable to the movie, you probably would have a tendency to challenge your friend's claim. Rather than merely questioning why the friend was recommending the movie, you would say, "From what I've heard earlier, I'm puzzled about why you think I should go," or "I'm afraid that you're going to have to show me why I should go after all I've heard about the movie." In either of these hypothetical responses, you are doing more than merely asking for the reasoning behind the claim: you are presenting your present belief and then challenging your friend to somehow change your perspective. Your friend may answer your questioning response with a simple statement of why she thought the movie was a good idea, but it seems to me that she will have to answer a challenge more directly by defending (not merely explaining) her claim. Then, too, the choice to respond by challenge is available to your friend as well. In answer to your challenge, she may challenge the sources of your prior beliefs about the movie: "Who was it," she may ask, "who didn't like the movie? Did they see it—more than once? Where did you see the movie reviewed? How do you know the reviewer is competent (in contrast to me)?" In all those comments, the friend is challenging your skepticism and demanding some information and defense of her own. Though each of those statements ends in a question mark, they are not merely open and neutral questions that seek information; rather, they raise issues and demand a defense.

In certain situations, however, you may deem it appropriate to partially accept and to partially reject your friend's claim. In this potential argumentative choice of response, therefore, you may wish simply *to modify* the claim as it is presented. Hence, you may reply to your friend that "Yes, perhaps I should go to the movie, but I should not go this evening," or "Yes, I should see it, but I think that I will wait until it comes to television." In each instance, although you are not totally accepting the claim as presented, you also are not rejecting the claim totally either. In response to such a modified claim, your friend is presented with various options in the argumentation: to accept your modification of the claim, to question your reasoning in delaying your attendance, to challenge your delay, and so forth. In addition, though, she also may choose to modify the response that you have made. She may submit, for instance, "Well, perhaps you ought to delay seeing the movie, but tonight is the last night for the showing for the film." In this response as well, your friend would be accepting certain ideas that you advanced, but she would be modifying them to demonstrate some disagreement with how you responded.

Finally, you as the receiver of the claim to attend the movie can opt to respond by *countering* the claim;[7] that is, by asserting your own claim that is in direct opposition to the first claim. When you hear your friend say, "You really ought to go to the movie," you may simply reply, "No, I shouldn't. Nobody should go to see that movie."

---

[7]In quarrels, as illustrated by the latter part of the children's "shoot-out" in chapter 1, claims are often simply met by the receiver introducing a second claim that directly contradicts or is at least different from the original claim. In formal debate we refer to a *counter plan* when the negative team advances their own plan for change in the system rather than merely challenging the original plan.

That response, of course, is much stronger than either the questioning, challenging, or rejecting choices. Here, you are not asking for more information, you are not challenging the arguer to defend herself, nor are you merely signaling your complete rejection of the idea. Instead, you are advancing your own claim that no one—including you—ought to see the movie. In response to such a strong reply from you, your friend could choose from a number of strategies. She could accept your counterclaim and decide not to pursue the point further; she could reject your counterclaim and term it vague, exaggerated, or unfounded; she could question your new claim, hoping to get more information about it; she could challenge the merit of your claim and demand that you defend your unfavorable view of the movie; or she could ignore your counterclaim completely and continue to advance her claim. Finally, of course, she could choose to do what you have just done: she could present some sort of counterclaim to what it is that you have said. If, for example, you had countered her claim by contending that no one should see the movie, then your friend might counter that claim by suggesting that "You are always so negative about things," or "You always exaggerate," or "You don't know what you're talking about." Any of these would be a counterclaim advanced in opposition to your own counterclaim, so again, the choice to counter a claim is an available choice of both parties engaged in the process of argumentation.

Argumentative Choices about Other Argumentative Functions

Though I have discussed all these various argumentative options as argumentative choices primarily involving initial receiver responses to claims and arguer responses to those initial receiver choices, it is clear that all the argumentative functions of language that we discussed in the last chapter are equally relevant to the choices that participants in argumentation make. You as a receiver, for example, must decide what sort of response you will make to offered evidence: Will you ignore it? Challenge it? Counter it with other (contradictory) evidence? Accept it? A choice must be made either consciously and directly or by implication. Similarly, as an arguer, will you accept or challenge your receiver's modification of your statement of probability—your qualifier? If, as a receiver, you accept the offered evidence as being evident or acceptable, you face a choice of either ignoring the need for a warrant, of questioning the existence of an acceptable warrant, or of responding to something that the arguer has offered as a warrant: Will you reject it? Challenge it? Or modify it? In essence, the choice that either arguers or receivers make about the initial claim is only one of many choices that the participants will make as they become involved in a serious and thorough process of examining argumentation as it develops. In most argumentative situations, where the communication is likely to be unstructured and informal, the argumentation will arise from participants making choices to ignore, accept, reject, challenge, question, modify, or counter language that has been intended to function as claims, evidence, warrants, backing, qualifiers, or reservations.

While clearly there may be any number of combinations of responses that receiver and arguer might make to each other in an extended transaction, I feel that I can make certain predictions about the result of various sorts of argumentative choices. A preponderance of acceptances, it seems to me, normally indicates an amiable and fruitful process that will probably result in the general acceptance of the claim. The prevalence of choices to reject, ignore, or counter probably will result in the argumentation ending unresolved (you may leave the room upset, for example), in a digression to other topics (as when you let the matter drop), and/or in the development of hostile and unproductive argument or outright quarreling. In contrast to these options, it seems to me that a predominance of questioning and challenging probably will result in in-depth, well-thought, and constructive argument. In these last cases, you will ask for or demand reasons, evidence, warrants, objections, interpretations—and the product should be a thorough and deliberate analysis of the claim and its support.

In addition to the effect that a preponderance of choices can have on the nature of the argumentation that develops, certain individual choices can significantly affect the argumentative situation. One of the most important of these individual choices would be the decision by a receiver to reject completely the claim as advanced. In having a warrant or evidence rejected, the arguer can immediately offer some other idea, but that is not so simply the case when the claim itself is rejected completely. In the face of that sort of rejection, no other argumentation may be possible: indeed, the claim has been considered, but complete rejection may indicate the receiver's refusal even to engage in further discussion. The arguer, of course, may opt to attempt to modify and re-present his claim, but even that act may not be effective in encouraging the receiver to participate; thus, while rejection of evidence (etc.) may simply force the argumentation to develop in a different manner, outright and complete rejection of the claim may preclude the argumentation altogether.

A second individual choice that may significantly affect the entire process of argumentation, ironically, is the outright and complete acceptance of the claim by the receiver. In this situation, no argumentation occurs. A claim, you will recall, is a statement that is actually being challenged, questioned, and so forth. In that sense, though the arguer may intend something to function as a claim, it actually may function more like evidence than a claim: the receiver immediately decides that the statement is acceptable, and that is how we have conceived the function of evidence. Your reaction to this may be that a claim is a claim regardless of how it is judged by receivers—so long as there is a high probability of there being a challenge or question. That, however, would be an arguer orientation to argumentation. Seen from a receiver orientation, evidence is not evidence until it is perceived as acceptable by the receiver; a warrant does not connect claims and evidence until the receiver judges the connection between them to be sound; and—this is the issue here—claims do not function as claims until and unless the receiver chooses to question or challenge the statements. Though the immediate acceptance of the claim may be an important aspect of communication in general, I see the situation as generally irrelevant to our concerns for argumentation specifically.

The emphasis in this last discussion upon how various argumentative choices have different impacts upon the development of informal and unstructured argumentation, however, reintroduces the concern in the previous chapter for the functions of language in argumentation. Indeed, though in that chapter we stressed argumentation that was constructed as a message (in the mass media message, for example), we can now begin to understand argumentation as it exists most frequently: as a kind of interpersonal and unconstructed communication transaction. Let us, then, examine the relationship between argumentative functions and argumentative choices by studying a situation in which most of you have found (or will find) yourselves.

Case Study: The New Car

Though many of the case studies in this text are hypothetical, this study of the argumentation surrounding the purchase of a new automobile is not only factual, but autobiographical. I will describe, as accurately as possible, the main lines of argumentation that developed in my final contact with a new car salesman—immediately prior to my purchase of a different kind of car from some other salesman at another showroom. I, of course, have altered the names of people and products that are involved. As the case develops, I will interrupt the narrative at various places to discuss my interpretation and to ask your interpretation of the choices and the language functions of argumentation.

In early 1975, my wife, Ann, and I decided that the advent of a new baby and the traveling necessities of diapers, toys, baby chairs, strollers, blankets, and so forth, signaled the end of the days when we could travel the twelve-hour trip home to see parents and friends with two adults, a four-year-old boy, a cat, luggage, and sanity in a small, imported automobile. Hence, we decided, we should purchase a mid-sized station wagon for long,grueling trips and keep the import for most of our other driving. We had narrowed our decision to two possibilities which were nearly equal in cost and generally equal in attributes. After we made a final test drive of car A (and incidentally, *before* being able to test drive the car we eventually bought), we sat discussing the purchase, the deal, and the comparative advantages of both cars with George, the car A salesman. The following is, generally, how the discussion went.

GEORGE: Well, Dick, what did you think about it?

DICK: We did like it. It handles well, and it seems comfortable. It's big enough for all of us and luggage.

GEORGE: I was sure you'd like it.

DICK: Why don't you tell us what kind of deal we can get—how much would it cost to drive it off the lot, with taxes, license, and things?

What followed was a period when options were listed, a discount was given since we had no trade-in, and taxes and other factors were determined. Financing was discussed, along with an impending move out-of-state, and servicing at dealers other than the one from whom we bought the car.

GEORGE: Did you look at the B last night?

ANN: Yes, but we didn't get a chance to drive it. And we really want to do that before we buy.

GEORGE: How do we compare on price?

DICK: Well your 1975 A is about $500 more than the '75 B, so I guess that the crucial thing is the comparison between your leftover '74 and the '75 B. The '74 is about . . . well, it is $400 less than the B. The question is whether the $400 saving will be worth having a year older car when it's time to trade the thing in. I'm afraid I might end up losing money. So we're really comparing two things—the features and options of the cars themselves and the cost difference between the '74 and the '75.

Let me interrupt here to explain graphically what I had just told George. Realizing that the claim that I was examining was "We ought to buy the A," I did not merely demand evidence, warrants, and so forth. Instead, I stated that the evidence he supplied must be related to two specific warrants: one involving cost and one involving options. Consider figure 10.

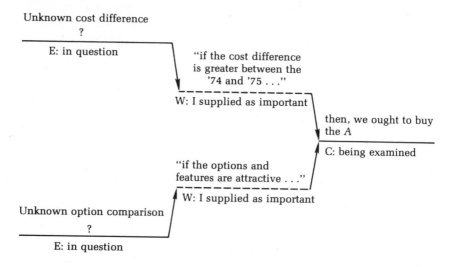

Unknown cost difference
?

E: in question

"if the cost difference is greater between the '74 and '75 ..."

W: I supplied as important

then, we ought to buy the A

C: being examined

"if the options and features are attractive ..."

W: I supplied as important

Unknown option comparison
?

E: in question

FIGURE 10

In essence, the claim was clear to all three of us, and I had just told George the warrants that would be relevant to us. The implication to George was clear: what he needed to do was to fill-in information that could function as evidence for those warrants—he needed to tell us what those question marks meant in terms of options, features, dollars, and cents.

GEORGE: Okay, let's talk about those things. We have some advantages over the B, and I think we can do something about the money difference. I think, Dick, that we can put together a better deal for you.

George's comment demonstrated that he was an experienced salesperson who knew that the reasons that might convince me to buy the car could vary tremendously depending upon my personal experience with automobiles, my belief system about As as automobiles, my personal value judgments about appearance, my relative concern for economy, and so forth. At that point in our discussion, however, he knew that I had narrowed my concerns to two: I had said, in essence, that the money difference between the '74 and the '75 and the car-to-car comparison were my chief interests. George wasted no time with reasoning that he assumes will be irrelevant to me; instead, he restated his claim that "I ought to buy the *A* and introduced two items of evidence suggested by my communication: first, that the monetary deal could be changed to a plus factor, and, second, that his car was a better one. He did not express anything that functioned as a warrant simply because I had literally told him that if I agreed that those two items of evidence were present in his deal, then I acknowledged that I would be favorable to the claim. The warrants, then, were beliefs that I had already supplied for him.

You now can begin to understand the relationship between argumentative choices and argumentative functions of language. As a receiver, I had chosen to ignore all other items that might function as evidence; as an arguer, he accepted that position and also ignored any item that he might otherwise have used, such as the appearance of the automobile, its color, and so forth. Moreover, since I had selected and accepted the warrants beforehand, he saw no advantage in doing anything other than ignoring them. Consequently, we both ignored any mention of support for the warrants; indeed, when the warrant has been accepted, it is not subject to attack or in need of support-for-the-warrant or backing. In other reference to language functions, it is important, but hardly surprising, that George chose to ignore completely any attention to a qualifier or reservation. Subconsciously, or by design, he knew that if I accepted the items of evidence, that I would accept his claim, buy the car, and provide him with a commission.

In essence, the entire purchase began to hinge on my judgment about his evidence and whether he could get rid of the question marks. It is at that point that what I call a magical thing happened: the two items of evidence, since I challenged them, did not function as evidence, but, instead, began to function as claims themselves. Their form or content did not alter, but their function was affected by my judgment as a receiver. Had I merely accepted the $400 cost factor and the available options as evidence—as things that were evident to me—then those ideas about the cost difference and the options would have been able to serve their function as evidence. Such, however, was not the case. Instead, I challenged the amount of the cost difference and the importance of the options, and I ignored the importance of reservations, qualifiers, and support and, tacitly at least, accepted a belief that functioned as a warrant. Thus, the relationship between argumentative choices and argumentative function is clear: our argumentative choices determine the function that the language serves. My choice to pick cost and options as key items constituted a challenge to George to show that those items could function as evidence. With that choice, the things that might have been offered as evidence (magically) became claims that, themselves, needed evidence and perhaps warrants, backing, and so forth.

Realizing (at least subconsciously) that he now had two claims to support, George began to develop his argumentative position as our discussion continued. He began with the cost difference, claiming that the cost factor was attractive.

GEORGE: So what you're saying is that if I can sweeten the deal a little, you'll buy the A.

DICK: Well, that is one of the major . . .

GEORGE: Okay, how much more than $400 do you need between the '75 and our '74? How much do I need to help you with?

DICK: I guess that $200 more would make it a lot more worthwhile for me. I'd feel better about it.

Let me illustrate (figure 11) the situation in relation to this first new claim. Note that he had just asked me to supply another warrant, which he would try to match with a dollar figure (evidence):

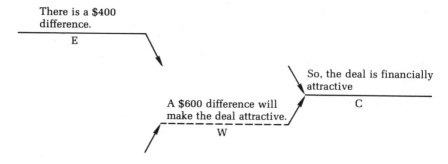

There is a $400 difference.

E

A $600 difference will make the deal attractive.

W

So, the deal is financially attractive

C

Note that, though there is a claim, a warrant, and a statement of evidence, the three are not compatible because of the different dollar amounts; the claim, thus, is unacceptable.

FIGURE 11

Note that the dollar figure in the evidence and the dollar figure in the warrant I just supplied are not consistent; hence, my rejection (at this point) of the new claim. As you are about to see, George found that he probably could up the figure that served as evidence to $600 as my warrant demanded. At the outset, that would seem to allow the evidence, via the warrant, to support the claim. But, as you shall see also, another problem arose: his raising of the dollar amount had a reservation attached to it. Observe:

GEORGE: Let's see. What's the price of the B? Oh, I see. Well . . . hm . . . okay, now I think I can do it, but I would have to get this approved by the new car manager. I can give it to him, and if he approves it, it will be a contract, okay?

DICK: No.

GEORGE: What do you mean?

ANN: We haven't even driven the B yet and we want to.

DICK: The cost was one of the factors, but not the only one.

At this point, it is interesting to explore in more detail what George was doing from an argumentative perspective. The claim (which he hoped could function again as evidence later for the claim that I should buy the car) was that financially the deal was a good one. What makes that claim evident? George knew that the most direct way of establishing that monetary figure was to ask me what I wanted. He was asking me for a response that would function as a warrant, and I supplied the statement "If I had $200 more as a difference between the two (making it a $600 difference), then the deal would be a good one." With that as a warrant, all George needed to do was to supply the evidence: "Surprise," he said, "I can drop the price of our car another $200." Thus, George's argument to support his evidence-turned-claim is this: this is a good financial deal (claim). What makes that evident? A $200 discount (the evidence he was ready to give me). What is the connecting idea or warrant? That $200 more would make it more attractive (again, he had asked what warrant I would *accept*, and then he offered an amount of evidence or money that was covered by the warrant). Since I had already suggested the warrant, and he supplied the price evidence, he felt his claim was well supported.

George, however, made a critical mistake: he attached a reservation to the argument; that is, he could offer the lower cost, *unless* I refused to be committed to the deal. Because I had no desire to be committed to the deal before test driving the '75 B, I chose to ignore his offer. I reasoned that I would always be able to get the $200 drop in price from him, so I ignored the offer and moved to the other item of evidence that I had challenged earlier. I said, in effect, that we have resolved (but not committed ourselves to) the cost claim, which can now function for me as evidence. If George could support the car-to-car option comparison, then it also could act as evidence for the prior claim that I should buy his A.

In making his comparison, George offered several items that he wished to function as evidence for the claim that his A was better than the B. Let me recount those attempts and describe our reaction to them.

GEORGE: Looking at the equipment, the B has much the same as far as options . . . ours doesn't have a luggage rack, but it does have a thermostat-type air-conditioning system and cruise control so that you can just set your speed and stay there . . .

ANN: (who accepted those items as evident, but rejected the warrant—the controls—as being unrelated to the claim) We'd really like to have the rack, but we're not that excited about those controls.

Note Ann's reaction (figure 12) to his "we have these controls" evidence:

Note that, though we accepted the evidence as accurate, we saw no way for that to influence our acceptance or rejection of the claim; without the acceptance of warrant, the claim is unacceptable.

FIGURE 12

GEORGE: (who wisely ignored her comment and went on to other possible areas to find evidence that would relate to the claim) I can give you the car without radial tires and save another fifty dollars.

DICK: (who challenged the offered evidence) Won't that cost us gas mileage?

GEORGE: (who countered the remark) Yes, but you will eat the savings up when you have to replace the more expensive tires.

Thus, that item ended in a stalemate and could not function for us as evidence at all: it simply was not evident. Can you diagram what that dialogue would look like?

Consequently, George dropped the point and looked for other items of evidence.

GEORGE: I think our tailgate is really a lot better than the B's. It can open three different ways. The B has a tailgate that slides down and sometimes gets stuck.

DICK: (who accepts the three ways as being evident, but rejects the warrant that if the tailgate is better, then the car is significantly better) Well, okay, but I don't see that as a major point.

Can you diagram what just took place?

ANN: George, how do you compare the ease with which you can see behind and sideways from the front seat?

This of course set up a chance for George to focus upon something that might make his option claim evident.

GEORGE: (avoiding the comparison and losing his chance) Well, what did you think about it?

ANN: (demonstrating another mistake by George) Well, I won't be sure until we drive the other one.

GEORGE: (choosing to ignore another unproductive strategy) I don't know whether you know it, but A has been really ahead for sometime in the automobile industry. They came out with Sparrow and then a year later, B had a car the same size; in 1973, we came out with the Hawk, and two years later, they had their Eagle. A has just always been out there in front.

DICK: (who accepted that as being evident, but couldn't accept it as a warrant that "this station wagon should be bought if the company is progressive") Humph . . . I didn't know that.

GEORGE: Yeah.

DICK: Listen, I think we've taken up too much of your time. We're planning to test drive the B, and we'll let you know what decision we make.

The claim that we should buy the A was neither well supported for the buyers, nor had the claim been rejected since one of the two items of challenged evidence (now claims) remained unable to function as evidence.

Just for your information we test drove the B and decided that it handled better than the A, was more stable on the road, and had better back and side visibility. We bought the B.

Implications of the Case Study

The case study illustrates the relationship between the argumentative functions and argumentative choices. Indeed, the choice made

by the receiver or the arguer will determine how the language functions and *if* the idea succeeds in functioning as the communicator
(receiver or arguer) desires. If the receiver, for example, accepts
something as evidence, but chooses to challenge the connection
between the claim and the evidence (as when I accepted that the *A*
company may have been more progressive, but failed to see the
relationship between that idea and the claim that their cars were
better), then the argumentation centers upon the warrant and not the
evidence or the claim directly. In this case, the argumentative choice
of the receiver dictated what function the arguer's language needed
to serve; it needed to warrant the relationship between the accepted
evidence and the claim in question. Similarly, when the receiver
accepts the warrant (as I did when I stated what amount of money
would make the deal worthwhile), then the arguer need only strive
to supply the evidence (I can drop the price $200), and the rest of the
argumentation should progress smoothly to an acceptance of the
claim. If, in still a third case, the arguer chooses to advance a new
reservation ($200 less, un*less* you decide not to make a contract), the
receiver is placed in the position to choose between accepting a deal
with strings attached or rejecting the offer, at least for the time being.
In all these instances, the choice that the arguers and receivers make
will dictate, not only how the language is functioning for the other,
but what will be the next appropriate response: argumentative
choices and argumentative functions of language are inherently in-
terdependent.

Secondly, it seems to me that the case illustrates the most common
sort of argumentation: argumentation that simply arises from a
communication situation. The arguments are not preplanned,
though experience can mean fewer mistakes; the arguments are not
well structured, though it will help to be aware of what functions are
being served by the kind of things said; and the arguments are not in
formal settings, though they can determine the course of important
actions, like engaging in premarital sex, pursuing a particular career,
adopting a certain life philosophy, or, yes, spending several
thousand dollars to buy a new car.

Finally, I submit that the case study exemplifies a concept from an
earlier part of this chapter: argumentation may be interpersonal, and
it may be conducted (as in this case) among three participants, but
inevitably it will be affected by receivers, arguers, or influences other
than the ones immediately present. Communication, as we discussed earlier, occurs within a large and complex human system of
mutually interacting forces. Was it unusual that we made a decision
on the basis of a test drive—without giving George a chance to

respond to our newly formed beliefs and attitudes? I think not. We left his office and showroom with his claim that we should buy the A still undecided. George's problem was that he had been unable to create enough support for the two items of evidence that we had challenged: show us that the car-to-car comparison is favorable to the A and that the monetary difference can be worked out (we said), and we will accept them, not as claims, but as things which make the claim that we buy an A evident. As the argument developed, it was clear that we had not accepted those items as evidence, and so the major claim had little chance. Instead, we accepted the evidence of our senses of sight and touch as support for the claim that we should buy the '75 B. Indeed, then, the case study capsulizes this chapter's concern for the complicated process of argumentation in addition to illustrating our specific concern for the relationship between argumentative functions and argumentative choices.

Summary

I began this chapter with the acknowledgement that, while chapter 2 had stressed the argumentative functions of language (rather than forms of language), the emphasis in chapter 2 was still upon argumentation as a preplanned and earlier constructed message. Such an interpretation, I argued, needed to be modified since most of your argumentation would occur in relatively unstructured and informal situations. You needed, in essence, to learn about argumentation that develops and progresses in all sorts of communication situations.

To begin that study of argumentation conceived as a process, we discussed a basic model of argumentation which clearly identified argumentation as a kind of communication activity. The elements that are crucial to a basic understanding of argumentation include arguers, receivers, messages, channels, feedback, and conceptual screens. Next, we expanded our model to demonstrate that argumentation, even that involving only one or two people, inevitably will be affected by receivers, arguers, and other influences that are not immediately present. The argumentation will be affected by what we have heard before, what we already have said to others, what others hear about us, and so forth. Argumentation, therefore, must be conceived as a process that occurs within a whole complex of mutually interacting forces: argumentation occurs within a system of human communication and influences.

Thirdly, we examined a more complete model of argumentative communication, stressing the subprocesses of argumentation that were common to arguers and receivers alike. We discussed the subprocesses of reception, interpretation, choice, symbolization, and transmission as constructs that can be helpful in understanding the complexity of the argumentative process and the reason for the difficulty in arguing successfully. Finally, we focused specifically upon the sorts of argumentative choices that are available to both arguers and receivers, including accepting, ignoring, rejecting, questioning, modifying, challenging, and countering. These options were discussed as they related directly to our earlier concern about the argumentative functions of language.

The end of the chapter was devoted to a factual and reconstructed case study of part of the argumentation in which my wife and I were involved in the purchase of a new automobile. I interrupted the dialogue at various times to describe my interpretation of what sorts of argumentative choices were made and what those choices implied for how the communication was functioning argumentatively. Because the ultimate decision to purchase a car was made on the basis of issues raised after that session with the car salesman, the case study became an appropriate place to reiterate, not only the relationship between argumentative choices and argumentative functions, but also the idea that argumentation occurs as communication within a complex human system of transacting forces.

Programmed Questions

To test your understanding of the material presented in this chapter, you may wish to answer the following questions. In the multiple-choice questions, the answers may be all correct, all incorrect, or several may be correct. The suggested answers to the questions appear on the last page of this chapter. If you fail to answer the questions correctly, you may wish to review the material to increase your understanding and/or to discuss the items in class.

1. Elements that are absolutely necessary to a basic model of the argumentation process include:
    a. an arguer
    b. a receiver
    c. an oral message
    d. verbal feedback
    e. appropriate channels
    f. conceptual screens

2. When we speak of conceptual screens in argumentation, we must stress that the backgrounds, experiences, and values of the individuals:
   a. overlap in certain relevant areas
   b. be identical
   c. be completely separate

3. Argumentation should be viewed as:
   a. an activity that is affected by a whole complex of forces outside the immediate situation
   b. a part of a whole communication system
   c. an activity that is influenced only by the two or more parties directly involved
   d. being synonymous with communication in general
   e. only affecting the parties directly involved

In items 4 through 8, match the term on the right with its description on the left.

4. _____ reception | a. the decision about what sort of response to make to the message

5. _____ symbolization | b. the process of translating the choice of response into a meaningful message

6. _____ interpretation | c. a physical process such as seeing, hearing, and so forth.

7. _____ choice | d. the process of sending the message to the other participant

8. _____ transmission | e. the attachment of meaning or significance to a received message

9. The subprocesses of argumentation listed in items 4 through 8 are activities conducted by:
   a. the arguer, exclusively
   b. the receiver, exclusively
   c. neither arguer nor receiver
   d. both arguer and receiver

10. In response to a part of an argumentative message, an arguer or receiver may choose from a number of options, including:
    a. to accept
    b. to ignore
    c. to modify
    d. to reject
    e. to question
    f. to challenge
    g. to counter

11. Two argumentative choices that, in immediate response to a *claim*, actually keep the argumentation from developing are the decisions to:
    a. question or challenge the claim
    b. accept or reject the claim
    c. counter or modify the claim
    d. accept or modify the claim

Discussion Questions for Appendix Case Studies

To test your understanding of the material in this chapter, you may wish to answer the following questions that refer to the case studies in the Appendix of this book. You may wish to (a) work on the questions individually; (b) work on the questions in pairs or in groups in or before class: (c) develop written answers to the questions; (d) have class discussion based upon the questions; (e) prepare an extended paper on several related questions; or (f) develop a major paper about one case study (using the questions related to it that appear in various chapters).

1. Study "Satisfaction (Almost) Assured" beginning on page 258. Use the models in chapter 4 to diagram what the argumentation was between Deal and the manager. Are there elements that need to be added to the model to explain the situation? Are there elements that are unnecessary?

2. Study "Address to the Catholic Lawyers' Guild" beginning on page 259, and "How Free is Free Will?" beginning on page 254. Diagram each, using the models in chapter 4. Which of your models highlight the importance of communication elements that others of your models de-emphasize? What similarities do you note as you study the models of the two settings for argumentation?

3. Study "You Find Good Assets in Des Moines and Iowa" by John R. Fitzgibbon beginning on page 256. Diagram the argumentative situation. What problems do you encounter when you try to determine the receivers or groups of receivers? How do you think your difficulty in diagramming the situation might be shared by someone creating an argumentative pamphlet that would *function* equally well for receivers that include the public, stockholders, bank employees, customers, city and state officials, and so forth?

4. Study "The Success of the Program" beginning on page 264. How does Wallace's *choice* of response to the administrator's evidence affect how the administrator's language *functioned* for Wallace? In general, in what ways do the administrator's choices as an arguer differ from Wallace's choices of response as a receiver?

Research Project for Advanced Students

What is often said of models of communication or argumentation processes is that the model is incapable of demonstrating the complexity and, especially, the dynamism of the process. Research how various authors view the strengths and shortcomings of models in general or certain types of models.

Though it may be difficult at first, you may want to begin by studying Abraham Kaplan, *The Conduct of Inquiry: Methodolgy for Behavioral Science* (Scranton, Pa.: Intext Educational Publishers, 1964), especially chapter 3.

Answers to Programmed Questions

1. a, b, e, f   2. a   3. a, b   4. c   5. b   6. e   7. a

8. d   9. d   10. a, b, c, d, e, f, g   •11. b

5

Arguer Intent and Receiver Judgment

My *general objective* in this chapter is to refine the discussion of the argumentative functions of language by illustrating the potential difference between how an arguer might intend the language to function and how a receiver judges the language to function.

My *specific objectives* are

to examine various types of claims that arguers may intend to make—and how receivers may judge the claim to be something else

to examine various types of evidence that arguers may use—and how receivers may choose to deny that it is evident

to examine various warrants that arguers may submit—and how receivers may choose to deny that they justify the movement to the claim's acceptance

to examine intended backing—and how receivers either may force different backing to be used or may prompt the arguer to try to put off the discussion of the point until later

to examine various types of qualifiers that arguers may use—and how receivers may demand varying strengths of evidence depending upon their interpretation of the qualifier to examine various reservations that arguers may express—and how receivers may demand more detail depending upon their judgments of the intent of the qualifier

In chapter 4 we discussed the process of argumentation as being a dynamic activity involving a whole system of potential influences and subprocesses such as reception, interpretation, choice, symbolization, and transmission. The case study which constituted the chapter's last phase illustrated how that process occurs in something as simple, informal, and unstructured as the purchase of a new automobile. I assume that, as you studied the parenthetical explanations, you began to appreciate the relationship between the concern for communicative functions of argument (chapter 3) and the stress upon argumentative choice (chapter 4). Indeed, both arguer and receiver continually are called upon to choose a response to certain ideas related to the basic claim: we choose, for example, to accept or ignore language that is intended to function as a warrant or some other argumentative language unit. It is the choice of the receiver that determines whether the language, in fact, functions for him in the situation in the manner intended.[1] Clearly, how the arguer intends to have the language function is of interest to us, but what is overwhelmingly important is the response to that intended message by receivers.

Let me illustrate my point with the following hypothetical dialogue that might have transpired in the mid-sixties when the widely read pediatrician, Dr. Benjamin Spock, began demonstrating against the war in Vietnam. The dialogue involves two students, one who is aware of the doctor's political position and the other who knows Spock only through his mother's belief in him as a pediatrician.

1st STUDENT: You know, we really ought to be getting out of that war in Vietnam—Dr. Benjamin Spock says that we just keep getting deeper and deeper into a situation where we shouldn't be in the first place.

---

[1] Though the discussion in this chapter will focus upon the importance of the receiver's judgment, this is not to say that the judgment should be made without guidelines or good reasons. As we discussed in chapter one, something is meaningful and significant partly because of individual interpretations and partly because of the collective significance dictated by the individual's background and his awareness of the situation. Chapter 7 will make clear certain productive standards that receivers can utilize in determining how something functions, and chapter 8 will deal with the ever-present ethical demands of argumentation.

2nd STUDENT:	What in the world are you talking about? (the student is confused somehow)
1st STUDENT:	(thinking that his friend had not heard or was questioning the evidence) Well, Spock said that we were getting...
2nd STUDENT:	(accepting the evidence as being evident but making it clear that he was challenging the warrant) No, no, no. Okay, I can believe that Spock said that. What I meant is, what in the world does his statement have to do with anything related to the international political scene? What does he know about it?
1st STUDENT:	Haven't you been listening to the news? Spock knows a lot about the situation over there. He's...
2nd STUDENT:	Oh, come now. Anybody can read about the situation. What makes him so expert in the area? (as they walk on) Spock may be a good baby doctor, but that doesn't mean that...

Obviously, the first student, whom we may label the arguer, intended that Spock's comment should function as evidence for the claim about Vietnam. The problem is that the intended function cannot be our chief concern: we must stress whether the idea in question functioned for the receiver as evidence, and clearly it did not. Although the receiver acknowledged the probable authenticity of the evidence, she denied any link (warrant) between the evidence and the claim being advanced. Hence, while she admitted that the authentic comment could be evidence for some claim, the receiver denied that it could function as support for the claim in question. Does this mean that the receiver was at fault as somehow arbitrary or narrow-minded? No, the failure of Spock's opinion to function as evidence indicates that when you engage in argumentation, you must be prepared to have your argumentation accepted or rejected, not on the basis of what you intend, but on the basis of what your receiver judges to be the case.

To illustrate this approach to the study of argumentation, we shall reexamine the concepts of claims, evidence, warrants, backing for warrants, reservations, and qualifiers. We shall discuss these in traditional terms as to what the arguer intends, and then we shall reexamine them in light of what might be the difference between these intentions and the judgments made by receivers.

Claims in Argumentative Communication

Traditionally, students of argumentation are taught that there are four classifications of propositions or claims:[2] declarative, evaluative, policy, and classificatory claims. Though it is traditionally acknowledged that any particular claim might be difficult to "put into" one of these categories, it is assumed that such labeling can be done, and that the result will be an insight into the argument. Let us investigate each of those claims.

Declarative claims refer to claims that are advanced when the arguer is prepared to defend the idea that something is the case, has been the case, or will be the case.[3] Note that, in all those situations, we are referring to something that is, something that is about to be, or something that was once: the emphasis is upon "what is the case" whether we refer to the present, the past, or the future. Let us take a simple situation in which you and I are looking at an apple to illustrate, first, the nature of declarative claims, and, second, the different time labels for such claims. You might look at the apple and say to me, "Professor Crable, my father grows apples like this," meaning that at the *present* time it is the case that apples like the one before us are being grown by your father. On the other hand, you might look at the apple and say wistfully, "My father used to grow apples just like this," meaning that at some unspecified point in the *past* it was the case that your father grew apples of this sort. Finally, of course, you and I might be walking in an orchard, and you might point to an apple blossom, saying, "You know, these apples will be just like the kind my father grows," meaning that at some point in the *future* you fully expect it to be the case that these trees will produce the kind of apple grown by your father. In all these instances, you would be making what you intend to be a claim that we can label declarative: something is, was, or will be the case.

Theoretically, at least, declarative claims are statements that are made about "what is the case" when we do not have direct (sensory) data about the situation. On the other hand, while we do not have the needed data, we assume the matter could be settled if somehow we

---

[2]Some of the analysis in this section is based on ideas in Douglas Ehninger and Wayne Brockriede, *Decision by Debate* (New York: Dodd, Mead and Co., 1963), especially p. 102; and Douglas Ehninger, *Influence, Belief, and Argument* (Glenview, Ill.: Scott Foresman, 1974), chapter 3.

[3]Ibid. Ehninger, for example, uses the term *declarative claims*, rather than the more traditional *factual claims*. I agree that the term declarative avoids the difficult discussion of the nature of facts, although later we shall examine the nature of facts in more detail.

did acquire the necessary data. Frequently, we assume that the data could be supplied by direct sensory information gained through sight, touch, taste, hearing, or smell. If it were possible for me to visit the orchard in which you claim your father grows these apples, then I should be able to discover for myself the accuracy of your claim. Similarly, if I am interested in the accuracy of your prediction that the apples on these trees will be of the kind grown by your father, I could visit his orchard and then come back later to this orchard to see if the apples are of the same variety. I would have a more difficult time in assessing your claim concerning what your father once had in his orchard: I cannot reverse the clock in order to verify your claim. Indeed, it may be that at times we simply will never be able to verify the claim of what is, was, or will be the case: we must rely upon argumentation. Then, too, even if it were possible to verify the claim (for example, by looking at the orchard 400 miles away), we may still choose to rely upon argumentation.

Though we may usually expect to be able to verify claims about the future and the past less easily than we do claims about the present (since the present can be examined most simply by sense perception), at times even claims concerning the present must be verified by making judgments based on other kinds of data. We would expect data sources such as records, histories, and so forth, to provide us with information about claims about the past or to serve to support predictions about the future. Yet this sort of data is at times necessary to help verify claims about what is currently the case. You may claim, for example, that the moon is made of rock and sand rather than green cheese, and I can judge that claim about something that is the case only indirectly: information from moon landings, scientific articles and denials of the cheese hypothesis, or televised pictures of the moon. Moreover, even when the object of the claim is present, and I can use my sensory powers, I may still be depending largely upon judgment. You may hand me a sandwich, for example, and you may claim that "On the table there is a ham sandwich." I may look at it, smell it, and taste it and agree with you. As I eat the sandwich, however, it is entirely possible that you will laugh and make me aware that what I agreed was a ham sandwich, in reality, is composed of a soybean meal mixture that has been treated to look, smell, and taste like ham. In essence, then, while declarative claims theoretically are subject to sense verification, we shall find that the examination of such claims about what is, was, or will be the case is not conducted so simply as we might at first think.

Evaluative claims refer to claims that imply certain value judgments about what is the case, what was the case, or what will be the case. At one time or another, everyone assumes something to be the case and then evaluates it in terms of (among other standards) its quality, its degree of goodness, its effectiveness, its strength, or its worth. Referring to the apple mentioned earlier, you may refer to the present condition of the apple as you eat it and say, "This is a very good apple." Clearly, this would be a claim that involves an evaluation on your part. Similarly, you might look hungrily at an apple core and contend, "This was obviously a good apple: look at how little is left on the core." Finally, of course, you might refer to the future rather than the present or the past by observing a well-developed apple blossom and claim, "Surely, this will be a good apple."

In situations where the claim involves an evaluation, the examination of the claim is more difficult. By definition, evaluative claims are not verifiable by empirical or sensory means. Certainly, I might taste the apple and agree with you that it is a "good" apple, but I simply would be sharing your value judgment. Even though you and I might be tempted to reinforce one another to the extent that we say, "Well, it is a good apple," we would not be discussing a declarative claim. Our value judgments merely would be the same: we would not be arguing about the state or condition of the apple; instead, we would be arguing about our tastes in apples. Others might disagree with us if they, for example, valued tartness rather than sweetness in an apple. Thus, if they disagreed with us, they would be arguing against our taste and not against the apple itself.

Policy claims are claims that are advanced to defend the idea that something (e.g., a policy, program, procedure) should be made the case now, should have been made the case in the past, or should be made the case in the future. Note again that such claims can refer to any time frame, and that these claims differ in principle from both declarative and evaluative claims. Referring to our now-familiar apple, you may be so overwhelmed by the taste of the apple that you may claim, "You know, all apples should taste this way," or more directly related to the common conception of "policies," you may contend that "More growers ought to be growing this kind of apple tree." In doing so, you would make clear your contention that something should be the case in the *present.* Then, too, you may state a policy claim related to the *past* by contending, "Hey, more farmers should have planted orchards of this kind of apple." Similarly, you may claim that a policy should be adopted in the *future* by saying, "Anybody starting an orchard certainly ought to plant this kind of apple." Whether you are claiming that a policy should be in force now, should have been in force in the past, or should be in force in the future, the contention is a policy claim.

One of the main ideas traditionally advanced by writers of argumentation, however, is that policy claims refer exclusively to the future by advocating a change from the present situation. In contrast, I believe that frequently our claims that "something should be" will also refer to either the present (and what should be the policy now) or the past (and what should have been the policy). Often, we will observe the events of the present and wish a rule or activity to be in force in the present: for example, "We should be living like Ghandi," or "We should be living under better police protection." Similarly, it seems to me that we will often look to the past and wish that a certain policy had been in effect at that time: "We should have withdrawn from Vietnam earlier," or "We should have been on the metric system long ago." We indulge in such argumentation frequently, and such claims seem to me to qualify as policy claims. Perhaps the traditional belief that policy claims refer exclusively to the future is explained by the fact that most argumentation texts are also debate texts, where policies for change in the status quo are the central concern. Regardless of the explanation, when we approach argumentation as it exists in a diversity of communication situations, we ought to expect to encounter policy claims that refer to the present and the past, as well as the future.

Classificatory claims are those that contend that something is, was, or will be of a particular kind, category, type, or classification.[4] In one last treatment of our well-used apple, you may scrutinize the apple and decide that "This is a Jonathan apple," meaning that it presently is of the type that we call "Jonathan." Then, too, you may look at an apple core you find in the orchard, and after examining its shape, size, and color, say to me, "Professor Crable, this was once a Jonathan apple." Finally, you may look up at a particular type of apple blossom and contend that "This will become a Jonathan apple." In all these instances, you will have looked at something before you and claimed that something is, was, or will be of a particular variety or classification. The categories or classes of apples are well established, and you use those labels as a method of classifying what it is that you see. You would do the same thing if you were to observe a certain automobile and claim, "This car is a Ford"; if you see a bird and contend that it is a member of the blackbird family; or if you looked at this book and said, "This is an argumentation book." In

---

[4]Ehninger, *Influence, Belief, and Argument.* Again, I agree with Ehninger that the term *classificatory* is more practical than *definitive*, another term sometimes used.

each case you would be identifying the object based upon what you know to be the established classes, kinds, or types.

At this point, there are several important and traditionally mentioned ideas that will aid your grasp of the types of argumentative claims. First, each one of the types necessitates *judgment* on the part of both arguer and receiver. The arguer judges that something is the case and proceeds to create an argument advancing that idea as a claim. The receiver, in turn, judges the merits of the claim. The same sort of mutual judging and evaluation is involved in all types of intended claims. My reason for stressing this similarity among claims is because of the possible confusion between evaluative claims and all other types: though all claims require some sort of judgment or evaluation, that *evaluation* is about different kinds of things. In examining declarative claims, we shall judge what is (was, will be) the case; in policy claims, we shall look at what should be (should have been, or should be in the future) the case; and in classificatory claims, we shall judge the category of a particular thing. Although all those involve judgments, they differ from the evaluative claims which stress evaluations of quality, worth, and so forth, rather than policy, classification, or what is the case.

A second helpful, traditional comment is that the argumentation you engage in may involve more than one sort of claim. Policy claims, for example, typically will be based upon certain evaluative claims. The reason for discussing any policy probably would be that some judgments had been made about other matters: you claim that the university is experiencing a drop in enrollments (declarative), and, further, you claim that the drop in enrollment is unhealthy (an evaluative claim about your declarative claim). On the basis of these, you may well feel justified in advancing the (policy) claim that your university needs to change its student admission procedures. Clearly, the development of the whole line of reasoning would require that you support those claims with evidence and any other argumentative elements that are demanded. Yet, one of the situations you will find is that, for example, the *declarative claim* that enrollments are dropping (if supported adequately and accepted by the receiver) can later be used as *evidence* to support the *evaluative claim* that the situation is unhealthy: recall that the difference between claims and evidence is their function, since (by our conception) evidence is accepted, and claims are the subject of controversy. Then, if that *evaluative claim* becomes accepted also, it can be presented to the receiver as *evidence* to support the *policy claim*. This development in how claims and evidence function explains the traditional comment that your argumentation may involve more than one sort of claim, even if your basic claim is of only one type.

It seems to me, then, that the usual advice given to students of argumentation is generally helpful and crucial in such activities as debate where rules, procedures, and conventions abound and are normally heeded. Our concern for argumentation as communication in various sorts of situations, however, necessitates that we acknowledge the relative indistinctness of these categories of claims. For example, you may advance an argumentative claim such as: President Lincoln was a good President. If you did so, you probably would intend for the claim to be an evaluative one: it makes a value judgment about Lincoln, who was "in fact" a President (a declarative claim). Yet, you must be alerted that some degree of ambiguity will exist in your claim. It can be interpreted by a receiver as a claim that puts Lincoln into the category of "good" as opposed to "bad" Presidents"; the claim can be seen as a classificatory claim. If such an interpretation is advanced, then your receiver will misunderstand your claim and possibly your whole intent in stating the argument. On the other hand, the fact that you are arguing about such a well-known, well-studied, and popular President (can you conceive of Harding's birthday as a national holiday?), you are vulnerable to the interpretation that your claim is declarative in nature: Wasn't he, *in fact*, a good President? My point is simply that regardless of the kind of claim you intend to advance, your receiver(s) will respond to it as the kind of claim they judge it to be. Frequently, your intent and their judgment will not be consistent.

The discussion of the potential difference between the intent and judgment of the type of claim, though, serves to introduce another variable in the complex process of argumentation. The language that you intend to have function as a certain type of claim may not be interpreted by your receiver as a claim at all. From the point of view of function, your proposed evidence may magically turn into a claim if it is challenged rather than taken as being evident; this is the point here. You may advance (what you intend as) a claim for which you are prepared to present support, but you may find that your statement is accepted with no further support. Your intended claim simply does not function as a claim, because of the judgment of your receiver. Certainly, you could term your statement a claim (since you were willing to defend it), but it would still be largely irrelevant to the process of argumentation. Let me illustrate: you come into your dormitory room angry about something that happened earlier. You are seeking an argument to give vent to an emotional state, so you immediately launch an attack upon your roommate by saying, "Hey, you really ought to pick up your things better. This room is really a mess." Your roommate may take the statement as an argumentative claim and may challenge you to support it: your intended claim would begin functioning as a claim. On the other hand, your room-mate may reply, "Oh" and walk out of the room. Your intended claim fades into insignificance, simply because your receiver has failed (at least we think) to judge it a claim (as we have conceived it) and respond accordingly. Again, just as the type of claim advanced is primarily a matter of receiver judgment, the question as to whether the intended claim really serves as a claim at all is a matter of the receiver's choice of response.

One final comment must be made about the difference between arguer intent and receiver judgment concerning claims: although we have discussed the difficulty of argumentative claims because of the impact of receiver judgment, I continually alluded to the relatively simple situation of dyadic (one-to-one) communication and argu-ment. When we add the variable of a group of receivers, the problems become even more complex. When the intended claim is presented to a group of receivers, the possibility—no, the probability—exists that various receivers will judge the claim in vastly different ways. One may agree completely with the claim and consider the matter above question: the statement would not function as a claim at all. Others might judge the claim to be a classificatory claim and demand appropriate support, and still others may perceive the claim to be a declarative one and demand other kinds of support. The difference in receivers' judgments, then, can become one further way of ex-plaining the complexity of argumentation and the difficulty in insur-ing its success: How do you "support" something that is being interpreted in widely different ways by various receivers all at the same time?

Evidence in Argumentative Communication

Just as certain statements and treatments about claims or proposi-tions have become traditional, particular ways of conceptualizing evidence have also become rather conventionalized. Such concepts as opinion, statistics, and testimony are normally included in dis-cussions of argumentative evidence. For reasons that will become clear in our treatment of warrants,[5] I think it will be easier for you to conceptualize evidence by asking, "What are the general types of 'things' which can be assumed to be 'evident' to a receiver, and therefore, used as evidence by arguers to build argumentative sup-port?" Though the following may not be exhaustive, it seems to me that your question might well be answered by "things" such as unplanned, contrived, and hypothetical occurrences; reports of un-

[5]Suffice it here to say that such things as testimony will be treated more in terms of warrant than in terms of evidence. Our next section in this chapter involves warrants.

planned and contrived occurrences; objects and artifacts; and expressions of belief and reports of expressions of belief. To explain how any of these classes of things may be perceived as evident, let us explore and illustrate each. In order to compare the types of potential evidence, I shall incur the risk of overworking a claim by demonstrating how any one claim might be supported by any of the evidence types. Let us assume that you are in the extremely comfortable position of being sought for employment by a large and successful business organization. The personnel director of the organization has invited you to the place of business for an interview aimed at persuading you that you ought to accept their job offer. In that situation, what are the kinds of evidence that the director, Mr. Russell, might present to you to support his claim that you would like the job? Let us explore the possibilities together.

Occurrences: Unplanned, Contrived, and Hypothetical

One of the most obvious strategies that Mr. Russell might use is to guide you through the place of business, Roan, Inc., in areas meant to expose you to the actual day-to-day activities of the company. In this manner, he would be attempted to make his claim credible by having you witness *unplanned occurrences*: activities that occur or states that exist in unstaged settings, whether social or physical. Your acceptance that these (hopefully) attractive activities, in fact, were happening as they appeared to be would constitute your acceptance that the occurrences he guided you to may soon be used by Mr. Russell as evidence for his claim. Just as your touring of a natural disaster area such as a tornado-struck city might enhance your acceptance of the claim that aid should be offered, Russell expects your observation of the occurrences in Roan, Inc. may enhance your acceptance of his claim that you would like the job.

Not all occurrences, of course, occur naturally; sometimes they are the result of manipulation. Russell, for example, may include a cocktail party in your honor later in the evening. The scene and the activity at such an employment-related party are not without preset objectives or preplanning: they are *contrived occurrences*: activities that occur or states that exist because they have been staged to occur or exist that way. The goal of such a party may well be to "let you get to know everyone," but Russell undoubtedly would hope that your reaction to the party will be a favorable acceptance of the occurrence, so that you will be even more disposed toward the claim.

A related type of potential evidence is what we can call a *hypothetical occurrence*: an activity or state of affairs which is envisioned as a possibility. Instead of merely allowing you to observe the natural occurrences at the office or the contrived occurrences at a party, Russell might describe for you what sort of activity you would be involved in if you were to accept the position. "If you were to come here," he might say, "you would be in this sort of office with a secretarial and clerical pool to support you. Your duties would typically include. . . . " In essence, he would hope that you would accept his visions as plausible, acceptable, and constructive in supporting his claim that you would enjoy the position.

Reports of Occurrences: Unplanned and Contrived

Russell, of course, probably would not rely upon your observation of occurrences, unplanned or contrived, or his description of a hypothetical occurrence. He would probably seek the aid of various other employees who could relate to you their perceptions of the situation at Roan, Inc. You might have an interview schedule set up which would include visits with people who would be working with you on a steady basis. These visits would allow you (Russell hopes) to gain whole new sources of evidence from *reports of unplanned occurrences:* statements from other observers about activities or states of affairs as they occur or exist. These people would provide you with potential evidence by virtue of their having been in the organization for varying lengths of time, having different perspectives than the personnel director himself may have, or having more age or experience than you might. If you handled these interviews well, you might gain whole new views of the organization with which to examine Russell's claim that you would like working at Roan, Inc.

If Russell were more scientist than humanist in outlook, he might present potential evidence in terms of experimental results of studies done inside the company. Companies sometimes participate in laboratory sessions aimed at exploring various situations within the organization or comparing certain companies. These studies would be another sort of contrived occurrence, but since the experiment would need an experimenter and a statement of the results, we would call the distributed information a *report of a contrived occurrence:* a statement about activities or states of existence that have been contrived, created, or manipulated. From this perspective, the results of experimental research would be reports of contrived occurrences, every bit as much as would the report of the party in your honor made by one of Russell's other employees. Regardless of the nature of the occurrence, when an understanding of it can be gained only through someone's secondhand report or commentary, we shall classify the potential evidence in this group.

Objects and Artifacts

Frequently, though, potential evidence exists in the form of some physical item or article such as a rifle in a courtroom, a baseball in a neighbor's living room that has entered through a picture window, or a lipstick stain on a collar. In each of these instances, the intended evidence is in the form of an *object*: a physical article that relates directly to the essence of the claim. The rifle, for example, can be assumed to be directly related to the commission of a crime; the baseball to a broken window; and the lipstick stain to almost anything from a clumsy salesperson to an unfaithful husband. In his attempt to present as much potential evidence as possible, Mr. Russell also might submit some object such as the automobile to which you would have access for business purposes if you took the position. His indicating of the automobile, your future office, or your nameplate would all be included in the category of potential evidence that we shall call objects. On the other hand, if none of these objects were available for your scrutiny, Russell might rely upon a man-made (with or without the aid of machines) reproduction or picture of the car, office, or nameplate. When the offered evidence is such a reproduction and not the object itself, we shall call it an *artifact*: a man-created facsimile, copy, document, or graph. Instead of presenting those tangible objects or related artifacts mentioned earlier, Russell might use other types of artifacts: charts of the company's production increase, financial statements, or letters from respected institutions that are pleased with their relationship with Roan. Though these items are only reproductions or representations of objects such as capital assets, and so forth, these artifacts function similarly to objects in supporting argumentative claims.

Expressions of Beliefs: Personal and Reported

Russell, though, might choose to utilize Roan employees instead of objects or artifacts, but use them in a way different from when they reported to you their perceptions or reports of the occurrences at the company. He may hope that they present their own *expressions of belief*: self-reports of their personal convictions, attitudes, and judgments.[6] Indeed, whether Russell intended that you use your

[6]As we begin discussing such "evidence" as expressions of belief, reports of expressions of belief, and the like, it should be noted that these expressions are sometimes said to be *based* perhaps on evidence, but not on evidence itself. Since, however, we are approaching argumentation from the perspective of receivers, we must realize that a multitude of different judgments and reports can be accepted as evident, or obvious, by receivers—allowing these to be used to support a disputed claim. Thus, although they may not take the *form* of what we traditionally speak of as evidence, they do (or at least can) *function* as evidence in realistic argumentative situations. Hence, such reports and judgments are discussed in this section as potential evidence.

interviews with other employees in this way or not, it seems reasonable to suppose that when you asked these people about what occurred in the organization (reports of occurrences), you would also attempt to have them express their attitudes and judgments about the organization. If you did, however, you would be asking them to go far beyond any mere report of the occurrences during the working day; you would be asking for their judgments (probably) about employee-management relations, working conditions, and organizational climate. You would not be expecting, nor would you accept, simple reporting of activities or occurrences; you would be seeking personal convictions to serve as evidence as to whether, in fact, you would be happy working at Roan, Inc.

What normally happens when you begin seeking such reports, though, is that your interviewee will step across the boundary of his or her self-reports and begin "reporting" other persons' feelings and perceptions. This secondhand information is what we shall call *reports of expression of beliefs:* hearsay accounts of personal convictions, attitudes, and judgments. Though you may gain a great deal of useful information from self-reports from talking with Roan employees, you will also be confronted with the task of determining how much of the belief is self-report and how much is hearsay. When John R. contends, "Everyone here is happy and pleased with the company," you may need to examine the statement more carefully to find out how it is that John knows enough about the personal judgments and beliefs of "everyone" to provide an accurate picture of what "they" think. Such secondhand accounts might be entirely valid, but they may also be prompted by John's assumption that everyone is as contented with the company as he is. Those reports of expressions of belief may be simply John's own self-reports, generalized to the entire staff at Roan. If the reports are accurate, however, they may become important sources of evidence for your evaluation of Russell's claim.

In sum, I have suggested that for any one claim, such as the one advanced by the personnel director, the types of potential evidence are several, including unplanned, contrived, or hypothetical occurrences, reports of unplanned or contrived occurrences, objects or artifacts, and expressions and reports of expressions of belief. Although we normally would not expect to find any one claim supported by intended evidence of all these types, we certainly could expect to find several different sorts of evidence being presented. Indeed, it seems reasonable to suppose that the claim will be supported more strongly if the evidence is of more than one type. If several types are provided, it seems again reasonable to suppose that one or more will be judged self-evident by the receiver.

Here, again, we confront the potential conflict between what the arguer presents as *intended evidence*, and whether the receiver judges it to be actually something that *functions as evidence*. An arguer, certainly, is free to contend that anything she presents is in fact evidence, but all she would be saying is if she were the receiver, it would function as evidence, and that sort of comment would reveal that the arguer knows little about argumentation. Her argumentation will never be successful if she formulates an argumentative claim and supports it with evidence that is not acceptable to the receiver. For if the receiver rejects or challenges the authenticity or accuracy of the evidence, then it really begins to function as a claim (for the receiver), and this new claim will have to be supported—hopefully better than the original claim was. Clearly, the crucial variable in the effect of evidence is what the receiver judges to be the case.

Warrants in Argumentative Communication

As we observed in chapter 4 in relation to the purchase of a new automobile, warrants can be tremendously important to the development of argumentation in interpersonal communication situations. Claims may be understandable and intended evidence may be evident to the receiver, but he may not be clear as to what the evidence has to do with the claim: the arguer may be called upon to supply a warrant that demonstrates the relationship between the evidence and the claim, or how our acceptance of the evidence leads us toward acceptance of the claim. In the midst of the argumentation about the new car, my wife and I at times chose to accept the evidence, but we rejected or at least challenged the warrant that would allow the evidence to make the claim evident. At other times, the salesman asked what warrant we would accept, and then he tried to develop his deal to provide evidence that would be consistent with our warrant: in such a situation, he assumed, we would also accept the evidence and later the claim. In essence, whether you are confronted with a claim and evidence and you demand a warrant, or whether you are confronted with a claim and asked to provide a warrant that would be suitable, the concept of warrant is critical to your understanding of how argumentation develops in communication situations.

Realizing that warrants are statements of relationships between claims and evidence, we are now faced with the task of analyzing any potential differences between the arguer's intent in providing warrants and the receiver's judgment of whether the warrants function appropriately. As we have done with both claims and evidence, let us first examine some classifications of how warrants might relate evidence to claims and then discuss the impact of receiver judgment upon these arguer intentions. For ease in understanding these warrant classifications, I will focus upon one particular claim, "parliamentary system of government is best for the United States," and discuss what different sorts of warrants might be demanded— depending, in part, upon the kind of evidence offered in support.[7]

Warrants of Comparison: Parallelism and Analogy

First, then, if a friend were advancing the claim that a parliamentary form of government is best for the United States, you might be tempted to reply, "Why, of all things, a parliamentary form of government?" In response to your question, your friend probably would provide some sort of evidence: she might say, "because a parliamentary form of government has been so good for Great Britain." Since this is an expression of belief, you might challenge the evidence and allude to Britain's current problems. On the other hand, you might accept the evidence as being "evident" to you, but you might ask for a warrant: "Okay, but what does that have to do with the best government for the United States?" Clearly, some warrant is demanded, but what type? What sort of language could function as a warrant between the claim and this evidence about Great Britain? The answer, most probably, is that your friend would need to supply what we shall call a *warrant by parallelism:* something that says that the two ideas (what is in the claim and what is in the evidence) are so "literally" similar that we assume that what is true for one is true for the other. In this case, a warrant by parallelism might be something such as, "You know, of course, that the two countries are so similar that what is good for one is good for both." That warrant, combined with the evidence that the parliamentary form has been good for Britain, (hopefully) makes clear why parliamentary government is best for the United States. The term "literal" is important since a parallel warrant is based on the actual similarities that exist. In law, we would call such a parallelism a "precedent," and one attorney would argue that the precedent and the case decision in question are

[7]Ehninger deals with several of these ideas as warrants (see Ehninger, chapter 6), although his discussion differs substantially from that here.

so similar (parallel) that the decision made in the precedent should be the verdict here. Your friend would be doing the same thing in citing the literal comparison of Great Britain and arguing that what is good for them is good for us now. Keep in mind, however, that the example of Great Britain is merely a report of a state of affairs: it is the warrant that relates evidence to claim by parallelism.

Instead of relating the ideas by parallelism, however, your friend may be more poetically or metaphorically oriented, and so she may cite as evidence, "The commander-in-chief works best when his supply officer agrees with his policies." Again you might disagree with that as evidence, but let us assume you accept it for the time being. You might ask, though, "What does the claim have to do with that statement about the commander-in-chief?" When your friend replied that the commander-in-chief was something like the President (or Prime Minister) and the supply officer was somewhat like the Congress (or Parliament), she would be supplying a *warrant by analogy:* something that says that the two ideas (what is in the claim and what is in the evidence) are somewhat alike or so metaphorically or figuratively similar that what is true for one is, in some respects, true for both. In contrast to warrants that assert parallel and literal similarities, the warrant by analogy simply says that the two ideas share a basic principle or enough attributes that one is useful as evidence for the other, which is the claim. When someone argues that people inevitably "turn out" to be what they were when they were young (claim) and supports it with the saying, "As the twig is bent, so grows the tree," he is using a similar strategy: the warrant that makes the argument "make sense" is your understanding that there is just enough similarity between people and trees that what is true for one, in some respects, will be true for the other—even though no one would say that the tree and a person are "literally parallel."

Warrants of Grouping: Classification,
Generalization, and Residual

Another possibility as your friend supports her claim is that she will offer a statement that refers to an entire group of similar situations or cases. She may say to your need for evidence, "Well, modernized, advanced democracies function better with a parliamentary form of government." Such a statement, if accepted as being evident in itself, might still prompt you to ask for a warrant: "What does that have to do with the United States?" She might then reply that the United States is indeed a modernized, advanced democracy, and she would be supplying a *warrant by classification:* a statement that the idea in the claim is in the group, classification, or category expressed in the warrant. In the closest thing to a categorical syllogism (as discussed in chapter 3) that we will discuss, she says since all countries that are modernized, advanced democracies function better with a parliamentary government (evidence), and since the United States is one such country (warrant), then it would also function best with a parliamentary form of government (claim). The warrant merely asserts that the idea in the claim "fits into" the category discussed in the evidence; thus, the claim and the evidence are related by category or by classification.

Warrants by classification, then, relate the evidence about a group to a claim about a specific case. Related, but nearly opposite in effect, is what we shall call a *warrant by generalization*: a statement that a claim and evidence are related since an idea expressed in the claim is merely the culmination of the things alluded to in the evidence. Your friend may attempt to support her claim about parliamentary government by suggesting a number of ideas (intended evidence), including that foreign affairs are conducted best with a parliamentary form of government, as are domestic and social policies, economic affairs, and defense concerns. After she lists those areas, she may conclude: "See, a parliamentary government is best for the United States." Assuming that you take her ideas as "evident," again, you may challenge the link between those examples and the claim. Her most appropriate response would be a warrant by generalization: "If parliamentary government is best in foreign, domestic, social, economic, and defense affairs, then it must be best in all the affairs of a nation state." Here, the warrant would connect all the specific instances (much like the inductive process of "adding" that we discussed earlier) into a generalization that you claim.

Another option that your friend would have available as a method of supporting her claim is related somewhat to warrants by classification and generalization. She may point out to you that, in actuality, there are only a limited number of governmental types, including parliamentary forms, dictatorships, pure democracy, socialist states, the present form in the United States, and anarchies. After you listen to her enumeration of these, you may find yourself acknowledging the lists (finding them evident), but wondering what it all means. You may pause, and finding no response forthcoming, you may say impatiently, "So?" She would probably need to supply some sort of *warrant by residual*: a statement indicating that since all the ideas mentioned in the evidence, except one, are unacceptable, the remaining one is the reasonable choice. Specifically, then, she may provide the necessary warrant by asserting that, since "everyone" knows the problems of other forms of government, logically the parliamentary form of government is the best choice. Just as you might examine your evening's plans by saying, "I could do a, b, c, or d, but I don't want to do a, b, or c, so I'll do what's left," your friend may present you with evidence that supports the claim by eliminating all but the choice embodied in the claim. Warrants by residual, then, stress that evidence and claim are related, since the idea in the claim is all that is left (the residual choice) from the options in the evidence.

Warrants and the Question of Causality: Correlation, Circumstance, and Cause

Most of the argumentative options for warrants that we have discussed involve relationships of categories, kinds, types, choices, and so forth. Not all warrants, however, are of that nature. Three related types of warrants, for example, involve varying degrees of the general idea of causality or the idea of effect: warrants of correlation, circumstance, and cause. Let us examine each of these by focusing upon one item of intended evidence.

Your friend may support her claim by stating that she feels that shorter terms for national public figures are desirable. You may listen to this expression of personal belief and agree with her judgment, but you may fail to see how such intended evidence applies to the claim. She may reply with a *warrant by correlation*: a statement that what is in the evidence and what is in the claim often occur simultaneously—but not causally. The assumption is that since the one is desirable and occurs frequently with the other, the other is also desirable. Your friend would not be asserting any real causal connection between the idea in the claim and the idea in the evidence; rather, she is noting that they are often found together, and both, then, are desirable. Just as a survey revealing that the incidence of suicide is high among single men may not argue that one causes the other, your friend stops short of declaring that either parliamentary government or short terms cause one another.

You may agree with her intended evidence, but you may be unmoved by the idea that the two things are often found together. In essence, you may want her to provide some reason to believe that if a parliamentary form of government, in fact, were adopted, there would be a good chance of having shorter terms for elected officials. You may ask, that is, for a stronger warrant, *warrant by circumstance*: a statement that what is in the claim or what is in the evidence *may* have caused the other to occur. Just as a prosecuting attorney argues that the defendant's presence at the scene of the crime is "circumstantial evidence" that he *may also have caused* the crime to occur, your friend may argue that the fact that parliamentary government and shorter terms exist together *may* be reason to believe the one can cause the other to occur. She would be contending that since the short term (a desirable outcome) may be caused by the parliamentary form of government, this form of government is best: it *may* cause the desirable effect to occur.

Still, you may not be satisfied, since you are dealing with what might occur should you opt for parliamentary government. You may demand a *warrant by cause*: a statement that what is in the claim or what is in the evidence, in fact, does cause the other to occur. This is a demand for a much stronger warrant; one that confidently asserts that one will result from the other, or that one caused the other. Though it would be unreasonable to assume that such a judgment would be "fact" or "beyond all doubt," it is reasonable to expect a tremendously high probability that if you have one occurrence (parliamentary government), that you will have the other (shorter terms). In law, we would say that such direct causality must be "beyond any reasonable doubt," and in the case of your friend, you would be demanding that she virtually guarantee a parliamentary government would cause the shorter terms to exist. Warrant by cause, then, represents the ultimate demand that arises from dissatisfaction from stating a correlation or a circumstantial situation.

Warrant of Authority

Beyond such options of causality, a final alternative that your friend might choose involves *warrant of authority*: a statement asserting that the claim is acceptable because of the *expertise* of the *source* of the evidence. In supporting her claim, your friend may relate a reported expression of belief, such as "Ralph Jones contends that the parliamentary system is best for the United States." Again, you may accept as evident that Jones said that, but you may demand to know what his statement has to do with the claim. In response, your friend probably would rely upon a warrant by authority by arguing that if Jones, a political science professor, says it, then it must be true. That sort of warrant with that sort of expressed belief (or reported expressed belief) is commonly called "testimony," but it is the report or expression related by the idea of authority that makes it such: without the warrant asserting expertise, the evidence simply would be a report of belief or a belief. Clearly, though, not all warrants of authority refer to academic experts. Instead, some will involve witnesses (who are "expert" because of what they saw or heard); the

Bible (which is "expert" because of its perceived divine origin); or a child (who is "expert" in toy selection because of his total submersion in the topic). In all such cases, the evidence is brought to bear upon the claim because someone or something related to the evidence carries with it some sort of authority to some receivers.

In sum, we have examined a number of ways in which evidence can relate to claims. For the sake of simplicity, we have assumed that, in all cases, the evidence is accepted as being evident in itself but unclear in its relation to the claim. When evidence is questioned or challenged, then it functions not as support for a claim, but as a claim needing support for itself. Yet even when the evidence itself is accepted, the argumentation may be just beginning as receivers attempt to see how what they take as "evident" is related to what they are asked to accept as a claim. The concern for language that functions as warrants, then, is a critical focus for your understanding of argumentation as communication.

What we must add, of course, is that our discussion has emphasized the warrant as the arguer would like it to function. Just as we contended that the functioning of claims and evidence will be determined by the arguer's choice of response to them, we must suggest that the successful functioning of warrants is based upon similar choices by receivers. Only the arguer who was naive about the complexity of the argumentative communication process would assume that since he himself accepted the warrant connection between the evidence and claim, the receiver must somehow see the relationship. As an arguer, you can expect receivers at times to reject or question a claim; you can expect them to question the self-evidence of intended evidence; and, as we have just discussed, you can expect receivers to demand a warrant, to examine it critically, and then to decide (perhaps) that it does not function for them as it was intended by you. In that situation, they either may be rejecting the idea expressed in the warrant, or they may be interpreting the warrant in some way other than in the desired manner. In the latter case, although we may be tempted to call the interpretation a misinterpretation, the result is much the same as when the warrant is rejected, but understood accurately: we may substitute a different warrant, we may choose to explain the warrant in different terms, or we must supply backing for the warrant as stated.

Backing in Argumentative Communication

Once a warrant has been judged in need of support, the arguer should be prepared to provide the necessary backing. If I claim that the Yankees will win the pennant this year, I may choose to offer evidence that their pitching staff is superb. You may accept the evidence, challenge the claim, and force me to provide a warrant such as "Well, they have the pitching staff they need." If you press me to support such a warrant, I probably would provide the names of those pitchers who comprise the staff. I would intend these pitchers to serve as backing for the warrant that the pitching staff is what they need to win the pennant. Yet, as with the other argumentative functions that we have discussed, the course of the transaction would be controlled more by you, the receiver, than by me: you may be out of touch with baseball this year and say, "Well, the names don't help; what are their earned run averages?" In essence, you would ask for a different kind of backing than I had intended to provide. Instead of that response, you might say, "Yes, but are these really great pitchers?" If you directly question the backing—or, really, the backing-warrant relationship—then you, as a receiver, have begun to present a different sort of problem: you are switching the whole discussion from the Yankees and their staff to a more general and abstract argumentative discussion about "What does it take to be a great pitcher?" My answer to such a general question, then, would succeed, most probably, in simply taking us farther away from the discussion at hand. Thus I probably would point out (as I indicated in chapter 4) that your judgment of the backing has created the need for an entirely different discussion—at some future date—about the criteria for being a great pitcher. Still, whether I succeed in having you accept my backing, whether I must provide different backing (earned run averages instead of names), or whether I might have to say that the argumentation is getting too far afield will depend, not on my intention, but on the judgment of the receiver.

Qualifiers in Argumentative Communication

Although argumentative claims can be presented as absolute, certain, or unqualified, the claims in our communication typically will be somewhat less positive than such phrases imply. We may say, "The United States simply must get out of some foreign commitment," but if we were forced to defend our "simply must" claim, we probably would admit that the phrase is perhaps exaggerated: we really meant that in all probability, we ought to end the agreement. We are not discussing here something that weakens your argumentative point (students generally feel a qualification weakens their case); instead, we are adjusting what it is you claim to what it is that you can defend: we are supplying a reasonable warrant to an idea that, at best, is highly probable. When the adjustment is made, we no longer face the same possibility of a challenge or question that will force us to weasel or water-down what it was we said originally.

In discussing qualifiers in more detail, even from the initial standpoint of what is intended by the arguer, we must acknowledge a distinction among three perspectives on the degree of probability or qualification: first, probability defined as odds arising from the situation or data itself; second, probability conceived as a nonstatistical interpretation of probability (even intuitive); and finally, probability defined as the degree of confidence the arguer tells his receivers that they can have in the claim. Let me illustrate those distinctions by relating an incident that occurred to me several years ago.

Case Study: The Fifth Six in the Fourth Game

Several years ago, I was visiting my sister and brother-in-law who live in my hometown of Circleville, Ohio. The three of us and my wife were playing a game called Yahtzee late into the evening and discussing the kinds of things that people discuss when they get to visit only infrequently. We were seated at a round table in their kitchen, and, as the fourth game approached, we realized that everyone had won a game but me, and that the order of winning was in sequence all around the table: Donna, Abe, and Ann. As the fourth game began to be completed, it was evident that in terms of the *statistical odds* as generated by the situation itself, I had almost no chance of winning "my game": Yahtzee requires five dice to be thrown which, when thrown, act as poker hands—two pair, three-of-a-kind, full houses, four-of-a-kind, and so forth. As the game developed, the only roll of the dice that would allow me to win the game was (in a combination of three throws) to roll *all* sixes with the five dice, resulting in a "Yahtzee." A five-of-a-kind is considered rare; even rarer is getting a "Yahtzee" with precisely the number you need: and I needed one in sixes to win the fourth game. Realistically, I said to myself, I probably would not roll such a combination of sixes: the mathematical odds against it were just too great to assume that I had much chance.

Orally, however, I did not reflect this doubt in my claim to the others that "I think that I'm going to get the fifth six." Indeed, there was a great difference between the probability based on the odds and the probability based on the confidence that I felt and expressed to the others. Because of a feeling I had about the final die, I rejected the degree of probability that was based upon statistics and chose instead to claim that I was going to win because of other factors: a feeling, a hunch, the factor of faith. I felt somehow certain that I would win, and so I rejected the probability of the dice and claimed my impending victory on the basis of my interpretation.

And, indeed, I did receive the fifth six on the third (and last) throw of the fourth game. Fate? Luck? Whatever it was, my own interpretation of probability and my statement to receivers about the confidence they could have in my claim emerged as being more accurate in this case than the probability that was implied in the statistical odds. Yet, this is the essence of probability as it will function in common argumentation: statements such as probably, possibly, almost surely, and so forth, will frequently not function to state the statistical odds of the claim being accurate, but rather to express the *degree of confidence* that the arguer tells his receivers they can have in the claim. When a receiver asks, "How sure of this are you?" the arguer will reply by saying, "I am (this) certain . . . and you can be, too."

Yet, what we must say about claims, evidence, warrants, and backing (if we call it that), we must add about qualifiers: there is a great, potential difference between what the arguer intends to be the expression of confidence and what the receiver actually judges to be the degree of confidence that she would place upon the claim. Just as the arguer (for example, me in relation to the fifth six) can choose to ignore the statistical probability and place his confidence in a nonstatistical interpretation, the receiver may reinterpret the arguer's qualification or demand that the arguer himself do so. To a claim that "Lincoln was, without doubt, the greatest American President," we may ask if the arguer is prepared to present all the evidence he would need to support a "without a doubt" qualifier (really an absence of a qualifier). Most probably, either we as receivers will say, "You mean he *almost* without a doubt, was the greatest President—which I can accept"; or we will say, "Okay, prove that to me without a doubt—if you think you can." Indeed, our study of qualification, like the analysis of claims, evidence, and warrants, must focus more upon receiver judgment and less upon mere arguer intent.

Reservations in Argumentative Communication

The final function of language in argumentative communication that we should allude to, at least briefly, is the function of reservation. Just as an arguer may be called upon to state the level of confidence that he attaches to his claim, he may also be required to list the situations in which the claim may be something he would retract. As receivers, we might ask, "But is this true in all cases?" (Are there no exceptions?); "How often is this the case?" (What is the percentage rate of such exceptions?); or, "What would happen if . . . ?" (Is this an exception?) In each instance, the receiver is demanding that, since the arguer has acknowledged the *lack* of the claim's certainty, the arguer also state those conditions under which the claim is irrelevant, not helpful, or no longer applicable.[8] I may ask a car dealer if his automobile *really* delivers thirty-three miles per gallon of gasoline, and he may soften his original claim with a reservation: "Well, unless you floor it every time you pull away from a traffic light, . . . " I have asked him for his assessment of the instances in which the claim might need modification, and he has responded appropriately.

As a receiver, obviously, I do not have to accept his reservation as being the *only* reservation. Exercising my receiver judgment, I may add to the car dealer, "Or unless you drive with a heavy load, or if you drive in town, or if you ever idle in traffic, or if you ever drive over forty miles per hour, or if. . . . " In essence, I am under no obligation to accept the reservation as he intends it. I examine the claim, his evidence, the evidence of others, the warrants, and the qualifications (some made by law or dictated by the fair-trade agencies), and I interpret my own statement of reservation: my judgment as a receiver will always affect the development of the process of argumentation much more than anything merely intended by the arguer.

Summary

Whereas chapter 3 dealt with the nature of argumentative functions of language, and chapter 4 dealt with how those functions are developed by arguers and receivers as they engage in the process of argumentation, this chapter sought to relate those two concerns by stressing the potential difference between how an arguer might intend something to function and how the receiver might judge it to actually function for him: this chapter discussed the relationship between arguer intent and receiver judgment.

We examined language that could function as claims, evidence, warrants, backing, qualifiers, and reservations in processes of argumentation. Our consistent approach was to examine those argumentative functions in terms of (at times traditional) types of classes or categories, and then we reexamined the importance of

---

[8]Clearly, of course, what an arguer might do is to state the reservations early in the process and then attempt to minimize their significance as the argumentation developed; there is no reason why an arguer must wait to supply any relevant reservations until they become challenged, unless he feels that the reservations are likely not to be demanded.

these functions in terms of how receivers might react differently from the way arguers would like them to. Indeed, though students of argumentation can be aided by a conceptual distinction between declarative and evaluative claims, the important variable is how the receiver interprets the statement—regardless of the arguer's intent. Similarly, it is the receiver's judgment of the evidence—its type and whether it really is evident—that dictates how and if the intended evidence will function in the argumentative process. Then too, the nature, functioning, and success of warrants as connections between claims and evidence; of qualifiers as statements of confidence; and of reservations as the admission of exceptions will depend much more upon the judgment of receivers than the intent of the arguers themselves.

We have now examined functions in argumentation and the process of argumentation, and we have seen the burden of decision, judgment, and choice fall squarely upon the shoulders of the receiver. The most reasonable next questions are, "But how is the receiver to judge?" "What can he demand?" or "What are the standards for evaluation by receivers?" We shall answer these questions in the following chapters.

Supplemental Information

Though chapters 7 and 8 will deal with a variety of productive demands and standards that can be used to evaluate claims more clearly, you may wish to use the following questions about claims, warrants, evidence, backing, reservations, and qualifiers as preliminary guidelines in examining argumentation—or as guidelines in preparing argumentation.

I.   In examining claims:
    A.   In general, ask whether the claim is:
        1.   *positive* (e.g., something *is* the case; *was* of a certain kind or class; *should be* the case in the future; or *was* of a quality) or *negative* (e.g., *wasn't* the case; *is not* of a particular kind; *should not have been* done; or *will not be* of a particular quality)?
        2.   *qualified* (e.g., probably; possibly) or *unqualified* (e.g. certainly is; or absolutely should not be)?
        3.   stated *with reservations* (e.g., unless; until) or *free from reservations* (e.g., under all conditions)?
        4.   relevant to the present, the future, or the past?
    B.   Specifically, you may wish to ask:
        1.   declarative claims
            a.   Is it an occurrence, a situation, or a behavior that is, was, or will be the case?

      b.   How will we know (by what standards) whether this occurrence (etc.) is, was, or will be the case?

  2. evaluative claims

      a.   What is the nature of the quality, characteristic, and so forth?

      b.   By what standards is the quality or characteristic being judged?

      c.   What other objects, ideas, or events are used for comparison or contrast?

  3. classificatory claims

      a.   What is the category of things that is relevant?

      b.   What are the characteristics that cause something to be outside or not a part of that category?

  4. policy claims

      a.   What is or was the current situation, policy, procedure, and so forth?

      b.   In what ways is, was, or will be the new policy a departure from the present or past one?

      c.   What are or were the alternatives to this new or different policy?

      d.   By what standards are we to judge the new or different policy?

II. In examining evidence, you may wish to ask:

  A. Artifacts

    1. Is it an accurate representation of the object or situation?

    2. Is it a proportionately fair representation of the situation (or is it out of proportion and misleadingly represented)?

    3. Is it clear and relatively unambiguous?

    4. By what specific standards should this artifact be judged?

  B. Objects

    1. Is it verifiable by senses (sight, etc.) or more indirectly?

    2. Did it occur, was it found naturally, or was it somehow manipulated?

  C. Occurrences

    1. Is it an unplanned occurrence or was it somehow contrived?

    2. By what means was it perceived? By whom was it perceived?

    3. Are there factors affecting the accuracy of the perception?

    4. Is the occurrence common or unusual?

    5. Is the occurrence still the case or has it somehow changed?

  D. Reports of occurrence

    1. Is it reported in a relatively clear and unambiguous way?

    2. Is it reported in a fair or biased manner?

    3. Have all relevant aspects (positive and negative) been reported?

    4. Is this report consistent with all others?

    5. Was the reporter physically, emotionally, and intellectually in a position to make the report?

    6. By what standards should the report be judged?

E. Contrived occurrences
  1. Does it accurately reflect the actual occurrence?
  2. What aspects of the actual occurrence are omitted or added to?
  3. By what standards should the occurrence be judged as accurate?
F. Reports of contrived occurrences (especially experiments)
  1. Is it clear and relatively unambiguous?
  2. Does it utilize a consistent method of assessing or comparing?
  3. Are the standards by which to judge the report clearly stated?
  4. Was the reporter physically, emotionally, and intellectually in a position to make the report?
  5. Is the report fair and reasonably unbiased?
  6. Is the report consistent with other such reports?
  7. Are any inconsistencies in the report or in the findings explained?
G. Hypothetical occurrences
  1. How likely is the occurrence to occur? And under what circumstances might it occur?
  2. How likely is the occurrence to occur in the manner described? And under what circumstances might it occur that way?
  3. What are the consequences, costs, or results if the occurrence does occur?
H. Expressions of belief
  1. Is the belief expressed freely or under some sort of coercion?
  2. Is the belief expressed in a manner relatively free from undue bias?
  3. Is the expression clear and relatively unambiguous?
  4. Is the reporter physically, emotionally, and intellectually in a position to express such a belief?
  5. By what standards should the belief be judged or evaluated?
  6. Is the expression consistent with expressions made by others—or by the same person earlier?
I. Reports of expressions of belief
  1. Is the report secondhand, thirdhand, or what?
  2. Is the report clear and relatively unambiguous?
  3. Is the report a fair and reasonable report of someone else's belief or expression?
  4. Was the reporter physically, emotionally, and intellectually in a position to make the report?
  5. Does the report contain all the aspects expressed by another—or is the report unfairly selective?

III. In examining warrants, you will benefit from using the guidelines for the particular kind of evidence listed above, and then you may ask specific questions of the warrant, including:
  A. Parallelism
    1. What are the similarities between the two (or more) instances or objects?

    2. What characteristics does one have that the other fails to exhibit?

B. Analogy
1. What basic principle or idea do the two (or more) instances or objects share? How important to each is this principle?
2. In what important ways do the instances, objects, or events vary from one another?
3. Are there only certain circumstances within which the similarity in the principle exists?
4. Are there situations in which the principle or idea is not shared?

C. Classification
1. Ask the questions found under classificatory claims in the earlier section.
2. Under what special circumstances will the idea or object *not* be considered a part of the class?
3. Are there other classifications under which the object, idea, or event would be more appropriately placed?

D. Generalization
1. How many instances or objects make up the entire group?
2. How many instances are represented in the evidence?
3. If the evidence is only a sample or a part of the group, is the sample fair and representative of the whole?
4. Are there exceptions in the group of things that make the generalization inaccurate?

E. Residual
1. How many alternatives exist for the claim? Have they all been considered?
2. In what ways are all but the one unacceptable?
3. What are the potential problems or disadvantages of the remaining alternative?
4. What are the additional advantages of the remaining alternative?

F. Correlation
1. How often do the things occur at the same time?
2. How often does one occur without the other?
3. What are the indications that they will occur at the same time this time?

G. Circumstance
1. How often do the things occur at the same time?
2. How often does it appear that the one causes the other?
3. How often does the one not seem to cause the other?
4. What are the indications that the one may cause or have caused the other this time?
5. By what standards are we to judge the likelihood of the one perhaps being responsible for the other (in law, for example, probable cause)?

H. Cause
1. Does the second thing *always* follow the first thing?

    2. Does the first thing *never* occur except in the presence of the other?

    3. What *other* factors may be a part of or the major cause for the thing to happen? Do the first two things simply occur at the same time with no causal link between them?

    4. By what standards are we to judge the extent of the causal link (in law, for example, beyond all reasonable doubt)?

  I. Authority

    1. What are the *positive* qualifications (background, opportunity, knowledge, attitude, etc.) that make the statement "expert"?

    2. What are the *negative* factors (bias, attitude, prejudice, conflict of interest, lack of opportunity) that may counteract the "expertness" of the statement?

IV. In examining qualifiers, you may wish to ask:

  A. Is the qualifier consistent with the statistical chances or odds of the thing being the case?

  B. Does the qualifier reflect only an intuitive confidence of the person, or is it a well-studied and expert expression of confidence?

  C. Does it reflect only on an expression of how confident the receiver should be of the claim—or does it combine with *A* or *B* above?

V. In examining backing, you may wish to ask:

  A. Does the backing explain in detail the general statement contained in the warrant?

  B. Are there other sorts of relevant ways to back the warrant?

  C. Is the backing clearly stated and relatively free from ambiguity?

VI. In examining reservations, you may wish to ask:

  A. Have the stated reservations been expressed clearly?

  B. Are there other reservations that should have been stated?

  C. How likely are the reservations to occur—and thus provide a situation in which the claim should be abandoned?

  D. Are the statements of reservations dealt with and taken into consideration when the claim is advanced?

  E. Is the statement of reservations related appropriately to the stated qualifier?

Programmed Questions

To test your understanding of the material presented in this chapter, you may wish to answer the following questions. In the multiple-choice questions, the answers may be all correct, all incorrect, or several may be correct. The suggested answers to the questions appear on the last page of this chapter. If you fail to answer the questions correctly, you may wish to review the material to increase your understanding and/or to discuss the items in class.

1. What a receiver judges to be the function of something in argumentation is:
   a. less important than what the arguer intended
   b. a decision with no guidelines whatsoever
   c. partly a matter of personal interpretation, partly a matter of the shared situation, and partly a matter of the receiver's culture, training, and background
   d. more important than what the arguer intended
   e. something the arguer will be able to predict with complete accuracy

Match the type of claim on the left with an example of it from the right column in items 2-5. A question may have more than one answer.

2.__declarative claim	a. the colonists should have revolted earlier
	b. Linda is better looking than Fred
3.__evaluative claim	c. the Celtics will win the play-off
	d. this is a tasty apple
4.__classificatory claim	e. this is a Golden Delicious apple
	f. I should study more
5.__policy claim	g. this is a pipe wrench

6. It is the case with claims that:
   a. all claims involve a judgment of sorts
   b. once a claim is accepted, it may be used as evidence to support another claim
   c. claims are highly susceptible to various interpretations
   d. receivers will respond to claims based upon their interpretation of them

Match the type of evidence in the right-hand column with an example of its use in the left-hand column in items 7-15. Mark only one answer for each item.

7.__artifact	a. "Yes, Jane said she felt better today."
8.__unplanned occurrence	b. a handgun (introduced into a courtroom)
9.__contrived occurrence	c. a spontaneous protest against higher meat prices
10.__report of contrived occurrence	d. a graph showing a current balance of payment deficit
11.__hypothetical occurrence	e. "It is my opinion that socialized medicine is in the future for this country."
12.__object	f. "Picture yourself in your own pool, spending the day in cool relaxation."
13.__expression of belief	g. a psychological laboratory experiment
14.__report of expression of belief	h. findings from a psychological experiment
15.__report of occurrence	i. "I found the defendant standing over the body."

Match the type of warrant (a through i) with an example of how the *warrant* (*italicized* in questions 16-24) might relate to the claim (not italicized in questions 16-24). THEN, in the parentheses, state the sort of thing that would seem to function as *evidence* in the situation. For example:

0. __c__ (evidence: Harriet gains $100,000 in insurance now that her husband is dead.)
Anyone who gains $100,000 at the death of another person must be considered a suspect in the murder, so Harriet is a suspect in the murder.

a. parallelism   d. generalization   g. circumstance
b. analogy   e. residual   h. cause
c. classification   f. correlation   i. authority

16. _____ (evidence:)
Johnson is the state's leading scholar in the area, so clearly the bus service can be considered inadequate.

17. _____ (evidence:)
Spring always comes at the same time that my wife insists on cleaning the attic, so I guess spring has finally come.

18. _____ (evidence:)
Whenever someone deliberately sticks out a leg, and the other person falls, the first person has been the reason for the fall; obviously, then, Jill was the one who made Jack fall down the hill.

19. _____ (evidence:)
Since a nation is so much like a ship at sea, we can be sure that a sudden change in our president or "national captain" will be disastrous for the country.

20. _____ (evidence:)
Since anything that has seeds should be termed a fruit, we must consider the tomato a fruit.

21. _____ (evidence:)
Because price controls are the only options that do not have significant disadvantages, we clearly should institute them as soon as possible.

22. _____ (evidence:)
Since there are only five members in the group who have voting privileges, we must consider the nomination to be unanimous.

23. _____ (evidence:)
We know that John occasionally says whatever he thinks will be accepted by his social group, so John probably did not really mean what he said.

24. _____ (evidence:)
The Waffle Company's frying pans are made by the same company that makes Jones, Inc.'s pans, so we can be sure that Waffle's pans will be good ones.

Consider the claim: "Jim is a prime candidate for graduate school in mathematics." The claim can be supported by a number of kinds of evidence, but each bit of evidence may require a different sort of warrant. Below, the claim is repeated and followed by a series of *statements of evidence*. Decide what sort of warrant would be necessary (a through i) and then, in the parentheses, give an *example* of such a warrant that would serve the appropriate function.

a. parallelism   d. generalization   g. circumstance
b. analogy   e. residual   h. cause
c. classification   f. correlation   i. authority

"Jim is a prime candidate for graduate school in mathematics,

25. _____ (warrant:)
           because Jim is weak in social sciences, sciences, humanities, fine arts, and languages, but excellent in mathematics."
26. _____ (warrant:)
           because Jim graduated from Clarkson University."
27. _____ (warrant:)
           because Jim is skilled in algebra, trigonometry, geometry, analytic geometry, and calculus."
28. _____ (warrant:)
           because Jim has good scores in mathematics on the GRE, the SAT, and the ACT."
29. _____ (warrant:)
           because Dr. Fred Lewis has said that Jim is a prime candidate for graduate work in mathematics."
30. _____ (warrant:)
           because his brother, Jack, is an excellent graduate student in mathematics."

31. In what three ways do we expect to find qualifiers functioning in argumentation?
    a. as a way of arguing in a weak manner
    b. as a way of revealing the statistical odds of something occurring
    c. as a way of expressing our own confidence in a claim
    d. as a way of avoiding responsible argumentative positions
    e. as a way of expressing how confident our receiver can be in the claim

32. Reservations in argumentation:
    a. should never be admitted until absolutely necessary
    b. may be stated immediately in the argumentation
    c. explain the conditions under which the claim might no longer be defended
    d. often begin with unless, until, etc.
    e. should be expressed in a way that makes them appropriate to the qualifier

33. Backing in argumentative communication:
   a.   supports the warrant in some way
   b.   cannot ever be challenged
   c.   gives the details of the general statement that is the warrant
   d.   may have to be replaced by other backing if the receiver demands different detail for the warrant

Discussion Questions for Appendix Case Studies

To test your understanding of the material in this chapter, you may wish to answer the following questions that refer to the case studies in the Appendix of this book. You may wish to (a) work on the questions individually; (b) work on the questions in pairs or in groups in or before class; (c) develop written answers to the questions; (d) have class discussion based upon the questions; (e) prepare an extended paper on several related questions; or (f) develop a major paper about one case study (using the questions related to it that appear in various chapters).

1. Study "A 2 or a 4?" beginning on page 266. What claim did Alice make in the interview? What claim did Stoner make in the interview? What kind of claims were they? What evidence did Alice provide for her claim? What evidence did Stoner provide? What different kinds of evidence were used? What warrants were either expressed or implied in the argumentation? What kinds were they? Do you find instances of the use of reservations? Of backing for warrants? Of qualifiers? How were Stoner and Alice's evidence, warrants, and so forth, interpreted by the other?

2. Study "How Free is Free Will?" beginning on page 254. When Ellen questions her interpretation of Tom's interpretation of Skinner, why is her attention drawn to the difference between whether freedom of will "can" but "usually doesn't" mean a conditioned choice? Why is she concerned about whether the conditioned choice occurred most of the time? What one argumentative function are these two concerns related to? What other kind of argumentative function is she referring to when she says that the claim of the conditioned freedom should not be accepted if Skinner is only seeking publicity?

3. Study "Address to the Catholic Lawyers' Guild" by Senator Clark beginning on page 259. What claim does the Senator make about the lack of trust in public officials? What kind of claim is it? Once he supports that claim, how does he use it to support other claims? The Senator alludes to arguments that have been submitted against his proposals and attempts to answer those charges. Can you consider these arguments against the proposals to be reservations which he denies?

4. Study "Letter-to-the-Editor" beginning on page 254. What is Elbarc's major claim? What kind of claim is it? It seems as if three more specific claims are used to lead to the major claim. What three claims are they? What kind of claims are they? Once these specific claims are supported, do they begin (Elbarc hopes) to function as evidence for the major claim? Is there a warrant in the last paragraph that shows the relationship or allows the movement to that major claim? Is there backing for that warrant?

5. Study "The Success of the Program" beginning on page 264. What are the kinds of evidence that the administrator uses to support his claim that the program is a success? Are there warrants to justify that claim based upon this evidence? What kinds of evidence does it seem that Wallace wants? Can you get some idea of what sorts of warrants he is envisioning?

Research Project for Advanced Students

In the text, as I have mentioned, I have attempted to approach good reasons, significance, and meaning with what I consider a proper balance between saying that these are purely individualistic and saying that they are affected by shared situations and common group identity. In all cases, however, I have attempted to avoid all positions that were absolutist. The absolutist, the individualistic, and the sociological viewpoints can be considered as basic *philosophical* perspectives from which to view man, language, communication, and (thus) argumentation. Research these and other philosophical views—and distinctions among them. A good place to begin a study of a variety of philosophical positions on communication, argumentation, and rhetoric is a collection of essays, edited by Donald G. Douglas, *Philosophers on Rhetoric: Traditional and Emerging Views* (Skokie, Ill.: National Textbook Co., 1973), especially the sections on Wittgenstein, Kierkegaard, Buber, and Burke.

SELECTED REFERENCES

Ehninger, Douglas. *Influence, Belief, and Argument.* Glenview, Ill.: Scott Foresman, 1974.

Ehninger, Douglas and Brockriede, Wayne. *Decision by Debate.* New York: Dodd, Mead and Co., 1963.

Toulmin, Stephen. *The Uses of Argument.* 2nd ed. Cambridge: Cambridge University Press, 1969.

Answers to Programmed Questions

1. c, d   2. c   3. b, d   4. e, g   5. a, f   6. a, b, c, d

7. d   8. c   9. g   10. h   11. f   12. b   13. e

14. a   15. i

16. i   (Johnson has complained about the inadequacy of the bus service.)

17. f   (My wife has just demanded that I clean the attic.)

18. h   (Jill stuck out her leg and Jack fell down.)

19. b   (A change in ship's captain in the midst of a voyage spells disaster for the vessel.)

20. c   (The tomato has seeds.)

21. e   (Wage controls have been shown to be counter-productive, spending curbs have resulted in higher levels of unemployment, tax increases have not worked well, but price controls seem to present no major problems.)

22. d   (Jon voted for the proposal, as did Fred, Mabel, Ginger, and Harry.)

23. g   (At that time John was in the presence of his social group.)

24. a   (Jones, Inc.'s pans have proved themselves to be superior products.)

25. e   (Mathematics seem to be the one major area where Jim excels.)

26. g   (Clarkson University has proven itself capable of producing excellent mathematics majors.)

27. d   (The skills in algebra, trigonometry, geometry, analytic geometry, and calculus are the various skills that are important to a mathematics major.)

28.　f　(There is a high correlation between people who score well on the SAT, the ACT, and the GRE in math, and people who perform well as math graduate students.)

29.　i　(Dr. Fred Lewis is qualified to speak about success in mathematics at the graduate level since he is a distinguished professor of mathematics and Graduate Dean of Thessel University.)

30.　a　(Jack and Jim have always performed equally well at everything, especially at math at the various levels.)

31.　b, c, e　　32.　b, c, d, e　　33.　a, c, d

6

Problematic Receiver Demands

My *general objective* in this chapter is to discuss several commonly used but problematic demands that receivers can make of arguers and argumentation.

My *specific objectives* are to discuss, illustrate, and assess:

the demand for personal reinforcement

the demand for logicality

the demand for certainty

the demand for causal force

the demand for real reasons

In chapter 5, we investigated the variances that can exist between how an arguer intends some phrase to function and how a receiver may interpret that phrase to function. Whether we are concerned about evidence, warrants, claims, or any other name for how language may function, we, as students of argumentation, must be prepared to realize the potential divergence of arguer intent and receiver judgment. Moreover, my position has been that in the everyday argumentative situations in which you will find yourself, the judgments made by receivers will be more crucial than what was intended by the arguer; indeed, the primacy of the receiver in argumentative communication has been a central theme of this text.

My emphasis upon the judgments of receivers, however, *does not* entail the belief that argumentation is completely a matter of whatever the receiver wants it to be. Although I am convinced that we must always stress the interpretation of argumentative language, I am also persuaded that not all judgments by receivers are equally helpful or desirable in the process of argumentation. Certain demands can be made of argumentation which I consider *problematic* in one way or another. At times receivers make demands of arguers or invoke certain standards for judging argumentation which are impossible to fulfill, which are simply too stringent, or reflect what I consider to be an unproductive or misleading attitude toward the process of argumentation. Since some of these demands and standards are so commonly used or so well established, it seems to me that they cannot be ignored: they should be discussed, illustrated, and assessed as a way of creating a framework within which to understand more productive demands in argumentation. Consequently, while chapter 7 will deal with recommended approaches to the study of receiver demands, and chapter 8 will deal specifically with the ethical nature of argumentation, the present chapter will discuss these problematic demands and standards. In this chapter, we will examine the demands for personal reinforcement, logicality, certainty, causal force in argumentation, and real reasons. Though, again, I consider each of these demands problematic in ways we shall discuss, and though my comments will appear negative during the entire chapter, the discussion is necessary because of the pervasiveness of the demands, and because these demands will provide a valuable context for understanding the following two (more positive) chapters.

The Demand for Personal Reinforcement

Perhaps the most common and simplistic standard that you as a receiver might use in argumentation is a standard characterized by similarity to your own position. Although you may realize the possible divergencies in opinion at an intellectual level, you still may be tempted to judge argumentative communication from the standpoint of whether it is consistent with a position you maintain on the matter at hand: whether, for you, it is *personally reinforcing*. A case study will illustrate the familiarity of this sort of receiver demand.

Case Study: I Wanna Cookie

Consider the following dialogues, each involving a conversation between my 4 1/2-year-old son, Bryan, and myself. In each case you will note that the time of day is of utmost importance, and that my son reacts in a highly predictable and consistent manner. Note also that at the outset of the conversation, I advance a claim and support it with a single bit of evidence, and my degree of success is also predictable, but by no means consistent.

Time: middle of the afternoon

BRYAN: Daddy, can I have a cookie?

DADDY: Sure, you can have a cookie. Mama just said that you could have one if you wanted it.

BRYAN: Okay; good . . . thanks, Dad.

Time: just before lunch

BRYAN: Daddy, can I have a cookie?

DADDY: Sorry, buddy, you shouldn't have one. Mama said that it was too close to lunch.

BRYAN: But I want one . . . I really do, really . . . it isn't too late.

DADDY: Sorry, but Mama said no, and she's the keeper of the cookies.

BRYAN: But, Daddy, I wanna cookie!

Though the second discussion was not completely finished, let me summarize it by suggesting that Bryan did not receive a cookie, and Bryan was somewhat less pleased with the process than he had been with the earlier transaction. The point here is that Bryan's (the receiver's) reactions to the two situations were predictable. In the first instance, I advanced the claim that a cookie was accessible to him and supported it with the something that I hoped would function as evidence: Mama said you could have one. The evidence was accepted as coming from an authoritative source, and Bryan perceived it as being enough to accept the claim that he could have the cookie. Was he a discriminating receiver wise in the intricacies of reports of positions and authoritative warrants? Hardly. Basically, in the first instance, his primary standard for judging the merit of my claim was that it was consistent with what he already wanted to do: it served as personal reinforcement. In such a situation, he could be expected to agree with any implied or explicit warrant, any offered evidence, and the highly agreeable claim.

The second situation presented Bryan with an entirely different context. When Bryan found my claim to be inconsistent with his own position, he judged the claim and its offered evidence extremely differently . . . and much more harshly. No longer was Mama's statement acceptable as support for my claim; in fact, he challenged it directly by contending, "It isn't too late." Since my claim depended upon his acceptance of the evidence (or my physical effort to get him to accept the idea), I found it necessary to present something I hoped would function as a warrant: after all, I said, Mama is the cookie keeper, and (thus) she should know. Yet, in the context of Bryan judging the argument by its similarity to his own position, he refused the warrant, continued to refuse the evidence, and therefore failed to accept the claim as advanced. Without being able to verbalize all of this, he merely concluded, "But, Daddy, I wanna cookie."

The particular situation in which Bryan found himself is not at all unusual. The demand that argument conform to our established position is the most fundamental demand that arguers make and the most obvious explanation for numerous choices that arguers and receivers make. We ignore arguments advanced by a speaker by refusing to hear her or by rejecting completely (and without a great deal of thought) a position she may advance. We counter the arguments of a writer immediately with claims of our own—and we leave the rest of the article unread. We challenge the reasoning of a friend who cites a particular columnist's report as evidence; our rationale is that we have never agreed with that columnist before. We accept the argumentation of a political speaker simply because she expresses what we already believe. In all these instances—and when cookies are the prize to be won—our assessment of the merits of the argumentation may have less to do with the strength of the argument and more to do with the degree to which the argument is personally reinforcing to us; and the receiver's judgment is made by using the standard best characterized as similarity to our own position.

Although the demand for personal reinforcement is common and understandable, I consider such a demand unproductive in the development of thoughtful, circumspect argumentation. If the claims involved are significant, then they should be approached and evaluated on the basis of some standard other than mere similarity to what is already accepted. True, dissonance theory and other types of attitude theory describe how people are drawn toward reinforcing people, ideas, and beliefs,[1] but the existence of such phenomena does not demonstrate its desirability. Whether the argument is accepted or rejected is of little consequence: an unthinking and au-

---

[1]See, for example, Leon Festinger, *A Theory of Cognitive Dissonance* (Evanston, Ill.: Row, Peterson and Co., 1957); and Robert Zajonc, "The Concepts of Balance, Congruity, and Dissonance," *Public Opinion Quarterly* 24, 1960, pp. 280-96.

tomatic acceptance of a claim because it provides personal reinforcement is as unacceptable to me as an unthinking and automatic rejection of the claim simply because of its divergence from what is already believed. Both situations involve cognitive "short circuits" that preclude the participants from engaging in a fair and thoughtful consideration of the claim at hand. The demand for personal reinforcement, then, seems to me to be unproductive to the development of worthwhile argumentation.

The Demand for Logicality, Not Emotionality

To receivers unsatisfied with the superficiality of the demand for personal reinforcement, the demand for logicality might seem an acceptable, alternative standard for evaluating argumentation. Indeed, once the primary forms, rules, and procedures of something like formal logic are learned, any argument can be examined—and given a formal evaluation of validity. The receiver's judgment, it would appear at first, is an automatic product of the application of the rules of formal logic. Associated with that apparent result is the idea that emotionality or irrationality can be avoided in argumentation. Yet let us examine a case in which the demand is made of the arguer to be logical, unemotional, and (thus) reasonable.

Case Study: Withdrawal from the Ross Dependency

Envision a discussion between you and a friend concerning the current military conflict over possession of the Ross Dependency. Your friend is vociferously denouncing the plans of the United States to withdraw its troops and support from the Ross regime, an act which will mean the collapse of the regime and a turnover of the resources of that area to unfriendly forces. You have not really been concerned about the imminent fall of the regime, partly because you do not even know where the Ross Dependency is. However, since he is your friend, and since you pride yourself in your grasp of logical argument, you listen to your friend as he proposes what seems to him to be a logical argument. He argues that since "withdrawals from wars lead to a lessening of foreign confidence in the withdrawing nation, and since the United States is about to withdraw from the war in the Dependency, that, therefore, there will be a lessening of foreign confidence in the United States." Your friend is pleased with his convincingly stated argument and awaits your response.

As you analyze your friend's case, some things are obviously consistent with the concerns of formal logic: if you have a background in formal logic, you will realize that there seem to be a major premise, minor premise, and conclusion—all with the appropriate amount and placement of major, minor, and middle terms. In essence, whether or not you have a background in formal logic, be assured that none of the procedures of formal logic appear to be violated. Yet, as anyone who knows anything about formal logic realizes, one must always examine the meaning and reliability of the premises themselves: the rules of formal logic answer only the question of whether the appropriate steps have been taken *after you have examined the premises*. What about the premises themselves? The minor premise (that the United States is preparing to withdraw) is well substantiated by the President and the Congress as well as independent reports on the scene; the minor premise seems in order.

As you analyze the argumentation further you recall that, although premises and terms are in the appropriate places, logicality as a standard requires the lack of ambiguity and emotionality in argumentation. The terms should have one established meaning, and that meaning should be as factual, descriptive, and unemotional as possible. Consequently, as you examine the argumentation, you demand certain answers to questions as a method of deciding the logicality of the argumentation. What of the major premise? Are levels of foreign confidence indeed lowered by withdrawals from wars? You begin to ask yourself logical-sounding questions: What, logically, is a war? What, logically, is a withdrawal? What, logically, is foreign confidence? What, logically, is a lowering of such confidence? How, logically, is that confidence measured? And most crucially, what, logically, is the Ross Dependency?

Such demands, by you or any other receiver, will prompt nonlogical-sounding answers to logical-sounding questions. Your friend will begin to attempt definitions of withdrawal, of war, of confidence, of lessening of confidence, and of the Ross Dependency. Although his answer that the Ross Dependency is an area of Antarctica may satisfy you, his other answers will fall far short of your standard of logicality. His definitions will involve agreed upon conceptions and traditional connotations—all of which will sound very illogical to you since they are simply matters of interpretation of terms. You will demand terms and ideas that are validly arrived at and formally demonstrable—and you will have totally destroyed any chance that he has to win his argument with you. If you begin accepting his traditional conceptions, you will abandon your logical standard; and if you do not, you will leave yourself feeling accomplished at formal logic and your friend frustrated—or irate.

Formal logic, like any other system of logic, is simply that: a system. The system will work flawlessly until you begin asking questions that refer to the flawed (I hesitate to say it) "real world." For that "real world" is not in itself systematized, and when you attempt to put the practical affairs of your life into that system, you will have to begin categorizing things, interpreting ideas, and accepting or stipulating definitions—and all those are nonstandardized and variable interpretations that do not fit appropriately in formal logic's concern for absoluteness and certainty. Thus, the demands for one and only one meaning of terms can be achieved only with such symbols as A's, B's, and C's or X's, Y's, and Z's—symbols that can be given fixed and standarized values. When most other terms, such as war or withdrawal or confidence, are relevant to the argument, the standard of logicality with its concerns for certainty and fixed meanings is less easily applied: though you may use it as a standard of judgment; the comforting aura of certainty will have vanished.

Even more disturbing to receivers wishing to invoke the standard of logicality (and its goal of avoiding emotion in argumentation) is the probability that the acceptance of definitions or traditional views of, for example, levels of foreign confidence will contain certain emotional issues. In the Ross example, for instance, if you were to demand of your friend a logical and unemotional conception of lowered levels of confidence in the United States, he would have difficulty avoiding the emotional component of words like respect, dignity, loyalty, and faith. Your choice would be clear, it seems to me: you could continue to invoke the standard of logicality—and thus reject his arguments; or you could accept his conceptions—with their variable interpretations and emotional aspects—and thus abandon your demands that his argumentation be logical, without multiple and human-determined meanings or emotional elements.

Students who approach argumentation as a kind of communication process, however, are not faced with such a forced-choice situation. Indeed, if we truly believe that symbols and language in general are man-created ways of trying to re-create or create meanings, then we should also be prepared to accept such terms as logicality and emotionality as symbols that have no real meaning, but that can have a variety of meanings attached to them. We should consider them as constructs: terms that *we use* for the sake of convenience. If we allow ourselves to act as if a construct such as logicality has a predetermined and invariable meaning, then we are permitting the term—in contrast—to use us. Certainly, some of the thinking and procedures from logic can be helpful, but if we insist upon the standard of logical exactness, it is my belief that we will be pursuing a less-than-productive effort to understand argumentation as it occurs in the world of everyday transactions. In argumentation, we must be prepared to deal with countless nonlogical-sounding ideas, beliefs, and circumstances. We, thus, will benefit from some standard of judgment other than logicality.

The Demand for the Certainty of
Facts, Truth, and Reality

While it is clear that a receiver may judge argumentative communication by the standard of logicality or may demand that the argument be personally reinforcing, receivers also frequently insist that all they need are the facts, the truth, or what is *really* the case. In essence, such demands share the quest for some sort of certain standard; a standard, much like logicality, that can be used whenever a claim is being interpreted and evaluated. The assumption is apparent that no one can argue against the facts, the truth, or reality. In commonsense terms, we behave as if the facts, the truth, and reality existed independently of mankind—and that all we as arguers and receivers had to do was to "discover" them.[2] Let us examine a case in which the *facts* at hand, the *truth* of the matter, and the *reality* of the situation are probably not what we have always assumed them to be.

Case Study: Patrick Henry and His Speech

My first course in oral communication was a high-school speech class for seniors, where one of the assignments was to research thoroughly a speaker of our choice: we were to dig amid the holdings in oratory and such things in the Circleville High School Library, and to report historical, biographical, and, thus, factual information about our speaker. My speaker was Daniel Webster—only because I failed to raise my hand soon enough to get Patrick Henry. After all, Patrick Henry was an American institution and few Americans could forget the famous "Give Me Liberty or Give Me Death Speech" that Henry presented in Virginia. Though I worked as hard as I could on Webster, I was always left with a feeling of jealousy about my friend who "got" Patrick Henry.

Though that class was the first fairly in-depth treatment of Henry's "Liberty" speech that I had been exposed to, it was by no means the

[2]The argument concerning the nature of reality and man's role in relation to reality is, of course, a traditional argument in philosophy and related disciplines such as theoretical physics and the philosophy of the physical sciences. This present perspective on facts, reality, and so forth, is consistent with the philosophical approach described in John Dewey and Arthur Bentley, *Knowing and the Known* (Boston: The Beacon Press, 1949).

last. In an undergraduate English composition class, I have studied the speech as a major piece of American literature; on television, I have seen the masterful Henry portrayed—complete with the fateful ring of the speech; and in a magazine published by a famed American museum, I have read parts of the speech quoted and integrated into a saga of Revolutionary War roots. Indeed, Henry and his speech are American institutions: we assume the speech to be *factual*, since Henry in fact existed, wrote, and delivered the speech; we assume the speech to be *truthful*, since all the history texts, television programs, and popular lore have reinforced beliefs about the speech; and we assume the speech to be a part of the American *reality*, since the event is accorded the aura of certainty reserved normally for such things as statues and buildings. Yet, it is almost certainly the case that Patrick Henry's speech was written by his biographer, William Wirt.

My introduction to Wirt came in a graduate class at The Ohio State University where Professor Goodwin Berquist, Jr. of the Department of Communication and Professor Paul Bowers of the Department of History were coteaching a seminar that focused upon historical methods of research. The explicit problem of the instructors and graduate students was to determine the authenticity of the Henry speech, which has traditionally been in doubt among scholars: we searched for historical evidence that would support or deny the suspicion that the text was not really the work of Henry. The search led through many old bound volumes of several libraries, many discussions of clues by intense students of communication and history, and, finally, a trip to Virginia to get as close to the original documents and data as possible. For us, the search seemed to be ended when one of the group discovered a letter which is included in the biographer William Wirt's memoirs saying that, at that point, he had found no substantive or detailed reports of the speech, no text of the speech—in short, no valid way of reconstructing the speech. Ironically, the letter was written to a friend and was communicated *after* the time when Wirt produced a "text" of the speech.[3] Wirt does not actually admit that he created the speech himself from small bits of remembrances, but the evidence of his own research reports indicates that such was probably the case.

The goals of the seminar and this case study are not simply to debunk an established part of American history. Instead, we need to

[3]Though for years there had been suspicion about the authenticity of the Henry speech, as far as I know, the letter from Wirt uncovered and analyzed by a graduate seminar group at The Ohio State University in the spring of 1972 is the most direct evidence of the fabrication of the speech. The seminar and its research trip to Virginia were guided by Professor Goodwin Berquist, Jr. of the Department of Communication and Professor Paul Bowers of the History Department.

understand the implications of such a firmly held belief resting on such insecure footing: if you were to ask nearly anyone, "Who wrote and gave Patrick Henry's Liberty or Death Speech?" your receiver probably would chuckle and reply, "I don't know, but what was the color of George Washington's white horse?" Indeed, in classes where I have discussed this case, I have had students who have difficulty believing the new information; as one student put it, "In an English composition class, we just studied that speech and how he gave it. . . . " It is at that point (or in response to a similar reply) that I ask an important series of questions: What is a fact? What is truth? What is reality?

The rationale for such a series of questions, of course, is that the Henry speech seems to violate previous conceptions of the answers to these questions. Is it not a "fact" that Henry made the speech? Is it not "true" that the speech was written and delivered in the manner described in school texts? What *is* the "reality" of the Henry speech? Our discussion here will not solve the philosophical questions about facts, truth, and reality of the sort that have troubled and challenged thinkers for years; moreover, solving such questions is not really our main focus anyway. We are concerned with the nature of facts, truth, and reality only to the extent that we must understand as best we can what a receiver means when he demands that an argument meet the standard of factuality, truth, and reality. Thus, our specific concern for argumentation and receiver-judging standards necessitates that we arrive at some useful conceptions of fact, truth, and reality that can help us understand such receiver judgments.

The Demand for Factualness

The demand for factuality in argumentation, for example, implies that there are such things as timeless, immutable statements that can serve as the foundation of argumentative judgments. Yet, despite the seeming absoluteness of what we refer to as facts, they are continually being revised, retracted, or expanded. Dentists, for instance, have cautioned their patients for years about the advisability of brushing their teeth with up-and-down rather than horizontal motions of the toothbrush; now, dentists seem to advocate a diagonal motion as the way in which teeth should be brushed. Which procedure, in *fact*, is best? For centuries it was believed that the earth was flat; then, for several centuries, it was believed that the earth was round; and, with the advent of the satellite age, it seems that, in *fact*, the earth is somewhat oblong: more like a pear than a sphere. What shape, in *fact*, is the earth? And, returning to Patrick and his speech, it was assumed for years that Henry, in *fact*, wrote and delivered the

"Give Me Liberty" speech. Not all of these statements can be the timeless, immutable sorts of ideas that we like to think that facts are, since they reflect that what was considered a fact today, almost literally, can be rejected tomorrow on the basis of the discovery of a new fact.

What can we make of the situation? Is it that the older beliefs were not really facts but rather opinions? That would be a comfortable answer except that it would imply that all the older beliefs were really not factual and that all our present beliefs are factual—and will never be rejected. Is it not possible that some other discoveries may reveal that what we think of as today's facts will someday be considered as unacceptable as a statement about the flatness of the earth? Is it not possible to look at certain present beliefs as, at best, facts-for-the-present? If such possibilities exist, then we must look at facts as something less than the absolute statements envisioned in commonsense usage.

Let us look at *facts*, therefore, as being those claims made by human beings that are so strongly accepted by the universe of normal people who are competent and qualified to judge the claim that they are not usually open to debate. As elsewhere phrased, facts are claims that become encased in a disciplinary or commonsense mold and protected from normal questioning or challenge.[4] What, though does all this mean to you as a student of argumentation? In part, it means that the statements that we call facts are, in actuality, merely claims that enjoy the support of virtually everyone who is of normal judging capabilities (not insane, severely retarded, and so forth), and who knows enough about the matter at hand to be a reasonable judge.[5] Moreover, since the claim is accepted by all such people, that claim is not normally subject to question; to challenge it would be to argue in the face of overwhelming agreement about the claim. It is, for the time being, safely protected from debate by the acceptance that it enjoys.

Your probable response to this highly theoretical and philosophical idea is that no such claim exists; that no claim enjoys the support of all people normal and competent to judge. But it seems to me that such is not the case. As I look out the window and see a nearby tree, I can safely say that "It is a fact that the tree is standing there." To such a claim, I would expect universal acceptance. As I look at the

[4]See Richard E. Crable, *Rhetoric as Architectonic: Burke, Perelman, and Toulmin on Valuing and Knowing* (unpublished dissertation, Department of Communication, The Ohio State University, 1973), pp. 90-102, for a discussion.

[5]These criteria of normality and competence define what the Belgian philosopher and legal scholar, Chaim Perelman, refers to as the "universal audience" in several of his works.

moon, I would safely say that "Ah, the moon is full," and if it seems completely round, I would expect universal agreement. If I say to you that two points determine a straight line, then, again I would expect to receive universal agreement. The first two statements would be safely encased in the commonsense mold of sensory perception, while the last statement is encased in the disciplinary mold known as Euclidean geometry.

Yet, my point is that such statements are merely claims that, for the time being, enjoy universal support; they are obviously facts. Such facts, however, are still not timeless or absolute. New discoveries may lead us to ultimately reject any or all of these facts. Researchers, mathematicians, or philosophers may eventually challenge how we have phrased those statements, the theories upon which they are based, or the validity of the sensory processes used to generate the claims. In which case, even these well-protected claims become claims that not only are subject to challenge but also are rejected in favor of new claims. Is there a different method of brushing teeth that, in fact, cleans teeth better? Is there a better description of the shape of the earth? Will we find that the letter from William Wirt about the Henry speech was misleading, and that the speech was not fabricated? Time—or rather, the events and discoveries over time—will provide us with these answers.

What, then, of the demand by a receiver to have the facts, and only the facts? My position is that if the receiver recognizes the *tentativeness* of the facts that he is demanding, then no problem arises. He simply will be asking for the claims commonly recognized by the universe of normal and competent people. In contrast, however, I do not believe that that is what is recognized when a demand is made to have the facts. Consequently, the demand for facts is generally made naively, with no thought given to the tentativeness of the claims the arguer offers as facts. In this light, such a demand seems as unproductive as the demands for either personal reinforcement or strict logicality. One should demand evidence, warrants, or some other such obviously argumentative language and avoid the demand for a certainty that cannot exist in human communication.

The Demand for Truth

My position is similar in relation to the demand for the certainty of truth. Again taking a cue from philosopher Chaim Perelman, I suggest that a *truth* is a statement of the relationships among agreed upon facts.[6] To demand that argumentation meet the standard of truth is unproductive if truth is conceived as a complex and absolute

---

[6]See, for example, Chaim Perelman and L. Olbrechts-Tyteca, *The New Rhetoric: A Treatise on Argumentation*, trans. by John Wilkinson and Purcell Weaver (Notre Dame: University of Notre Dame Press, 1969), pp. 68-69.

statement of what *is* the case. If we adopt the assumption that facts are alterable and change from time to time, then we can readily appreciate that truth can vary with the reevaluation of the facts: what is the truth can vary from era to era and from instance to instance. While that idea is philosophically liberal and may not appeal to you at first, such an idea explains why people can argue eternally about what is the truth of a given situation; it explains why people who purport to each have the truth may never be able to convince the other of their particular interpretation of truth. To demand the truth in argumentation as a standard of judgment is to demand that what the arguer provides will confirm your perceptions of truth. To make such a demand, again, would be to ask for an absolute standard for argumentation where no such absoluteness exists.

The Demand for Correspondence to Reality

Similarly, to demand that argumentation meet the standard of correspondence to reality can be misleading and unproductive. You would be asking for a reality with a capital R, as though one, and only one, reality exists in the context of communication. Again, my position is that such a demand puts the label of absolute upon a concept that simply is not absolute. For all we know, there may exist a *Reality*, but since human beings in the argumentative situation are forced to interpret that Reality, it becomes more a matter of all the individual realities created by human perception and thought. Indeed, Reality may exist, but in argumentation we shall be forced to deal with interpretations of that Reality: the result of demanding correspondence-to-Reality is to demand what human beings are incapable of providing for you. Thus, if you as a receiver were to demand an *interpreted reality* as a standard, then no problem exists—except that you would be demanding far less than what receivers commonly want when Reality is used as a standard. If, on the other hand, you were to demand correspondence-to-Reality of the situation as a standard, you would be pursuing what seems to me to be an unproductive standard of judgment.

In essence, I see the demands for facts, truth, and reality to be based upon the same misleading desire for certainty. Receiver judgments of argumentation should not be made in relation to standards that appear so deceptively absolute. No argumentation will be able to satisfy all that is entailed in that demand for certainty, unless, of course, the receiver and the arguer happen to agree upon an interpretation of the facts, a perception of the truth, or a statement of reality. Yet, even if that occurs, the standards that are being met are not so much the ones of fact, truth, and reality as those of personal reinforcement.

The Demand for Causal Force

Though receivers may demand that argumentation meet the standards of personal similarity, logicality, and certainty, they may also make other demands which seem generally problematic. You as a receiver, for example, might demand that the arguer somehow cause or make you accept the argumentative claim. Specifically, you would demand that the argumentation be so convincingly presented that you had little or no choice but to accept the claim as advanced. When a receiver demands that the arguer "prove it to me," he may be saying simply that "I will accept your claim only if I have no choice; I will choose your claim (ironically) only if that is the only choice I have." Let me illustrate this receiver demand with a case study that focuses upon the issue.

Case Study: Can You Make Me Believe It?

One of my teaching interests is organizational communication, the study of those communication situations in businesses and various other types of organizations. Relatedly, I often serve as a communication consultant to organizations concerned with maximizing the effectiveness of their communication system. Such consulting often involves a preliminary or in-depth survey of employee perceptions, feelings, and viewpoints. In one organization, I was beginning a preliminary interviewing process to lay the groundwork for a complete analysis of the organization, its problems, and its communication effectiveness with employees. Let me relate to you a near-verbatim account of a discussion I had with one senior vice-president: one, by the way, who was not famous for his interpersonal skills with employees. Certain names and some specific comments have been altered to protect the confidentiality of my client organization and the senior vice-president.

JONES: Well, Dick, I'm happy to meet you. I was in the meeting where you and your project were introduced. It sounds to me like it will be a good one.

CRABLE: Frank, it's good to see you; but I think we met earlier when I was here on other business . . . I had a full beard then, and I do look a bit different.

JONES: Oh, I think I do recall that. . . . Was it in the summer?

CRABLE: Yes, it was. I've been anxious to get back with you. As you remember, we really didn't get a chance to talk back then.

JONES: Right. Well, what can I do for you? Do you need some things . . . information or whatever from me?

CRABLE: No, in fact, all I want for the present is to have some discussion with a few of the employees in your department. I will be interested in getting a roughly representative sample of people with varying age, sex, years on the job, years here at the plant . . . different levels of responsibility, that kind of thing. Though I knew you were aware of the project, I always like to make contact with area heads, and so forth, before I begin talking with employees.

JONES: Talk with anybody you like. Just tell them that they are to give you complete cooperation. Sometimes, I think that employees are a little timid about talking with a consultant. You know, they may be afraid to speak openly. . . . Some of them, on the other hand, well . . . some are more than happy to express their feelings.

CRABLE: Well, I guess that's always the case.

JONES: Dick, what do you plan to do with the survey? I mean that the last one we had around here wasn't very good. We got some information, but no one really knew what to do with it.

CRABLE: Part of my task, as I see it, is to report general as well as specific findings—and my interpretation of them—to various areas and departments, as well as to top management.

JONES: Yes, that's the real problem, isn't it?

CRABLE: I'm sorry, I don't understand.

JONES: You know, we'll cooperate all we can, but some supervisors may not be so willing to accept the results of the study. How do you make them believe the results?

CRABLE: The survey will be rather well refined—specifically oriented to this plant. The processing of the data will be done by a friend and colleague at the computer center. . . .

JONES: But supervisors don't know much about that kind of thing generally. How do you make them accept what you find out if your results vary with what their own perceptions are? How do you force them to accept the results; to believe them?

CRABLE: The survey is designed with two major components—the first, a kind of straightforward survey with response categories; the second, however, is an analysis of an essay answer in response to an open-ended question. So, I'll really have three sets of data: the initial interviewing I did, the survey, and the essay. All this. . . .

JONES: But none of that will *make* me believe what you say. . . . Do you see what I mean? What if some of our managers and supervisors don't agree with your study? How can you make them believe what you say?

CRABLE: Well, I. . . .

JONES: Now I don't mean that, necessarily, someone would give you any problems, but what happens if they do? Does your survey do any good?

CRABLE: Frank, you see the point is, all I can do is conduct the best possible survey, with those two parts—and compare that to conversation I've had with employees and observations I've made about the plant. If that doesn't. . . .

JONES: You see my point, though? . . .

CRABLE: If that doesn't aid the acceptance of the findings; if the manager has made up his mind that the results are inaccurate, then I'm afraid I can't do a thing. You see, there is no way on earth for someone to "make" another accept a conclusion—even a well-substantiated one—if the person is not willing to ever accept it. I assume that no one in the plant will take that position.

JONES: Well, I'm sure not.

CRABLE: It is getting late, and I have an appointment to see someone else on the third floor. I'm happy that we had an opportunity to talk with one another. I'm sure that we'll be seeing one another again soon.

JONES: Certainly, Dick. Feel free to talk with anyone here and come see me again if that'll be helpful.

CRABLE: Good-bye.

I will allow you to speculate about the sort of information that I gathered about Frank's area of responsibility, because that, though interesting, is of secondary importance to the idea that Frank was so concerned about. How do you *make* someone accept a conclusion (or a claim) if he is determined to reject it? The answer, it seems to me, is clear: you cannot. Unless we physically force the receiver to accept our claim with threat of violence or harm (and that is not consistent with our conception of argumentation), we must rely upon the receiver's willingness to say "yes" when we have presented a strong argumentative case. Agreement to the claim comes only from acceptance of the reasons for the claim, and if the determination exists to never say "yes," then no such acceptance is possible.

This is the central issue that leads me to consider the receiver demand to be "made" or "caused" to accept the claim as an unproductive demand. Such a demand cannot produce much of anything constructive to the process of argumentation. From the arguer's point of view, he will have no chance of winning an acceptance from his receiver: since no way exists for him to "make" the receiver accept the claim, he might as well discontinue the struggle. Similarly, from the receiver's point of view, she might as well end the argumentation since she will never receive that which she demands of the arguer. The standard that the claim must be so overpowering that the receiver simply *must* accept it is unrealistic. Argumentation, as I understand it, is based upon the choices of the parties involved—and demanding that you be caused or made to accept a claim implies you want no choice. Such a situation is alien to the whole notion of argumentation.

The Demand for the Real Reasons

Even when you as a receiver realize that the demand for causal force in argumentation is unreasonable and unproductive, you may be tempted to focus upon the concept of reasons a bit too intensely. Though we shall develop the concept of a reason much more in the next chapter, let it suffice to say that a reason in argumentation is a major idea (consisting of language functioning as evidence, warrants, and any other components) that serves to support the claim by answering the question: "Why should I accept the claim?" If, for example, I were to submit that Herman Jackson should be elected mayor, you might ask me, "Okay, why should he be?" My answer might consist of the following "reason": "He's had the most experience of any of the potential candidates, and experience is probably the key to effectiveness in office." Indeed, my "reason" may be highly complex and incorporate language that functions as evidence, warrants, qualifiers, and the like, or it may consist simply of me saying "experience." Whatever its form, content, or complexity, the reason advanced for the claim will reveal why the claim should be adopted.

The major problem with a receiver's perspective on argumentation and reasons, however, is the temptation to demand *the* reason for a claim: that is, to ask, "Wait, what's the real reason that you think Jackson should be elected? I know what you said, but what's the *real* reason?" To a public bombarded by media advertisements which they distrust; to a public constantly doubting the "word" of politicians; to a public accustomed to being wary of others, the question is not surprising. On the other hand, the demand to know the real reason for a claim seems to me to be unproductive. The following case illustrates the point.

Case Study: She's a Friend of the Family

The scene is a news conference at the statehouse of a large midwestern state. The lieutenant governor of the state is appearing before the statehouse press corps to answer questions about a recent episode involving his arrest on charges of drunken driving and speeding.

Lt. Gov.:	Ladies and Gentlemen, I have a brief statement, after which you may ask any questions you might have. The statement is as follows: I am deeply sorry for the incident two nights ago on Interstate 70. To drive while under the influence of alcohol is an act that no citizen of our state or the nation should be guilty of; as lieutenant governor of your state, I had an even greater obligation to avoid such activity. Though I rarely drink to any substantial extent, I realize that even one evening's mistake could have cost loss of property, and, yes, even bodily injury to innocent drivers. For my actions, I am deeply sorry and deeply ashamed. I ask for understanding from this group and from the people of this state; and I pledge that such an act will never occur again. Thank you.
	Do you have questions? Yes . . . Mr. . . . uh. . . .
1st Reporter:	Sir, are you contemplating a resignation from office?
Lt. Gov.:	I sincerely believe that my actions in the past year-and-one-half have been commendable and have been an asset to the state. I do not wish to resign. . . .
2nd Reporter:	Sir, do you. . . .
Lt. Gov.:	Nor do I think that such an act is appropriate.
2nd Reporter:	(Starting again) Sir, do you confirm the reports that there was a lady with you that night?
Lt. Gov.:	Yes, there was—she is a friend of the family.
2nd Reporter:	Your wife has refused to comment on her; does that mean? . . .
Lt. Gov.:	That means only that my wife has no comment; I've said that the lady is a friend of the family. Next?
3rd Reporter:	Why were you traveling that night, when? . . .
Lt. Gov.:	We were going to my house where my wife was waiting. It was to be something of a party.
4th Reporter:	Your wife has refused to comment on that also. Did she know about the party that was to be at your house?
Lt. Gov.:	Why, certainly, Miss Webb.
2nd Reporter:	Have you and your wife known the Smith lady long?

Lt. GOV.:	Yes, . . . well, for some months now.
5th REPORTER:	Is there any truth to the story that you and Ms. Smith had been at a party at a friend's house?
Lt. GOV.:	Well, yes, my wife was feeling ill and didn't want to go, so she requested that I take Ms. Smith, who has no family in this state. It was only a short, informal gathering.
1st REPORTER:	Sir, were you taking Ms. Smith home . . . to your home at the time you were stopped by the officer?
Lt. GOV.:	I've answered that already. Other questions?
6th REPORTER:	Does Ms. Smith also work for you?
Lt. GOV.:	That's a matter of public record; all state employees are on public lists. She does research for our office.
7th REPORTER:	Sir, was Ms. Smith also intoxicated?
Lt. GOV.:	I think that also is a matter of public record. I'm afraid I have another meeting now. Thank you all for coming.

Although the case is hypothetical, it illustrates a kind of situation that has happened at various times in American history and no doubt in other countries as well. The point is that if you are like most people who have analyzed the case, you probably are not satisfied with the lieutenant governor's explanation of the "friend of the family." The question you probably are still asking is something like, "Why was he *really* with the lady?" If she was a friend of the family, why did the wife refuse to comment? If his wife was ill, why did she encourage him to go with a young lady on his staff—because she had no family? If the wife was ill, why was she going to have a party of her own at her house? And why did the wife refuse comment on the party at her home? The questions simply do not seem to have been answered. The crucial question remains: *Why* was he with the young lady, in a drunken condition, driving on Interstate 70? What was the *real* reason?

Again, if you are like most of the students who have grappled with the case, you probably think you know the real reason: the young lady and the politician were having an affair. Yet, there is virtually no way to "prove" your probable prediction. Only the two people involved (and perhaps the wife) would seem to know the real reason—only they have knowledge of the situation that would allow a certain judgment about the relationship. And, *several* factors may have been recognized by the lieutenant governor as being responsible for his action: alcohol, lust, friendship. He himself may not know the real reason, but, indeed, the lieutenant governor may have been telling the complete truth. The most incriminating evidence is the refusal of the wife to confirm anything her husband has said. Could it not be that she is the problem in the situation? Her unfounded suspicions of an affair might preclude her making any statement of confirmation; her embarassment over the issue might prompt her to simply remain out of the controversy; or, her ambition for her husband's political future might make her feel that the less developed about the story, the sooner that the incident will fade from memory. Unreasonable, you say? What would have happened if she had defended her husband? Would she have been believed, or would her confirmation have been labeled a "cover-up" for her husband's sake?

I submit that, under the circumstances of the case, there was no effective explanation. Whatever was said would have been interpreted as a lie, as a cover-up, or both. Whatever explanation was given for his presence with the young lady would have been an ineffective one. Most citizens—and most readers of the case—would demand a series of explanations, but would probably not be satisfied until *the real* reason was presented. What would be the real reason? The real reason would be that which *you* as a receiver were prepared to believe: you probably would not be satisfied with anything short of an admission that the pair of travelers were having an affair. If you were presented with *that* reason for the two being in the car, then you probably would relax and respond, "Aha, I knew it!"

My point is that the whole concept of real reason is difficult to grasp: How do you prove that you did *anything* for *any* reason? I might see you walking down the street, heading for the drugstore. I might stop you and ask, "Why are you going to the drugstore?" You might reply, "I'm going in there to buy a candy bar." What if I reply, "But what's the *real* reason?" You probably would look at me strangely, check the dilation of my eyes, and then say, "To get a candy bar." If I pursue the point, you might say, "Well, if you really want to, you can come in and watch me buy the candy bar." "No," I would respond, "if I do, I'm sure that you will go ahead and buy one just to trick me—then I'd never know the real reason you're going in."

I will admit that the purchase of a candy bar is a bit trivial in the context of the world, but, on the other hand, you would have difficulty in proving to me that the real reason you went into the store was to purchase a candy bar. If I think that there is some darker motivation behind your entering the drugstore, then I probably will not be satisfied with anything but an admission that the reason was something more sinister or bizarre or questionable than the purchase of the candy bar. How do you prove the real reason for the purchase?

Probably you cannot. How much more difficult, then, was the lieutenant governor's task in explaining the real reason for his companionship with the family "friend" to an audience who suspects darker reasons. How does he know and how can he prove the real reason? Again, probably, he cannot. If he made a choice about his real reason in this situation, he undoubtedly would reevaluate the reason later.

Generally, in argumentation, a receiver who demands the real reason behind a claim may be asking for too much; the standard of the real reason may be too strict. At worst, the receiver will discount the arguer's reason as not being the real one; at best, the receiver will accept the reason, not really knowing whether the reason given is real or whether it is just a reason that is acceptable to him. In either case, the insistence upon the real reason is a problematic demand that a receiver—in his zeal to "get at" the truth—would be best not making. The receiver has the right, and I think the obligation, to demand a reason, but the search for the unprovable real reason seems to me to be clearly an effort that should be channeled in other directions—as we shall see in the next chapter.

Summary

We began this chapter by noting the stress upon the judgments of receivers in chapter 5. Yet, the importance of the receivers' interpretations does not imply that the argumentative process develops equally well with all receiver judgments: some demands that receivers make are more productive than others; some standards of judgment are more effective than others. Although chapters 7 and 8 will be devoted to more productive demands, this particular chapter explored some commonly applied but generally problematic kinds of receiver demands and standards of judgment.

Using a variety of case studies ranging from cookie acquisition to consulting, we explored the demands that receivers make for personal reinforcement; for logicality; for the certainty of facts, truth, and reality; for causal force; and for the real reasons for claims. These standards of judgment or receiver demands were all explained as being impossible to meet, misleading, or in some other way problematic. Clearly, receivers must make demands of arguers, and arguers are obligated to meet appropriate standards of judgment if they can. On the other hand, to demand that a claim be personally reinforcing is to avoid any possibility of altering your position; to demand logicality is to give logic a purity that it does not have; to demand certainty in argumentation is to give facts, truth, and reality an aura of certainty and timelessness which they do not possess; to demand that you be caused to accept a claim is to insist on not having a choice in a process that is built upon choice; and to demand the real reasons for a claim is to ask something that cannot be proved to be the case—even if it is the case.

The standards by which receivers judge claims, then, should be understood and invoked, but you as a receiver should not demand things of arguers or argumentation that cannot be provided. You should be prepared to judge the claim at hand by the most productive and practical means available; those methods are the subject of the next two chapters.

Programmed Questions

To test your understanding of the material presented in this chapter, you may wish to answer the following questions. In the multiple-choice questions, the answers may be all correct, all incorrect, or several may be correct. The suggested answers to the questions appear on the last page of this chapter. If you fail to answer the questions correctly, you may wish to review the material to increase your understanding and/or to discuss the items in class.

1. The demand for personal reinforcement in argumentation:
    a. is perfectly justifiable
    b. is probably very common
    c. may inhibit our assessment of the strength of the argumentation
    d. may be considered a "shortcut" to a serious examination of the argumentation

2. The demand for logicality in argumentation:
    a. implies too much of a concern for the form of argumentation
    b. implies that emotions are irrelevant or undesirable in argumentation
    c. may prompt us to examine claims as they are—instead of whether they conform to the rules
    d. may prompt us to ignore certain "nonlogical-sounding" ideas that may be important to us

3. Facts, as human beings deal with them, should be considered:
    a. statements that are unaffected by the passage of time and the occurrence of events
    b. statements that are absolute and certain
    c. claims so strongly supported that they are not normally open to question
    d. claims accepted by (virtually) all normal and competent individuals
    e. tentative statements or claims that may be changed

4. Our perspective on the relationship between argumentation and truth is that:
   a. a truth is an agreed upon statement of the relationships between facts
   b. a truth *known* by an individual can be different from a truth *known* by a second individual
   c. we should always seek the absolute truth in argumentation
   d. what is the truth can vary from one era to another

5. Our perspective on the nature of reality has been that:
   a. we should search until we find the ultimate reality
   b. what people discuss as Reality actually will be an interpretation of what is reality
   c. conceptions of reality are the creations of human perception and thought
   d. the demand for correspondence-to-reality is a way of demanding "certainty" in argumentation

6. The demand for causal force in argumentation is a demand that:
   a. arguers leave no room for the receiver to choose a response
   b. is impossible to make of an arguer (unless the arguer abandons argumentation and uses physical force)
   c. is difficult but highly productive in the argumentative situation
   d. is contrary to the idea of choice in argumentation

7. The demand for real reasons in argumentation is:
   a. probably a common receiver demand
   b. based upon the belief that we can discover the real reasons for a thing occurring
   c. problematic because the real reason can never be proved
   d. problematic because what you take to be the real reason for something may be changed later: "No, this other thing was the real reason," you say.
   e. misleading because it seems that people do a thing for a variety of simultaneous reasons

Discussion Questions for Appendix Case Studies

To test your understanding of the material in this chapter, you may wish to answer the following questions that refer to the case studies in the Appendix of this book. You may wish to (a) work on the questions individually; (b) work on the questions in pairs or in groups in or before class; (c) develop written answers to the questions; (d) have class discussion based upon the questions; (e) prepare an extended paper on several related questions; or (f) develop a major paper about one case study (using the questions related to it that appear in various chapters).

1. Study "A 2 or a 4?" beginning on page 266. Alice obviously was frustrated by the interview situation. In what ways does Alice demonstrate that her desire to participate effectively in the appraisal is overshadowed by her demand for argumentative claims that are personally reinforcing?

2. Study "How Free is Free Will?" beginning on page 254. Clearly, Ellen is having difficulty in deciding whether this new perspective on freedom of the will should be accepted and integrated into her thinking. Could part of her problem be the emphasis that she places on being "logical" and the resultant frustration of not being able to deal with contradictions, difficult questions, and uncertain answers? Explain your answer.

3. Study "The Success of the Program" beginning on page 264. Although Wallace seems to have some serious reservations about the evidence of the effectiveness of the antismoking program, the administrator seems *certain* that his evidence is strong. What do you think the administrator considers to be "factual" in his report? What would you guess is his conception of the "truth" of the effectiveness of the program? Do you get the feeling that the administrator would object to this chapter's discussion of "interpretations" of "reality?" Why, or why not?

4. Study "Letter-to-the-Editor" beginning on page 254. Pay particularly close attention to how Elbarc identifies himself after his name. Are you tempted to say that "The *real* reason Elbarc wrote the letter was? . . . " Is it possible that he honestly was motivated by a civic concern as well as by political ambition? Would Elbarc himself be able to say once and for all what his "real" reason was? Why not?

5. Study "Address to the Catholic Lawyers' Guild" by Senator Clark beginning on page 259. What you may not know, as you read about the Senator's support of public financing, is that Clark, as a nonincumbent facing a strong opponent in his election to the Senate in 1972, suffered from an apparent lack of funds for his campaign. Are you tempted to say, "Ah, that's the *real* reason? . . . " I hope not: Why would such a conclusion be almost certainly misleading?

Research Project for Advanced Students

Some of the argumentation that I have advanced about the problems of demanding "logicality" from arguers are said to be answered in the logician's concern for material validity. Research this concept and the manner in which logicians attempt to separate material validity from the problems of formal validity. A place to begin is Monroe C. Beardsley, *Thinking Straight*, 3rd ed. (Englewood Cliffs, N.J.: Prentice-Hall, 1966).

SELECTED REFERENCES

Beardsley, Monroe C. *Thinking Straight*. 3rd ed. Englewood Cliffs, N.J.: Prentice-Hall, 1966.

Kaplan, Abraham. *The Conduct of Inquiry: Methodology for Behavioral Science*. Scranton, Penn.: Chandler Publishing Co., 1964.

Perelman, Chaim. *The Idea of Justice and the Problem of Argument*. New York: Humanities Press, 1963.

Perelman, Chaim and Olbrechts-Tyteca, L. *The New Rhetoric: A Treatise on Argumentation*. Translated by John Wilkinson and Purcell Weaver. Notre Dame: University of Notre Dame Press, 1969.

Toulmin, Stephen. *Reason in Ethics*. Cambridge: Cambridge University Press, 1968.

——."Reasons and Causes," in *Explanation in the Behavioral Sciences*, edited by M. Berger and F. Cioffi. New York: Cambridge University Press, 1969.

Answers to Programmed Questions

1. b, c, d   2. a, b, d   3. c, d, e   4. a, b, d   5. b, c, d

6. a, b, d   7. a, b, c, d, e

7

Productive Receiver Demands

My *general objective* in this chapter is to explain a related and sequential series of demands that should aid receivers who wish to participate productively in argumentative situations.

My *specific objectives* are

to explain the crucial demand for good reasons

to explain the importance of general communicative clarity in claims

to introduce the idea of fields in argumentation

to explain the demand to know a claim's field

to discuss the importance of arguable claims

to explain the demand for nontrivial claims

to discuss in detail the demand for rationality in argumentation

to explain the demand for field-related reasons

to explain the demand that field-related standards be met

The discussion in the last chapter concerning problematic receiver demands is crucial to your understanding of our present perspective on argumentation. For, while it seems to me that we must stress the importance of receivers and their judgment of argumentative language (as we did in chapter 5), it is clearly not the case that all receiver judgments are of equally high quality. Receivers need not and should not rely upon whim to guide their reactions to argumentation; instead, receivers may utilize certain guidelines for evaluation and should make certain demands upon the arguer with whom they are communicating. As we discovered in that last chapter, however, not all demands that receivers can make of arguers are equally productive or desirable: argumentation that is forced to focus upon an illusive standard of logic, that attempts to exclude emotionality from its concern, or that seeks what is called the real reason for a claim is apt to be problematic in its desirability, possibility, or productivity. Thus, although I submit that making demands based upon standards is an essential aspect of argumentation, receivers need to select the demands that lead to the most productive and practical results possible.

In this chapter, then, we shall examine what I consider to be the more productive receiver demands, so that this chapter becomes the *positive* complement to the treatment in chapter 6 of problematic demands by receivers. We, therefore, shall deal with those demands that receivers *should make* of argumentation and arguers and the demands that arguers *should anticipate* when they engage receivers in argumentation. We shall develop fairly specific guidelines for receivers who wish to make their participation in argumentation as practical, productive, and rigorous as they can, given the complex nature of argumentation. Similarly, we shall present these same guidelines for arguers to utilize as they seek to argue effectively and productively in that same difficult process. To accomplish these goals, this chapter will focus upon a related series of receiver demands: the demand for good reasons; the demand for general communicative clarity; the demand to know the claim's field; the demand for an arguable claim; the demand for a nontrivial claim; the demand for rationality; the demand for field-related reasons; the demand for field-related standards. The process of examining these related demands should bring us closer to the goal of understanding the productive demands that receivers should make and that arguers should anticipate.

The Demand for Good Reasons

The whole process of productive argumentation, it seems to me, is centered around the demand for "good" reasons to support a claim.

In commonsense terms, we have all experienced occasions when we have said, "Give me one *good* reason"; when we have explained, "Well, that isn't a *good* enough reason"; or when we have sought to explain our action by submitting that "It seemed like a *good* reason at the time." The concept of a good reason probably seems extremely common, functional, and practical to the study of argumentation, but you may not be so clear as to how you would conceptualize exactly what a "good reason" is.

Reasons and Significance

Let us begin to examine the nature of good reasons by denying that they exist apart from the people who interpret them: that is, good reasons do not exist as combinations of evidence, warrants, and so forth—they are created when an individual attaches significance to the ideas in relation to the claim advanced.[1] There is nothing magical, for instance, about the phrase "it is late" that automatically makes it a good reason, but it may *function* as a good reason if someone says, "It is late, so, I guess you are right: I should go to bed." Similarly, there is nothing inherently good in the idea that "it is raining," but it may function as a good reason if a receiver says, "You're right: it is raining, so I should go inside the house."

In essence, then, nearly (and perhaps) any expression can function as a good reason in the proper situation. Yet, the proper situation always will be a setting in which an individual perceives that *for him,* the idea has significance and merit in relation to a claim under consideration. In order, therefore, to determine what are good reasons, we must discover not what the reasons *look like,* but whether they function as acceptable ideas for individuals seeking support for a claim. Hence, in our commonsense examples of the use of the phrase "good reasons," we can realize the personal emphasis: "Give me just one good reason"; "Well, that isn't a good enough reason *for me*"; "It seemed (*to me*) like a good reason at the time." Good reasons, then, are primarily matters of interpretation by individuals involved in an argumentative process.

Factors in Judging Significance

Those individual interpretations, however, probably are not so individualistic as we might at first think. As I mentioned in chapter 1 during a discussion of meaning, and as I have since alluded to, these

[1]The analysis of "good" reasons that follows is based upon the writing of Stephen E. Toulmin. See especially his *Reason in Ethics* (Cambridge: Cambridge University Press, 1968), pp. 70-71 and his "Reasons and Causes," in *Explanation in the Social Sciences,* ed. by M. Berger and F. Cioffi (Cambridge: Cambridge University Press, 1970), p. 4.

individual interpretations of significance seem influenced by several types of factors. Part of the interpretation of significance is, for lack of a better term, *the product of idiosyncrasy;* individuals seem, to one degree or another, somewhat unlike other human beings. Such factors as individual beliefs, backgrounds, and so forth explain why we can say that a portion of the assignment of meaning or significance is individualistically determined. Yet, ironically, it is these same factors of belief and experience that explain why the assignment of significance is not purely an individual matter: beliefs, training, and experiences normally arise from situations involving other people. Part of the attachment of significance to a reason, therefore, is based upon the *prior influences* of important other individuals. Moreover, part of the significance of a reason will be *created by the situation itself:* a reason would seem to have *no* significance outside an argumentative situation—or without someone functioning as arguer and receiver. Thus, a great deal of this individual (and psychological-sounding) significance is because of our position as a member of a collective (and sociological-sounding) world of influential *other* individuals and *shared* situations.

The complication in all this, however, arises from the idea that we find more than one individual involved in an argumentative situation. Since the "goodness" of a reason is defined by an individual attaching significance to an idea in relation to a claim, we are apt to find different interpretations as to the significance of the reason advanced in support of a claim. Thus, arguers typically attempt to support their claims by presenting (what appear to them to be) good reasons. The problem they may confront, though, is that the receiver simply does not attach significance to the same idea: what the arguer has predicted to be a good reason turns out not to be considered as such by his receiver. So, the same particular idea may be considered as a good reason, a poor reason, or no reason at all—depending upon the varying degrees of merit or significance that different individuals attach to the idea in relation to the claim.

The implication is clear that receivers in an argumentative situation should demand ideas that *for them* are significant. As a receiver, you should demand that the arguer supply reasons that you personally can regard as good—not simply reasons that the arguer himself deems acceptable and significant. Similarly, arguers must anticipate that they will have to present reasons that are significant for the receiver: it is not enough that they personally regard the support as comprised of good reasons. If those implications are clear to receivers and arguers, then the argumentation should proceed with considerably less emotional trauma and frustration than is usually the case. Instead of arguers being shocked that what they have considered to be good reasons have been rejected, they should expect that possibility to arise and be prepared to present other reasons or at least an explanation as to why the reason is better than the receiver initially thought it was.[2] Correspondingly, instead of receivers being puzzled that the arguer is presenting reasons that they reject, they should be prepared at all times to have that occur. Although it is clearly the case that receivers and arguers may at times agree upon the value of a reason that is presented, it is also the case that such agreement may not occur: we should be prepared to have good reasons evaluated individually—and perhaps differently—by each of the participants in the argumentative process. Good reasons, then, are simply ideas and expressions that are judged to be significant and sound by the individuals involved in the argumentation.

The Nature of Bad Reasons

If we consider the "goodness" of reasons to be based upon whether individuals attach significance to the reasons, how are we to account for reasons that are often labeled "bad reasons?" We may consider bad reasons to be those ideas that frequently are labeled fallacies, irrelevancies, or faulty reasons. As you may know, textbooks in logic, debate, and argumentation normally devote considerable attention to these concepts, and how one can discover and avoid these pitfalls of argumentation. Notions such as post hoc fallacies, red herrings, and attacks upon the person are all derived from the stress which we in debate, logic, and argumentation place upon factors that are "bad reasons" for claims.[3] Though we shall spend little time on the established categories of argumentative fallacies, we will devote more effort to understanding *why* something becomes labeled a fallacy. Let me first explain what a "bad" reason is in relation to our discussion of "good" reasons.

We established "good reasons" to be simply ideas and expressions that are judged to be significant and sound by the individuals involved in the argumentation. We shall, of course, continue to highlight the importance of the receiver's attachment of significance to

[2]Though in general we assume the arguer will offer as reasons those factors that he himself feels are significant, that clearly is not always the case. Conceivably, and perhaps fairly often, an arguer may choose to present a reason which he feels is insignificant, but which he predicts will be assigned significance by his receiver. Some observers may consider this to be an ethical problem, but, in general, I do not.

[3]We shall not list and describe here those ideas that are normally considered fallacies. Indeed, as we shall soon see, most fallacies might be legitimate arguments in certain situations. It is my position that no reason—good or bad—can be judged automatically or without reference to its use and interpretation in the argumentation.

the reason, rather than the arguer's judgment of the reason as "good." Correspondingly, therefore, we shall label a reason a "bad" one whenever a participant in argumentation considers the reason to be irrelevant, weak, or counteracting, with most importance placed upon the judgment of the receiver. The arguer, thus, may judge the reason to be good (acceptable to himself) and offer it as a reason for his claim's acceptance (predicted to be judged good by the receiver); yet, that same reason may be judged as irrelevant and bad by the receiver. Though we are concerned about what the arguer takes to be a sound reason (his good reason), our communicative perspective on argumentation implies a primary concern for the judgments of receivers involved.

In essence, then, we shall not label any factor as being a good or bad reason without an examination of the situation: the relevance or irrelevance, strength or weakness of the reason is something that is created by the transaction that occurs between or among receivers, arguers, and the language that they are examining. Such relevance or irrelevance, strength or weakness cannot be determined beforehand, in a timeless and absolute manner. An *ad hominem* attack, or an attack upon the person or the person's character, for example, is always listed as a fallacy, an irrelevancy. Texts traditionally assume that any argumentation so directed is automatically irrelevant to the main issue under contention. Although that presumption may be accurate in general, it also is clear that such an attack is highly appropriate in argumentation that seeks to ascertain whether deliberate falsehoods are being told; whether someone is mentally capable of testifying; or whether a person is so biased because of conflict of interests that he cannot be presumed to be objective. All those instances, however, are as common to informal argumentation as they are legal argumentation: you wonder if your friend has your best interests at heart when she wants you to date her brother; you question the objectivity of a person who is totally embroiled in a controversy; or you question whether your instructor has given a "shaky" answer to avoid admitting that he could not answer your query. In those situations as well, you will challenge or at least question the personal characteristics or qualities of the person involved—and sometimes your analysis of certain behavior will lead to attacks against that person's morals, ethics, trustworthiness, or character. Will these attacks be automatically irrelevant? Automatically fallacious? I suspect not. Again, the relevance or irrelevance of a reason is given its force by the attachment of significance by the receivers involved.

Thus, our perspectives on good and bad reasons share the common assumption that we will not be able to tell if the reason is good or bad until we see the transaction that occurs between arguers and receivers.[4] We indeed may set about labeling reasons as either good or bad in an a priori (before the transaction) manner. However, we must be prepared to acknowledge that what we as arguers considered bad reasons may be the very ones accepted as good by receivers: the surprise may be pleasant. On the other hand, we as arguers must be equally prepared for what we considered to be good reasons to be completely rejected by the receiver: the surprise, of course, will not be so pleasant. Let us summarize this discussion by exploring a case study that involves good and bad reasons in an argumentative transaction.

Case Study: You Ought to Go to the Game

College students, some away from home for the first time on an extended basis, frequently find themselves faced with dilemmas concerning the relative advisability of studying or participating in a particular nonacademic activity. Where in the past, the student might have had a parent to help with those decisions ("Stay at home and get at those books!"), the student may find himself in a difficult situation where only he can make the decisions.

GEORGE: Hey, are you going to the game with us?

JACK: No, I guess not.

GEORGE: You are going, though, aren't you?

JACK: I guess not . . . I don't really want to.

GEORGE: What do you mean? Everybody's going. It's got to be the biggest game of the season, and a whole bunch of us are going together.

JACK: No, I really don't think so.

At this point, of course, the essential claim is apparent: Jack ought to go to the game. George, in his eagerness to support the claim with reasons, suggests that one good reason for going is that everybody else is going. That prediction of an occurrence is meant to function as evidence, probably with an implied warrant that Jack ought to go to something that everybody is going to. Jack, however, is apparently unmoved by the reason: he attaches no significance to the report—

---

[4]I have attempted to keep the discussion in this chapter about good reasons focusing upon the strength of the reasons, rather than their ethical quality—chapter 8 deals with ethics. My rationale for this separation is the confusion that can arise when we insist on having good reasons be both strong and ethical—with no provision for reasons that are one but not the other. For an example of someone who attempts to make the two judgments simultaneously, see Karl Wallace, "The Substance of Rhetoric: Good Reasons," in *The Rhetoric of Our Time*, ed. by J. Jeffrey Auer (New York: Appleton-Century Crofts, 1969), pp. 277-90.

perhaps because he is not a joiner or overly social—and so George's proposed reason does not function *for his receiver* as a good reason. Similarly, George's attempt at presenting the game as the "biggest of the season"—to some, an obviously significant reason—fails to move Jack any nearer to the game. Whether George realizes his strategy or not, he continues making what he considers good reasons, hoping that Jack will make a similar evaluation of one of them.

GEORGE: You really ought to get away from the books for awhile; too much studying without a break makes you start retaining less of what you read.

JACK: Well, maybe . . . no, I don't think so.

GEORGE: What are you studying for? Crable's class? The test will be a snap; you know he never gives us anything difficult to do. I'm going to take the same test, and I've got plenty of time to go to the game. I'll even help you study later if that'll help.

JACK: I don't know. I've got to keep my grade point up if I want to get into law school, I'm just not sure that I ought to go. I suppose I could study later . . . no, I better stay here.

Can you identify what is transpiring between these friends? What sorts of reasons is George presenting? How is Jack responding to them? Does Jack's response begin to change here? Why do you think he is suddenly explaining in more detail why he should not go to the game? Why is George explaining his reasons in more detail to Jack? What do you predict that George will do now?

GEORGE: Okay, Jack, I understand. Well, see you later, huh? I'll tell Bill, Kay, Janet, and the others you said, "Hello." 'Bye!

JACK: What did you say?

GEORGE: I said, "Good-bye."

JACK: No, before that . . . what about Janet?

GEORGE: Janet? Oh, I guess she's going to be there with the rest of us. See you later.

JACK: When will you be back? Early, do you think?

GEORGE: Yeah, I guess not too late; I have to get up for that test, too, you know.

JACK: Do you think we could study together later . . . I mean if I went to the game?

GEORGE: Are you going after all?

JACK: Oh, I suppose I might as well. We can study when we get back. C'mon.

Obviously, Jack's position was much different at the end of the exchange than it was at the beginning. What do you think was responsible? What reason or reasons do you think Jack may have attached some high degree of significance to? Thus, what were, for him, good reasons to go the game? Were several reasons considered somewhat significant? How did his reaction to one reason differ from his reactions to the others George offered for Jack's attendance at the game? Did George know that he was providing a predictably better reason for Jack toward the last? What makes you think so? Was this latter factor of the people attending the game the only good reason presented by George? Or was it merely the final good reason which tipped the scales? Was Janet even presented as a reason?

In answering these questions about the nature of the reasons presented, we have a convenient opportunity to contrast the concept of *good* reason with a concept that we discussed earlier in chapter 6: the term *real* reason. I predict that many of you even used the term real reason to describe what finally gave Jack reason enough to go to the game. Was not the presence of Janet the real reason? Was not the dialogue about the studying afterward simply a method for Jack to rationalize his guilt about attending a game rather than studying? Was not his desire to see Janet the real reason that he went to the game?

Even though these questions may arise in your analysis of the situation, I will contend again that we are deceived if we put too much stress upon *real* reasons. First, we cannot get inside Jack's head to find out for sure what it was that he was thinking. This leaves us no choice but to make a judgment about his reasons. Since he did seem to be weakening prior to the announcement that Janet would be attending the game, we may ask if Janet could merely have been the final (of several) factors which tilted an already leaning scale toward going to the game. If so, how much of a factor was Janet in contrast to the other factors—including Jack's probably existent desire to go? We simply cannot be sure. Clearly, we can cite Janet as a powerful incentive if we wish, but to speak of her as the *real* reason for his going is, as I argued in chapter 6, simply misleading. Let us, instead, speak of her as one of several "good" reasons that may have affected the decision—and as the reason that finally tipped the scale in favor of Jack's attending the game. This modified or qualified answer is more reasonable, it seems to me, and certainly easier to defend if we are challenged.

If you are still concerned about "real" reasons, though, you may submit that all we must do is ask Jack if Janet was, in fact, the "real" reason. This also seems to me to be unproductive. Have you not had the experience of stating why you did something—only to decide later that you really did it for some other reason? You may have challenged an instructor's comments in class, explaining to a friend afterward that you were confused about something. Later, when the instructor annoys you again, you may realize that the real reason that you challenged her was that you wanted to "catch" her. Yet, that second self-judgment is also open to reinterpretation. Later, you may decide that the reason you did it was to impress a friend, but later you may decide that. . . . My point, in sum, is that even the person himself will not be able to claim once-and-for-all why the thing was done. Indeed, you may look at the activity and decide that something-or-other was uppermost in your mind, but to call it the real reason is deceptive, given how subject such final judgments are to revision.

This final discussion of real reasons is an inevitable result of our study of good reasons. My position is that the receiver and the process of argumentation will benefit if the receiver demands good reasons—realizing that there cannot be a statement of real reasons, knowing that most things can be a reason for something, assuming that the arguer may present reasons that are intended to be good (for the receiver), but that they may not be judged so. Through this whole process, the receiver should demand reasons that he himself considers good, relevant, and strong. The arguer should approach the process with similar knowledge and attitudes: he should offer reasons which he predicts the receiver will consider good, but which he realizes may be completely rejected. In such a case the arguer may need to offer other reasons, until there is presented a reason to which the receiver can say, "Yes, that is a good reason," or "Yes, that is reason enough." To supply anything less would be folly on the part of the arguer; to demand anything less would be for the receiver to surrender his right to accept claims because they are supported by what he considers to be good reasons. The demand for a good reason, then, is one of the foundations of responsible and productive argumentation.

The problem with viewing the demand for a good reason as such an important foundation of argumentation, however, is that it is such a general demand. Are there no guidelines that might prove helpful in evaluating how good a reason is? Is it the case that a receiver's decision of what is a good reason is purely an individual interpretation? My position is that such decisions need not be merely idiosyncratic or haphazard, but instead can be guided by certain more specific demands that receivers should make of argumentation. That is, once we have demanded a good reason, we can make certain other demands that can enhance the quality of argumentation. We shall chart these demands from the most basic (related to claims) to the most specific (related to standards of judgment), as demands that together can help assure that we are presented with good reasons in the process of argumentation.

The Demand for General Communicative Clarity

One of the most basic demands that receivers should make of arguers is that the claim be presented as clearly and as unambiguously as possible. In the context of viewing argumentation as a kind of communication process, we should expect the sorts of problems to occur in argumentation that occur in communication in general. Ideas may be presented sketchily, important words may be misinterpreted, important qualifiers may be omitted. In any of these situations—and dozens more—where communication failure can occur, the demand for general communicative clarity is crucial. If, as a receiver, you were not to demand such specificity, you might find yourself contesting the claim of the arguer for fairly lengthy periods of time only to find that there really was no disagreement at all; there was simply a misinterpretation. On the other hand, in a similar situation where clarity is not demanded, you might find yourself immediately agreeing to the claim that was advanced or the evidence that was presented only to find later that you disagree with the fundamental position of the arguer. In either case, the argumentation is confused, misdirected, and unproductive from the outset.

As a receiver wishing to demand general communicative clarity from an arguer, you well may benefit from some of the techniques and skills relevant to the study of interpersonal communication in general or counseling communication in particular. An increase in your general listening skills will normally aid your effort to assure communicative clarity from your arguer. An attempt to paraphrase (i.e., restate in your own words) what an arguer has claimed, before you respond, can provide a check upon what the arguer meant to say: she as an arguer can be accorded the opportunity to say, "No, that is not what I meant," or "Yes, that is what I am prepared to defend. What is your reaction to it?" In addition to general listening and paraphrasing skills, your demand for argumentative clarity can be better fulfilled if you simply delay any response until the entire claim or the entire unit of claims and reasons have been presented before you respond. Though these suggestions may seem dreadfully fundamental, they can be useful in preventing a situation where, after a period of arguing, you are forced to say, "I beg your pardon—I thought you had said that "Six-year presidential terms should NOT be permitted. I see that I agree with you—I also feel that the six-year term is desirable." In essence, the most basic demand that a receiver should make of an arguer is for communicative clarity.[5]

The Demand to Know the Claim's Field

Unfortunately, once we have clarified the general intent or meaning of the claim that is before us, we may still need more information about the ideas involved. An arguer, for example, may claim that "You cannot play the piano." In general, we may realize that the claim concerns a musical instrument, you as an individual, and what you *cannot* do in relation to the piano. As Toulmin observes concerning such a situation, the *force* of the argumentative claim is clear: playing the piano clearly would violate the major thrust or force of the argument, since the arguer has said you "cannot." At this point, your problem as a receiver may be that you will assume too easily that you understand the claim as presented. After all, you will tell yourself, I have demanded a clearly communicated claim, and, at this time, I understand that I "cannot" play the piano.

What must be kept in mind by receivers wishing to demand the most productive argumentative process, however, is that the force (you "cannot") of the argumentation must be further clarified on the basis of what sort of criterion is relevant to the claimed "cannot." If I phrase the claim, "Based upon an *artistic* standard, you cannot play the piano," I shall have a much different claim from when I suggest, "*Physically*, you cannot play the piano." Similarly, if I claim that "*Legally*, you cannot play the piano," then I am claiming something different from when I claim that "Based upon the *norms* of the church, you cannot play the piano." The examples could be extended, but the crucial point is that in order to understand clearly the claim as presented, we must know the *criterion* (physically, legally, etc.) on which the claim is based as well as the general notion of the *force* (you "cannot") of the argumentation.[6] Just as we can see that claims mean different things depending upon the criteria by which we are to judge the "cannot," the "should," the "are," and so forth, it is clear that these criteria can be related to various fields of thought: the "Legally, you cannot ... " is of a different field of thought and argumentation from the "Physically,

[5]See, for example, the techniques discussed in David W. Johnson, *Reaching Out: Interpersonal Effectiveness and Self-Actualization* (Englewood Cliffs, N.J.: Prentice-Hall, 1972), especially chapters 4 and 7.

[6]The discussion of force and criteria is based upon that found in Stephen E. Toulmin, *The Uses of Argument* (Cambridge: University of Cambridge Press, 1969), especially chapter 1.

you cannot. . . ." Although we can consider the legally, or physically to be different *criteria* for the claim, we can also say that they represent different and varying *fields*.

Some of these fields can be related to occupational or professional activities or fields. If the claim is supposed to be interpreted by using a legal criterion, we naturally would expect the claim to fall within the field of law. If, on the other hand, the claim expressed a physiological impossibility, we would expect that criterion to be related to physics, physiology, or something of the sort. At other times the field is not well represented as a professional or occupational activity. If, for instance, our claim is based upon the criterion that "For reasons of mental challenge you should read the book," we have a much different claim from one based upon the criterion that "For reasons of light entertainment, you should read the book." Yet even when the criterion does not relate to a commonly accepted occupational or professional field, we still say that the claims involving light entertainment and mental challenge belong to different fields.

Some fields of argumentation can be further broken down into numerous subfields: when we speak of the field of law, do we mean British Common Law, American Corporate law, the Iowa Revised Code (or whatever), the Ten Commandments, or the Justinian Code, or any one of dozens of other possibilities? When we discuss a claim involving the phrase that "Socially, it was . . ," we find ourselves in a similar situation: though we know the field to be the area of thought concerned with social norms, we may not know whether the arguer means, "Socially according to Emily Post," "Socially according to Cro-Magnon precepts," "Socially according to East-coast tradition," or "Socially according to common sense in rural America."

In essence, to understand a claim we must demand more than general communicative clarity. We should demand that the arguer disclose the criterion by which we are to interpret his claim. If he does so, he will enhance our understanding of the claim, its field, and any subfields that might be relevant to the claim. The demand to know the claim's field, therefore, brings us a step closer to our goal of participating rigorously in the argumentative process.

The Demand for a Reasonably Arguable Claim

Once we have demanded a clear understanding of the claim in question, we can begin to determine whether the argumentative claim before us is worthy of our continued interest. Receivers, that is, should demand a reasonably arguable claim. Although I have taken the position that virtually any claim is challengeable, we certainly will hesitate before arguing about some sorts of things in most situations. We normally, for example, would not challenge a claim that seems to have impeccable support, such as, "The sun will rise tomorrow," "I am alive," or "The presidential election of 1960 was a close contest." Indeed, we take for granted—and normally without a thought of challenge—that the sun will "in fact" rise tomorrow; we assume that if you have made a claim that you are alive then you "in fact" must be alive; and our general knowledge of the Nixon-Kennedy election leads us to accept without question that the election was "in fact" a narrow victory for Kennedy. In sum, certain kinds of claims are not normally the focus of argumentation.

This is not to say, however, that there are not situations in which we might argue even these claims. If we are confident that the world will end tomorrow with a gigantic explosion that will disintegrate the earth—hence, preventing sunrise as we conceive of it—then we may want to argue the claim about the sun rising. If we find records revealing that several hundreds of thousands of ballots in the 1960 election (most apparently for Kennedy) have been discovered, we may even want to challenge the narrowness of the election victory. And, perhaps, we might even discover something that leads us to believe that you are, in fact, not alive. These, however, are clearly bizarre situations; they do not sound reasonable; and we would not expect to have them ever occur. In essence, even though all claims are potentially challengeable, receivers should demand that the claims advanced be reasonably, not theoretically, arguable claims. Receivers, then, will wish to reject certain claims as, for all practical purposes, not suitable for the process of argumentation: they will wish to demand a reasonably arguable claim and ignore claims that are arguable only under the strangest and most unusual circumstances.

The Demand for Nontrivial Claims

As we have just seen, some claims that may be advanced are so well established that to engage in argumentation concerning them would seem unproductive; receivers, thus, should demand that an arguer's claim be reasonably arguable. Frequently, however, claims may be advanced that, instead of being too well established, seem to be either unsupportable or so implausible that we deem it unworthy of further consideration. An arguer advancing the claim in the late twentieth century that the moon is made of green cheese, hardly deserves attention; an arguer claiming that the Vietnam War was caused entirely by one president or one secretary of state is apt to warrant no serious consideration. Just as we should refuse to engage in argumentation about matters we normally consider settled and beyond the scope of everyday argumentation, we should decline to entertain claims or reasons that are simply too implausible: we probably should question the arguer for the purpose of arguing such claims, but our most basic impulse might be to say, "nonsense," and walk away from the situation.

In addition to argumentation that should be rejected as trivial because the claims are too implausible or because they cannot be seriously supported, receivers should decline to argue claims that concern matters that are inherently trivial or of little actual consequence. Heated argumentation, for example, used to occur to help settle the ancient issue of how many angels could dance on the head of a pin. While, so far as I know, the issue was never settled, I suspect that that claim is one that never should have been debated: at least from our perspective, any gain from the argumentation would seem trivial. In more common argumentative situations, we may still encounter arguers who would argue about claims that are of little consequence. It frequently is the case that more argumentation is expended over situations where no one really cares which decision is made. For example, in an organization confronted with two choices of (say) a kind of equipment, more time will be spent in the decision process if the differences between the two kinds of equipment are slight. Clearly, the decision between the two will be immaterial to those involved, and so the claims that "Equipment A should be bought" and that "Equipment B should be bought" are trivial indeed. In another example, a friend may engage you in argumentation to help him assess the value of course X versus the value of course Y. If you have no information about either course and neither does he, then you would be justified in disengaging yourself from the process: indeed, it seems as though any decision you make would be as uneventful as discovering the size of the group of angels on the head of a pin. You should demand that argumentation in which you engage not be trivial, either because the claim is unsupportable or implausible, or because the claim itself is of so little consequence.

What we have observed in considering these first productive receiver demands is a process in which we have continually narrowed and made more rigorous our attempts at being given good reasons. At first, we simply were concerned that the usual barriers to *communicative clarity* were removed so that we understood the general intent of the claim. At that point, we were prepared to examine the claim more closely to determine the criteria, and, thus, the *field in which we were to interpret the claim:* was the cannot (or the can, or whatever) a legal, ethical, or a physical cannot, or any one of numerous other possibilities? Then, as we understood the field for the claim, we were able to ascertain whether the claim was something about which we were interested in arguing? We demanded that *the claim be reasonably arguable* in normal situations; we did not wish to engage in argumentation about something we usually took for granted. And, further, we demanded that the claim be *plausible*, have a *likelihood* of being *supportable*, and not in itself be of *little consequence*; that is, we demanded that the claim not be *trivial*. In essence, in making four concrete and productive demands of the arguer and his claim, we are now prepared to begin the examination of the reasons for the claim.

The Demand for the Rationality of Reasons

At the point that we have succeeded in making demands so that we understand the claim as a clear, field-oriented, arguable, and nontrivial statement, we still are far from having demanded good reasons.

Though it seems to me that we can understand argumentation best as being based upon a receiver's judgment of a good reason for a claim, it is also my position that demanding that a reason be a good one does not imply that the receiver should feel he has absolute and complete freedom in judging anything he wants to be a bad or good reason. Although receivers may defend their right to accept whatever they will as good and sufficient reason, the more serious receiver should compare what he thinks is a good reason with a rigorous standard: the standard of rationality. The goodness of a reason, then, would be based, not on whimsy, but on the standard of rationality. Let us examine the concept of rationality, as conceptualized by Toulmin, and then we shall apply the standard to the notion of good reasons as a way of making receiver demands more productive. First, therefore, let us look at two separate case studies that allow the illustration of the concept of rationality.

Case Study: Why I'm Afraid of Snakes

Despite the traditional stories about little boys with snakes in their pockets, let me assure you that I was not one of that breed. Snakes, to me, were not pocket-stuffers as much as they were the material of nightmares. My father never liked snakes, my mother never liked snakes, and my sister was not even friendly with earthworms. My fear of snakes, then, ran in the family . . . so to speak. I have never been near any dangerous snakes, and yet the fear has continued. I was the kind of little boy who did not laugh when all the girls were frightened by a snake brought into the classroom by a four-foot sponsor. Normally, I guess I smiled (I suspect a bit nervously) and tried to appear nonchalant—give or take my white knuckles.

Thus, without boring you with all the close calls that I have had with garter snakes, black snakes, and the like, let me say that I still retain the fear that I have nurtured for years. I still do not like the *idea* of snakes—let alone their actual existence.

I have had friends who have thought my fear was amazingly humorous. "They won't hurt you," they say, "they'll run from you." "Not if I see them first," I shoot back. "They're really not at all slimy—just dry and warm; they kind of tickle when you hold them," they say. "I'll bet," I reply. They respond, "Look, I'll hold it, and you just pet it." I do not even answer an invitation like that. As the years have gone by, and I have grown to where I am considerably larger than most garter snakes, my behavior has not altered. Cognitively, however, I am much improved. I know that snakes are afraid of me, smaller than I am, generally harmless, not slimy, kind of dry and are fun to hold (as long as I am not the holder). Yet, I am still not close to where I could actually touch one, hold one, or smile at one. In essence, I am afraid of snakes because I simply am afraid of snakes.

Unfortunately, I am something else besides afraid of snakes: I am irrational in my fear. Toulmin has established two criteria which he feels characterizes the study of irrationality in human fear. One is *inappropriate behavior* and the other is *a lack of ability to modify behavior* to an appropriate level or kind.[7] My fear of snakes can be described aptly by the application of these criteria for irrationality. As I said, my response to snakes, even those that are obviously not dangerous, is inappropriate: I realize that the snake will not hurt me, that it probably fears me, and that it is not distasteful to hold or touch. An appropriate response (one of the criteria of rationality) would be to touch it, to hold it, or at least to consider doing those things. Unfortunately, nothing is farther from my reactions to the matter: I realize my behavior is inappropriate, and therefore irrational, based upon the first criterion.

Secondly, and relatedly, I seem to be incapable of modifying my behavior, or at least I fail to modify it. I recognize the inappropriateness of my behavior, but somehow I cannot seem to change. The rational response would be to modify my behavior once I realize its inappropriateness, but, again, that rational modification of behavior

[7]This explanation and conception of rationality in terms of how concepts are accepted and modified by argumentation is at the heart of Toulmin's first volume of his work on human understanding. See Toulmin, *Human Understanding* (Princeton: Princeton University Press, 1972).

does not occur. From both the criteria of appropriateness and modifiability, then, my fear of snakes is indeed irrational.

While the criteria of appropriateness and modifiability can be utilized to judge rational and irrational fears, they also can be useful in serving as criteria to judge rational and irrational claims and argumentation. Let us explore a second case study which has less to do with fear and more to do with a receiver's judgment of argumentation.

Case Study: The Legalization of Marijuana

The situation below involves two students conversing about the class one of them attended the previous evening.

MARY: You'll never guess what happened last night in my organizational communication class.

FRED: You're probably right.

MARY: Well, this professor of sociology—Cleveland or someone like that—was a guest in the class and he brought something that looked like a joint to class. He passed it around and invited anyone to try it if he liked—it was really funny. The thing was some kind of tea or something, but it looked like a joint, and the professor said that if someone would have lit it, it would have smelled like it too. Isn't that funny? It was a way of examining norms and group conformity.

FRED: I don't think it's all that funny. All we need around here is another professor who has no sense of common values. There are other ways to make a point about group pressure, I think.

MARY: Oh, come on. It was just a joke—on us really. It wasn't anything all that sinister.

FRED: Did the professor end by advocating the legalization of marijuana? They usually do.

MARY: Are you kidding? It was just a demonstration—not a presentation to get votes for marijuana. Come to think of it, though, I wish he had been more persuasive about it. That would have stimulated some lively discussion.

FRED: It would also have been irrelevant to your class, but I don't suppose you'd care if it meant one step closer to pot for all.

MARY: Well, it is true that I think all this stuff about long jail sentences and stiff fines is a bit much. It really doesn't hurt you, and it does help you relax and forget about school for a little while.

FRED: I bet it does.

MARY: What do you mean by that?

FRED: I mean anything that affects your mind like that stuff does
           ought to take your thoughts away completely—let alone
           just away from school for awhile.

MARY: There's not one scrap of proven research about any bad
           effects of marijuana—if you'd look at the things that are
           written about grass, you'd know that.

FRED: Yeah? What about what they found . . .

MARY: Nothing you can mention has proved beyond doubt that
           there are any ill effects.

FRED: Did you hear about the research at . . .

MARY: I really don't care what you say, nothing will ever con-
           vince me that pot is anything worse than your dad's
           Scotch.

FRED: My dad doesn't drink.

MARY: Well, your mother's pain reliever.

FRED: Mary, do you see what you're doing? You're being
           irrational—some of the research does indicate that some-
           times there may be an ill effect—maybe even something
           that we don't know about. No matter what you say,
           marijuana shouldn't be legalized and won't be in this
           country.

MARY: What if they proved once and for all that there were no
           problems with using pot—what then?

FRED: Well, first, it's a philosophical impossibility to prove that
           a thing will never happen . . .

MARY: Honestly, Fred.

FRED: I mean that that's just not going to happen and I don't care
           what you say, I will never believe that marijuana should
           be legalized.

MARY: Fred, let me tell you that . . .

Perhaps we should interrupt Mary and Fred at this point to use
their conversation as an illustration of irrationality in argumentation.
If we were seeking appropriateness and modifiability in either of
their positions, we would be disappointed. Neither seems to be
basing his feelings about the legalization issue on the evidence
available. Each is so strongly convinced of his point of view on the
issue that tempers are flaring and little sound support is being
offered: their strong convictions are not what I would consider
appropriate given the scant and contradictory findings about
marijuana. If I were a receiver and either Fred or Mary were the
arguer, I would demand a good reason for accepting either of their

claims. Part of what would make it a good, rational reason for me would be its appropriateness, given the amount of research done, the quality of the research, and the conclusiveness of the findings; yet, none of that is available, and much less actually coming from the arguments of either Mary or Fred.

Secondly, of course, I would try to judge their reasons as good or bad by the rational criterion of modifiability. Has the arguer, whichever one it was, advanced the claim so that there is room for any change, alteration of the claim, or difference in the claim based on future research? Here again, neither Fred nor Mary has allowed for the advent of new research or findings: both have contended that, no matter what happens, they will not modify their positions. Just as I react to snakes, Fred and Mary have established beliefs, and they declare that nothing will alter their positions. Thus, if I were their receiver, I would be disappointed on the basis of both criteria; first, because their claims seem inappropriate, and, second, because their claims and arguments are not subject to modification. My application of these criteria of rationality help immensely in my judgment of the claim and whether the reasons advanced are good reasons or not.

I could become more specific about my critique of Fred's or Mary's claim. I could speak directly of how language functioned or did not function appropriately; I could speak to them as a receiver who was going to demand specific appropriateness and modifiability from evidence, warrants, claims, reservations, and qualifiers. With these criteria of rationality and these tools that express the argumentative functions of language, I could become exacting in my demand for a good reason to adopt a claim. I could demand that more appropriate evidence be presented; that a more appropriate warrant be made explicit; that a qualifier be produced that was appropriate for the kind of claim and evidence; that an appropriate reservation be mentioned which expressed those exceptions to the rule. In essence, I could become more clear about what I demanded from the arguer offering the claim; I would be demanding appropriateness in argumentative functions of language.

In addition, though, I could use these same standards of rationality and those terms for argumentative functions to demand a good reason based upon the rational *modifiability* of the argument. Most important here are the terms qualifier and reservation. As a receiver of argumentation, I should demand that the qualifier and reservation, functioning together, reveal those incidences in which the claim would be most susceptible to change. The qualifier, that is, should express the degree of confidence that I as a receiver should have in a claim, and, correspondingly, the reservation should cite those instances where the claim will no longer apply or where the situation is so different as to make the arguer no longer wish to make the claim. The qualifier and the reservation, even though we should demand their appropriateness, are primarily important because of the clues that they provide about the modifiability of the argumentation.

Thus, as a receiver of argumentation wishing to demand a good reason for a claim, I have two groups of especially helpful cognitive tools to aid in my assessment of the reason: one group is the series of terms (claim, evidence, warrant, etc.) for how language functions in argumentation, and the other is the pair of criteria (appropriateness and modifiability) that express the basic attributes of rationality. At this point in my judgment of argumentation, I can begin to demand good evidence, appropriate warrants, sound backing, and an appropriate degree of modifiability. I know that the determination of a good reason is clearly my task as a receiver in an argumentative situation, but I can be aided by the standards of rationality to aid in my assessment of these reasons.

Even though the demands that we have made of argumentation will be helpful in our efforts to enhance the quality of our examination of claims and their reasons, even the criteria of rationality may not be specific enough tools by which to assess the reasons for claims. The concept of modifiability may be clear enough: there should be an acknowledgement of the lack of certainty and a statement about the conditions under which the claim would be withdrawn. But what of the criterion of appropriateness? Is it enough to demand what, in general, seems appropriate? It seems to me that we can benefit from using procedures available for yet more specific demands of the appropriateness of reasons: the demand for field-related reasons and the demand that field-related standards be met. Let us examine each in turn.

The Demand for Field-Related Reasons

At the point that we as receivers have ascertained the meaning of the claim and decided that it is worthy of our consideration, we should demand we be presented with reasons to accept the claim that are field-related.[8] We may be told, to return to our example, that "You cannot play the piano," and we may discover that our arguer means

[8]The notion of field-dependent (or field-related) reasons and standards is implicit in a number of Toulmin's texts, but the discussion here is especially indebted to Toulmin, *Uses*, chapter 1.

that "Legally, you cannot play the piano." Our demand that the arguer state the criteria (legally) has done more than simply enhance the clarity of the claim; in addition, you see, it has revealed to us the *kind of reason* we should demand in order to accept the claim. That is, since our arguer has said, "Legally, you cannot play the piano," we as receivers should demand that we be given a legally oriented reason for why we cannot play. The evidence-part of a reason the arguer might present that would be relevant to the legal criteria would be: "You are in a hospital zone." If we were to demand what the hospital zone had to do with our playing, the arguer might continue his presentation of the reason by submitting a warrant: "Hospital zones, by law, preclude the playing of instruments or the making of similar noise." We may or may not be satisfied with the evidence and the warrant, but at least we shall have been presented with a reason that is consistent with the criteria for the claim.

To further explain the point, let us assume that instead of expressing the legal criterion for the claim, our arguer submitted, "Based upon the question of permission, you cannot play the piano." This, then, is a different meaning for the claim (based on a different *criterion*), and we as receivers should demand a different sort of evidence, warrant, and so forth; we should, that is, demand a reason consistent with this other field. As a field-related reason, our arguer might reply, "Mrs. Smith owns the piano, and she has forbidden anyone else to touch it (the field-related evidence). Since she has refused her permission to play (the warrant), I conclude that you cannot play the piano."

Consider yet another example, in which our arguer says, "According to the norms of this church, you cannot play the piano." We should demand that we be presented with a reason consistent with that new field: what is the norm that operates in the church? Or, if our arguer has suggested, "Physically, you cannot play the piano," we should demand a physical reason why we cannot play: Are we handicapped in some way? Is the piano in some locked room? Is the piano broken? Why is it that physically we cannot play the piano? Finally (though this obviously does not exhaust the possible fields), if our arguer says, "Artistically, you cannot play the piano," then we should demand an artistically oriented reason why we cannot. Is it because it so out of tune? Is it because we are basically untalented? In all these various cases, we as receivers have demanded that we be given reasons as to why we cannot play the piano based upon our understanding of the criterion (and thus, field) by which we understand what is meant by the claim, "You cannot play the piano."

This matter of demanding that the arguer provide a field-related reason hardly can be overstressed. If the arguer has claimed, "Artistically, you cannot play the piano," and then supported the claim by suggesting, "This is a hospital zone," we would hardly understand what he meant. A similar confusion would occur if the arguer submitted that "Legally, you cannot play the piano," and then presented a reason that stated, "The baby is asleep." Although these examples seem extreme, similar situations can arise if receivers do not demand, first, to know the field for a claim, and, then, to know the reasons that are consistent with that field.

Suppose you ask a friend whether you should elect to take a course from Professor Brown. Your friend becomes extremely excited and says that indeed you should take a course from the professor. Your friend even goes so far as to claim that the course will be a valuable step toward graduate school. You smile and assume that your friend means, "From the standpoint of your accumulative average, the course will be a valuable step toward graduate school." You enroll in the course, find it extremely difficult and challenging, and you earn a D in the course—something you interpret to be a backward step away from graduate school. You confront your friend, claiming that he was something less than accurate in his assessment of the course's worth in relation to graduate school. He then asks, "Didn't you learn a great deal?" and you may have to admit that, yes, you did. Then he asks whether you acquired experience in research skills and, again, you may have to answer affirmatively. Finally, he asks if you covered material that is valuable as background for graduate school, and still you answer affirmatively. At this point, he may be confused and say, "Well, as I told you, from the standpoint of preparing you for graduate school, the course is excellent." Just as he fails to understand your complaint, you may fail to see the problem. Yet the problem is simply, first, that you did not demand to know the field for the claim that the course would be a valuable step toward graduate school: he meant to imply a preparation-oriented area of concern for the claim, and you thought (but did not confirm) that he meant a grade-point-oriented area of concern. Secondly, you failed to demand a reason that was field-related. If you had, and if he had begun talking of challenges, difficulty, and research skills, then undoubtedly you would have more clearly understood his claim. You might have said, "Since these challenges and difficulties are not always consistent with good grade points, then he is *not* claiming that the step toward graduate school will be the rise in my scholastic average." Then, you might have asked him what he specifically meant by his claim—and avoided all the unhappiness (or at least, disillusionment) that came from your failures to demand to know both the field for the claim and the reasons consistent with the field.

Thus, I take the demands to know the claim's field and reasons consistent with that field to be crucial and productive demands that receivers should make of an arguer and his argumentation. Yet, those demands alone cannot assure that you as a receiver will be given good reasons for claims; they simply insure that you will be presented with relevant reasons. The matter of finally demanding good reasons is a related but separate concern.

The Demand That Field-Related Standards Be Met

As receivers, then, who understand the claim, have found it worthy of more consideration, and who have demanded the field-related reasons for the claim, we still may seek aid in judging what should be a good reason for us to accept the claim. Since any receiver who has taken the steps so far described is unlikely to be careless or irresponsible, it seems likely that he would wish as much guidance as possible about the reason under consideration: he would want to apply the most stringent, accepted, and productive standards to the reason that he can discover.

Such standards, I submit, are discoverable by continuing to note the importance of fields to our argumentation. Indeed, already we have stressed the demand for the criteria for the claim and have said that such criteria will relate to a kind of field. At this point, we can also add that these fields may provide certain fairly well-established standards which are expected to be generally acceptable in that field for the evaluation of claims and reasons; we shall call these standards *field-related* to suggest that the standards we should use to assess claims depend upon the field in which the claim occurs.[9] Let me illustrate.

If we discover the claim presented to us is that "Legally, you cannot go into that house," we know that the field relevant to the claim is in some way the field of law. A serious receiver, then, will demand a field-related (in this case, legally oriented) reason such as, "Well, the home belongs to a private citizen (evidence), and the houses of private citizens cannot be entered without permission" (warrant). Yet, as a serious receiver, I will want to decide if that is a good reason for my not going into the house—but I may want guidance in helping me to decide. So, I use my knowledge of the

[9]Again, for material in this section, I am indebted to Toulmin, *Uses*, chapter 1.

field in which we are arguing to seek certain standards of law that might serve as ways of assessing a reason such as this. While it may help in general to concentrate on the field of law, we shall find out that we have to do more: we must decide, as discussed earlier, which of the subfields of law is relevant. Is the matter one that must be decided by the standards of the Justinian Code, the British system of Common Law, the Ten Commandments, the American system of corporate statutes, or the American criminal code, or some other subfield of the major area of legal concern? Once we have isolated as specifically as we can what field (or subfield) we are dealing with, we will discover fairly well-developed guidelines about how to evaluate good reasons (evidence, warrants, backing, etc.) for claims in that field.

Let us take another example: we are presented with the claim that a certain accounting procedure is particularly good. To begin to evaluate this claim, we may ask the criterion by which it is good and be told that "From the point of view of efficiency, it is a good procedure." When we demand a field-related reason for this efficiency response, we may hear, "It saves paper (claim) and it saves enough paper to be considered efficient (warrant)." Though we, as receivers, may be satisfied that the reason is field-related, all that really tells us is that it is relevant to the field in question: how can you tell the strength of that reason—how good is it? If, as I suggest, you insist on the reason meeting certain field-dependent standards, then your problems are less severe. Accounting, as a field of thought and as a professional area, has certain standards by which claims and reasons are normally judged. As you explore these, is it generally accepted that the saving of paper equals efficiency, or are other factors (time, legal tangles, effort, etc.) more important? If paper saving is the standard for judging efficiency in accounting, then you probably should accept the reason as good; if time, for example, is of more importance, then you probably should demand other reasons to support the claim; how you decide the difference between a good reason and a bad reason can benefit greatly from a demand that field-related standards be met—in this case, standards of accounting.

If the field involves a less structured or less well-established area of thought, we may be somewhat less fortunate. Remember Jack's decision about going to the game; it presented an area where standards of law, accounting, or art seemed less than immediately relevant. Yet, even when that is the case—as it often will be, Jack would have benefited from first establishing the criterion and field for George's claim, then demanding reasons that were related to that field, and finally judging the reasons on the basis of field-related standards. If Jack found that, for example, George meant primarily that he should go to the game from the point of view of relaxation, then Jack could have demanded reasons related to the relaxation criterion. In his attempt to comply with Jack's demand, George might have suggested, "For the sake of relaxation, you should go to the game." To construct a reason, George might add the evidence that "The game will be relaxing," and the warrant that "It provides the relaxation that is needed." Even though Jack probably would not perceive the claim and its reason as being relevant to a well-established field such as law, physics, or art, he still may benefit from stressing relaxation-related standards for judging the reasons for a claim. Based upon experience, he may ask, Do I need the relaxation? Have the games in the past been relaxing? Will the game be relaxing enough to justify my study time? Will I become more tense if I fail to study? Note that Jack would not spend time assessing the claim that he (in general) should go to the game: his examination of the claim would be more efficient, more concise, and more immediately productive if he focused (as he is doing in this example) on field-related standards for reasons even when the field is so ill defined.

Indeed, a demand that field-related standards be met by the reasons that are advanced for a claim can be tremendously helpful in the argumentative situation. It can provide us with an approach that can aid our decision about how good a reason is. More importantly, perhaps, such a demand is an excellent compromise between one extreme where we rely simply on caprice to evaluate what is a good reason and another extreme where we insist that the reason conform to standardized logic. As such a healthy compromise, the demand that reasons meet field-related standards is a crucial part of the productive demands that receivers can make of arguers.

Summary

Our chapter began with the goal of trying to improve the quality and productivity of the demands that receivers make of arguers. In the previous chapter, we discussed some demands and standards of judging claims that seem to me either impossible to fulfill, misleading, or else simply unproductive. In this chapter, we focused upon several major demands that are more productive, including the demand for good reasons in general; the demand for communicative clarity; the demand to know the claim's field; the demand for an arguable claim; the demand for nontrivial claims; the demand for rationality of reasons; the demand for field-related reasons; and the demand that field-related standards be met.

The most basic demand that receivers should make of argumentation, we found, is the demand to be presented with good reasons for claims. Our perspective on good reasons is the same as our perception of so-called bad or fallacious reasons: good and bad reasons do not exist; instead, they are created when individuals attach significance or fail to attach significance to the expression.

Yet, though receivers may wish to demand good reasons in general from arguers, these same receivers may want to rely upon certain other demands to help them determine the meaning of claims as well as the significance of the factors offered as reasons. We found it to be the case that receivers may not understand the meaning of the claim presented unless they demand the sort of clarity appropriate in any sort of communication situation. Yet even though the claim may be understood in general, there exists the difficulty that the force of the claim may be clear, but the *criteria* by which we should understand the claim are obscure; hence, we will wish to demand to know the criterion for the claim and, thus, the *field* to which it belongs.

Once we are confident that we understand the meaning of the claim, then we shall demand that the claim be reasonably arguable, and we normally shall refuse to engage in argumentation about things we normally take for granted. On the other hand, we shall also demand that the claim be nontrivial. If it is implausible, unsupportable, or of little consequence, we should refuse again to engage in argumentation.

At the point that we are confident we understand the claim, and we determine that it is worthy of further attention, we can turn our attention to the support for the claim: we finally know enough about the claim to ask, "What is a good reason in this particular situation or in regard to this claim?" At its best, argumentation is what Toulmin calls rational: appropriate and modifiable. An important receiver demand, then, is that the claim and its reasons should be both appropriate and modifiable. We discussed appropriateness and modifiability related to fear and then to argumentation. While the concept of modifiability may be easily applicable, the notion of appropriateness may be more abstract—and will force us to return to the question of fields of argumentation. In order to demand that appropriate reasons be presented, we may reinterpret appropriate as meaning field-related. The idea of fields thus provided a key as to what is an appropriate and relevant reason: physiological (field-related) reasons, for instance, should be introduced only to support claims such as "Physically, you can. . . . "

Once we established the field-relatedness of the reason, we found that we should demand the reason to be good as well. The receiver, we found, can demand that the reason must meet what we termed field-related standards in order to be judged good. Established fields such as law may have well-developed sets of standards for judging particular evidence, warrants, backing, and so forth; but even in fields where that is not the case, we still can benefit by continually focusing upon the criteria for the claim, thus its field, and thus any standard of judgment or questions that seem relevant.

This chapter, then, has made it clear that our emphasis upon the receiver does not imply that we ignore the quality of an argument. Although it seems the case that rules for argumentation are too strict and generally difficult to apply in the practical affairs of human beings, we can certainly stress that receivers have a significant responsibility in the assessment of argumentation: we do not assume that the judgment of a "good" reason should be made by whimsy. Rather, those evaluations can best be made by demanding reasons judged by certain rigorous standards. All argumentation is not of equally high quality, but the demand for high quality argumentation is possible and practical—even without a strict allegiance to formal rules about what is and is not a good reason.

Our discussion about productive argumentation, however, has ignored the idea that, in addition to demanding good (i.e., sound) reasons, we can as both receivers and arguers demand that certain ethical standards be met. Ethical judgments are complex evaluations that deserve a separate treatment; a discussion of ethics and argumentation, then, will be our task in the next chapter.

Supplemental Information

Though I have taken the position that bad reasons, like good reasons, can be determined only in the context of how those reasons or ideas function in the argumentation, certain terms for bad reasons are so commonly referred to that you may benefit from knowing what are considered—in general—to be inadequate ways of engaging in argumentation. Here, then, is a selected list of fallacies, bad reasons, or irrelevancies that may help you to understand what someone "means" when they label an argument in a particular way.

1. Ad hominem argument or attack upon the person: "Jones said that, huh? Well, anyone who's working on his third marriage is apt to say anything." (Thrust: ignore the argumentation, and slur the person or something about him.)

2. Post hoc (ergo propter hoc) fallacy or faulty causal argumentation: "Jones was elected—and the economic situation improved immediately." (Thrust: anything that happened before something else obviously (?) caused the second thing to happen.)

3. Ad populum argument or an appeal to majority rule or opinion: "You simply have to vote for Jones—everyone is doing it." (Thrust: whatever is being done by most people should be done by all.)

4. Circular reasoning: "Sure, the state legislature should adopt the bill because it is a good one; it's a good one or else the state legislature shouldn't pass it." (Thrust: use the claim as a reason to support itself! The thing that is called into question is used as evidence to support itself, in a circular fashion.)

5. Reductio ad absurdum or reducing the idea to an absurd level: "Jones is for freedom of expression, huh? I suppose he thinks that there's nothing wrong in calling someone anything you want to, or advocating the overthrow of the government, or yelling 'Fire!' in a crowded building, or . . . ." (Thrust: when you cannot find an argumentative position against the claim, find some ridiculous example related to the claim that you do have an argument against.)

6. Appeal to unchallengeable authority: "Hey, Jones is President—how dare you question what he says." (Thrust: refuse to argue about a claim by saying that you should never argue with the claim or the arguer.)

7. Appeal to tradition or norm: "Quit rocking the boat; we've always done it that way." (Thrust: since you've never argued about it before, you can't argue about it now.)

8. Begging the question: "I think you ought to vote for Jones because, since you ought to vote for Jones, then he's the man for the job." (Thrust: treat the idea that is challenged as if it is something that is already accepted—then use it to support something else.)

9. False dilemma: "Well, you really have to vote for Jones or support the cause of worldwide communism." (Thrust: create two alternatives, one of which is obviously unacceptable, and show why the other is better.)

10. Hasty generalization: "Well, I know this crooked politician named Jones, and I know that all politicians are dishonest." (Thrust: take one particular instance and say that what is the case with that one instance is true of all the instances.)

11. Straw man argument: "I bet that the reason that you aren't going to vote for Jones is that he is a Republican, but let me tell you that. . . . " (Thrust: create your own argument—especially one you can defeat—and then defeat it; that is, build your own man of straw and then burn him down.)

Programmed Questions

To test your understanding of the material presented in this chapter, you may wish to answer the following questions. In the multiple-choice questions, the answers may be all correct, all incorrect, or several may be correct. The suggested answers to the questions appear on the last page of this chapter. If you fail to answer the questions correctly, you may wish to review the material to increase your understanding and/or to discuss the items in class.

1. "Good reasons" in argumentation:
   a. exist as particular combinations of evidence, claims, and warrants
   b. are exclusively an individualistic matter
   c. are created when individuals attach significance to ideas in relation to a claim
   d. are influenced partly by the situation as it is shared with others
   e. are influenced partly by the individual's background, training, and culture
   f. should be judged as they function in the argumentative context, rather than prior to the argumentation

2. What are sometimes called bad reasons in argumentation:
   a. are often called fallacies or irrelevancies
   b. should be judged as they function in the argumentative context, rather than prior to the argumentation
   c. might be good reasons in a particular argumentative situation
   d. are more accurately reasons that simply have not been considered significant
   e. exist as particular combinations of evidence, claims, and warrants

3. Receivers wishing to participate productively in argumentation should demand:
   a. general communicative clarity
   b. a claim that is at least normally subject to question; that is, arguable
   c. a claim that is clear, even if little support for it is possible.
   d. a claim that is important enough to merit further attention
   e. the real reasons for a claim
   f. the criterion, and thus the field, of the claim

4. When we come to know the claim's field, then we know:
   a. immediately whether the reasons for the claim are strong
   b. what reasons might be relevant
   c. what standards, generally, ought to be met by the claim's reasons
   d. what reasons might be irrelevant
   e. more specifically the meaning of the claim

5. The field of an argumentative claim:
    a. is not all that important to the argumentation
    b. is often related to an occupational, academic, or professional field or area of thought
    c. cannot be divided into subareas
    d. may exist as a comparatively unstructured or informal area of thought or argumentation
    e. will be known by the criteria by which we are supposed to understand the claim

6. The rationality of a reason, as we have conceived it, is:
    a. partly a matter of the appropriateness of the reason
    b. a matter of whether the reasoning is logical
    c. crucial to the demand for good reasons
    d. partly a matter of the modifiability of reasons and claims
    e. generally inconsistent with the functioning of reservations and qualifiers
    f. as applicable to argumentation as it is to fears

Discussion Questions for Appendix Case Studies

To test your understanding of the material in this chapter, you may wish to answer the following questions that refer to the case studies in the Appendix of this book. You may wish to (a) work on the questions individually; (b) work on the questions in pairs or in groups in or before class; (c) develop written answers to the questions; (d) have class discussion based upon the questions; (e) prepare an extended paper on several related questions; or (f) develop a major paper about one case study (using the questions related to it that appear in various chapters).

1. Study "Satisfaction (Almost) Assured" beginning on page 258. In what ways does the manager's reinterpretation of "the strongest vacuum" become something of a discussion of the fields for the word "strong?" Would John Deal have benefited from asking for the field of the word strong when he bought the first vacuum cleaner? Why or why not? Was the manager "trying to put something over on John" by way of the reinterpretation of strong, or was he being rationally modifiable? Defend your answer.

2. Study "Letter-to-the Editor" beginning on page 254. Elbarc's major claim seems to be that the present council members are unfit for office. In addition to his three other claims functioning to support that claim, explain how each of the three can be said to provide a different field for the major claim's interpretation. What field-related reasons does he provide for each field?

3. Study "A 2 or a 4?" beginning on page 266. Given Alice's reaction to the appraisal, how would you evaluate her on the basis of the rational criterion of modifiability? How do you evaluate Stoner's behavior when you use the same criterion? Which of their two positions seemed most appropriate given the information in the case?

4. Study "You Find Good Assets in Des Moines and Iowa" by John R. Fitzgibbon beginning on page 256. One of the claims that Mr. Fitzgibbon makes is that Iowa is a good place to live, despite a less than perfect national economic picture. How do phrases such as "From an environmental standpoint, . . . " "From an agricultural standpoint, . . . " and "From a sociological standpoint . . . " function in his argumentative pamphlet? How do the statistics and figures in each of those areas function? Are they field-related? Do you agree that he uses the success of the bank as a field-related reason to believe that life is good in Des Moines and Iowa in general? Why, or why not?

Research Project for Advanced Students

Whether you realize it or not, you are about to enter or already have entered an occupational or professional field; each of these fields has its own (often unconsciously applied) standards for judging good reasons for claims, proposals, and advances in what is known in the field. Physicists, for example, might agree that their field tends to judge claims by whether the claim (1) has the extensive and accurate power to predict other occurrences, (2) is coherent with what is already known, and (3) is the simplest explanation (most elegant) of occurrences. Research your present academic or future professional or occupational field to see if you can discover the field-related standards that you soon may have to use in the judgment of claims.

SELECTED REFERENCES

Crable, Richard E. *Rhetoric as Architectonic: Burke, Perelman, and Toulmin on Valuing and Knowing.* Unpublished doctoral dissertation, The Ohio State University, 1973.

Toulmin, Stephen. *Human Understanding.* Vol. 1. Princeton, N.J.: Princeton University Press, 1972.

————. *Reason in Ethics.* Cambridge: Cambridge University Press, 1968.

————. "Reasons and Causes." In *Explanation in the Behavioral Sciences,* edited by M. Berger and F. Cioffi. New York: Cambridge University Press, 1969.

————. *The Uses of Argument.* 2nd ed. Cambridge: Cambridge University Press, 1969.

Answers to Programmed Questions

1. c, d, e, f   2. a, b, c, d   3. a, b, d, f   4. b, c, d, e   5. b, d, e

6. a, c, d, f

8

Ethics and Argumentative Choices

My general *objective* in this chapter is to describe the relationships among argumentation, ethics, and the choices of arguers and receivers.

My *specific objectives* are

to discuss the various ways that the ethical nature of argumentation can be expressed

to introduce the idea of argumentation as an "omnimoral" process

to cite specific choices arguers may make that can become the focus for ethical evaluation

to cite the specific choices receivers may make that can become the focus for ethical evaluations

to discuss several ethical standards that can be used to guide ethical judgments

to discuss the variance in ethical judgment that can be the result of selecting one standard instead of another

Though I have chosen to treat the discussion of ethics rather late in the text, this does not mean that I consider the topic unimportant. On the contrary, it seems to me that the question of ethics in argumentation should be of crucial concern to argumentation students, since it underlies so many of the situations and topics that we have discussed in previous chapters. Let us, then, devote this chapter to the accomplishment of three major tasks: first, to formulate some impression of the general role of ethics in argumentation; second, to cite specific ethical choices that arguers and receivers are called upon to make; and, third, to present some practical guidelines for dealing with ethical problems in argumentation. First, then, let us examine various notions about the relationship between ethics and argumentation.[1]

Argumentation: Moral, Immoral, Amoral, or What?

In general, it seems helpful to say that argumentation can be viewed in several different perspectives from the point of view of ethical behavior. Consider the following case study by focusing, first, upon the media advertisement itself and, then, upon the various reactions to it.

Case Study: Would You Like All This to Be Yours?

As I was on my way to class one day, I noticed that the mail had arrived early. I stooped to pick it up, opened the door and closed the mail drop; then I tossed the usual collection of bills, unsolicited advertising, and magazines on the kitchen counter. One of the envelopes caught my attention, partly because of the gaudy, golden yellow cover and partly because of the words which asked in glorious script, "Would You Like All This To Be Yours?" Since I had a few minutes to spare, I opened the envelope and examined the contents. The advertisement was for the purchase of land in the sunny paradise of Florida—away from the hassle of northern life and the dreary cold of a midwestern winter. As I looked further, it occurred to me that this promotion was the same one being done on local television. The message was virtually the same as the television advertisement: thrill to the ownership of land in a tropical paradise; walk on your own beach-front property; enjoy the sun and surf year-round. Even visually, the mass-mail advertisement was consistent with the television promotion: sunshine yellow pages with pictures of brilliant white sand, incredibly blue seashore, and tantalizing sun worshippers soaking up enviable amounts of sunshine.

---

[1] A text that generally is consistent with the approach to ethics that we shall use and which may be referred to for more detailed discussion of certain issues is Richard L. Johannesen, *Ethics in Human Communication* (Columbus, Ohio: Charles E. Merrill Publishing Co., 1975).

The brochure promised good, usable land; well-landscaped lots; homes that would double in value after you owned them a few years; and the easiest financing anywhere. Indeed, I was invited to a free dinner-film meeting where films, slides, and more information would be presented.

Rather than recount my own reactions to the offer and to the land-developer company, let me attempt to predict what your response was to the message. In the context of all we have heard about land-swindles where the land was under water, completely devoid of water, or so sandy that construction was doomed to failure, I suspect that you began making some judgments of the claim and its reasons that were not mere assessments of how good the reasons for buying the land were for you as a receiver. Instead, I suspect that you began to make certain ethical-sounding judgments: Was there a catch to the dinner, was the land described falsely, was the phrasing of attributes exaggerated? If that sort of judgment occurred to you, then let me suggest that you are a step beyond where you actually should be in the study of argumentation and ethics. Prior to the time when we make those all-important ethical judgments about specific argumentative messages, we should be clear about the relationship between argumentation and ethics in general. Let us, then, examine several different perspectives of that relationship, including the views that argumentation as a process is immoral, amoral, moral, or finally, what I shall call "omnimoral." We shall analyze each of those views and demonstrate how each would differently affect our general perception of the land-purchase message.

Argumentation: Immoral?

First, it seems that we could view argumentation as being essentially *immoral*: something that, regardless of its use, is morally questionable. Such an idea may seem somewhat strange to you, but I see increasing signs, as I indicated in an earlier chapter, that people are often reluctant to express and support a particular point of view. In the context of our awareness that subliminal influence, propaganda, fallacious advertising, and tricky sales techniques are being used to make people do something they do not wish to do, a reluctance to be considered a persuader—even an arguer—is wholly understandable. I see people at parties who change a subject when it is clear that differences of opinion are present; a party is not a suitable place for argument. I see students in beginning communication classes who simply want to "relate the facts, so that you can decide"; the student, he feels, has no right to impose an opinion on others. Moreover, I see scattered research evidence that indicates most young couples (and I suspect individuals and older couples as well) watch television and make a game of "finding the misleading statement"; "You know," they say, "that the message will not be straight."

If we were to examine the land-purchase advertisement with the view that argumentation is inherently immoral, then our task in evaluating the message would be simple. Since we would assume that the effort to influence another person is essentially immoral, we would immediately judge the message as unethical. Certainly the whole reason for the mass mailing was to influence large numbers of people to commit substantial sums of money in retirement property. The land-development company was not merely presenting the facts and allowing us to decide in whichever way we wished. They presented reasons (for example, the investment value) for the decision they wished us to make and supplemented them with attractive pictures of desirable places and people—all of which became other sorts of reasons for our purchase of the land. In essence, when the ethical judgment of the message is based upon the belief that argumentation as a process is somehow immoral, then our judgment will be easy, clear, and immediate.

Clearly, indications exist that the students who don't want to talk you into anything, the couples watching for deceitful advertising, and the people who are wary of land-purchase offers are not without some reasons for believing that the intent to influence can be unethical. Certainly, the examples of unethical argumentation are sufficient to make anyone suspicious of the argumentation in the mass media or anywhere else, including his own communication. On the other hand, I reject the position that there is something intrinsic to argumentation, to the supporting of claims, that makes argumentation an automatically scorned process. When I consider the importance of argumentation in the political process, in the propagating of religions or philosophies, in the negotiation of international incidents, and in the spreading of new ideas about health care and nutrition, I must simply conclude that not all argumentation is inherently evil or unethical.

Argumentation: Amoral?

Philosophers and scholars who share my rejection of the first "argumentation is immoral" position sometimes refer to argumentation as being *amoral*: a neutral process which in itself is neither ethical nor unethical. The most common manner of arguing this position on the relationship between ethics and argumentation is to use the analogy of a tool or a weapon. A hammer, for example, is simply a tool for doing certain kinds of work; for working on houses, walls, floors. In that sense, we never would think to classify a hammer as an unethical instrument, even if it were used by a burglar to murder the homeowner who caught the burglar in his act of stealing. Certainly, we would not condone the use of the hammer for such a purpose, but, on the other hand, we would not begin a movement to have all the hammers taken out of the homes of citizens. We realize that an ethically neutral thing such as a hammer should not be condemned even though we may condemn the misuse of it. Similarly, opponents of gun control in this country have traditionally argued that "Guns don't kill; people do." Thus, they reason, how can you lock up all the guns simply because some have been misused by immoral people. As in the argument about the hammer, the tool (or in this case, weapon) should not be the object of ethical judgments; instead, the judgments should be made about the ethical or unethical use of an ethically neutral—or amoral—tool.

The analogies of the tool and weapon are meant as rational reasons to consider argumentation amoral as well. Like any tool or weapon, it can be used for good or evil depending upon the mental or emotional state of the user. So, far from considering all of argumentation to be inherently unethical, we must consider it amoral and make ethical judgments only about its use. These arguers would view the Florida promotion as possibly unethical (depending upon any misleading material), but it would be unethical only because the promoters had taken an ethically neutral process and somehow made it serve unethical ends. This single instance, they would say, might be unethical, but that has nothing to do with the intrinsic ethical qualities of the process of argumentation.

If we, therefore, assume that argumentation is not itself immoral, but rather is an amoral process, then our judgments of the ethical quality of any message—including the land-purchase advertisement—will not be as easy or as immediate as our earlier judgment was. Rather than simply identify the process as one designed to influence, and automatically label it unethical, we must examine the degree of accuracy of the message, any hidden cost or obligations, and the general merits of the land described in the advertisement. After making that more in-depth analysis and evaluation, we may still conclude that the message was unethical, but the judgment would be based upon a far different idea than if we immediately assume the message is unethical because influencing others is immoral.

Still, though the belief that argumentation is in itself amoral may be attractive and comfortable for you, I am inclined to reject the position that argumentation is as amoral as any other tool or weapon (even assuming that weapons are amoral). I reject, in fact, the premise that argumentation is like a tool: tools can be used by one individual acting in solitude, and argumentation usually involves more than one individual interacting with others. (Even when the argumentation is intrapersonal, the argument or decision made by way of intrapersonal argumentation most likely will affect other people.) Consequently, although tools can be comfortably spoken of as things affecting no one but the user, the same cannot be comfortably said about argumentation. Argumentation is, in fact, the name we have used for a particular human interaction; to speak of argumentation without discussing human beings and human activity, thus, seems almost a contradiction in terms. My rejection of the amoral viewpoint on argumentation is simply that argumentation is, by its nature, something affecting human beings—and that effect is far different and far more important than hammering a nail.

Argumentation: Moral?

Yet my personal discomfort with considering argumentation either immoral or amoral may surprise you since all that seems to be left is to consider argumentation *moral*: inherently good based upon the intrinsic qualities of the process. This third perspective on the relationship between argumentation and ethics, however, is also a viewpoint that I reject. I have seen too much argumentation that seemed to me to be either unethical in nature or to be serving unethical ends: a Hitler's admonition that members of the Jewish religion should be exterminated; a high-ranking government official's false and misleading statements; a student formulating a lie to explain why a paper was late. These kinds of argumentation, it seems to me, would be considered unethical by a large number of receivers. Moreover, if we assumed that argumentation as a process was inherently moral and good, then we should be at a loss to explain land-purchase offers in the past that were deceitful, dishonest, and generally considered unethical messages and advertising. Consequently, I personally reject the view that argumentation is inherently moral as strongly as I disagree that it is either immoral or amoral.

Argumentation: Omnimoral

In contrast, my position on the relationship between argumentation and ethics is that argumentation is, what I shall call, *omnimoral*: a process which, at every stage, involves decisions that observers can interpret as posing ethical questions. Two ideas are crucial to this perspective on argumentation and ethics: first, that the various and numerous *decisions* in argumentation are seen as most important; and, secondly, that these decisions are *potential* areas for ethical questioning and judgment. Let us examine each of these ideas as we seek to understand argumentation as an omnimoral process.

First, it seems to me that we should concentrate upon the various decisions that arguers and receivers make in the process of argumentation, rather than focus upon the process itself or merely the use of the process. If we stress the process itself, as we do if we view argumentation as being either moral or immoral, we would risk making impractical and unproductive judgments that are much too general about argumentation: we would be trying to consolidate all that could occur when people support claims with reasons. If, on the other hand, we emphasize the use of the process, as we do if we view argumentation as amoral, it seems to me we risk making a judgment that is far too specific and one-dimensional. In the study of argumentation, as we have conceptualized it, there are literally dozens of potential decisions made as receivers and arguers engage in argumentation. Surely each of these might merit attention—and, as we shall see in the next section, some of these decisions are made prior to the interaction among people. The position that argumentation is an omnimoral process, then, allows us to avoid highlighting either the process itself or the use of the process, and to concentrate, instead, upon the individual and numerous decisions that arguers and receivers make when engaging in argumentation.

In addition to the stress upon the decisions that are made in argumentation, our omnimoral perspective on the process suggests that these decisions can always be interpreted as posing ethical questions. Each of the decisions that arguers and receivers make, it seems to me, can become the focus of an observer wishing to assess the ethical quality of the interaction. On the contrary, though, it is just as reasonable to expect that many—and sometimes all—of these potential ethical judgments will be ignored by the participants in the process. Obviously, receivers and arguers alike have the ability to ignore completely a consideration of ethics when they assess argumentation. They can assume that ethics in argumentation are unimportant, difficult to judge, or simply overshadowed by other concerns in the process. No one is forced to make ethical evaluations about any of the decisions made in the conduct of argumentation; on the other hand, nothing prevents virtually every decision made in that same process from becoming a matter of ethical evaluation. This omnimoral perspective on the nature of argumentation, then, allows our attention to be turned to all those decisions within the process about which we may make ethical judgments.

My insistence on the omnimorality of argumentation—even when the participants in the process do not choose to make ethical judgments—can best be illustrated by examining the plethora of ethical-looking decisions that receivers and arguers are forced to make in argumentation. A survey of those decisions is our next task in this chapter.

Ethical Choices in Argumentation

As we examine those areas of argumentative activity about which we could make ethical judgments, remember that my goal is not to provide any automatic system by which receivers and arguers can evaluate one another's argumentation. Nor is my goal, at this point, to further the acceptance of any particular standard of ethical judgment. Instead, I shall simply attempt to sketch for you those choices made by arguers and receivers that seem pivotal to the study of argumentation and ethics. Although some of those instances of choice are traditionally dealt with in texts on argumentation, our treatment of argumentation and ethics is somewhat nontraditional, both in our isolation of several choices that are not normally examined and in our stress upon the role of ethics in receiving and judging argumentation.

The Choice to Engage in Argumentation

Let me suggest first, then, that the simple choice to engage or not engage in argumentation is a decision that can become a matter for ethical judgment. Argumentation, as we discussed in chapter 2's analysis of argumentative motivation, does not occur without a reason. Argumentative communication may be interpreted as arising from a number of factors, but it is the human agents who respond or fail to respond to those forces: they are the ones who determine if the argumentation will occur. Arguers can be confronted all day with the forces of frustration, disillusionment, and failure in a work climate; yet, they can refuse to engage in argument with anyone. When these same arguers return home from work, the argumentation process may begin immediately, leading eventually to quarreling, shouting, or physical violence. Yet, again, these arguers were not completely at the mercy of their emotions; they controlled them until a more appropriate, or at least less professionally disturbing, opportunity presented itself. Similarly, the decision to engage in argumentation is a matter of choice for receivers. Unless a physical threat is present (and that would remove the situation from the study of argumentation for me), the receiver has the option of engaging in argumentation or of refusing to do so: but either decision is a matter of choice. Clearly, we must be aware that the decision to engage in argumentation is a matter of argumentative choice.

You may ask, however, why this decision is so fertile an area for potential ethical judgments. The answer, it seems to me, lies in the participants' analysis of the consequences of either engaging or refusing to engage in argumentation. Consider the situation where you are a recent convert to one or another religious belief. You have become convinced that the belief you have acquired through an intelligent and circumspect analysis is the formula for saving society from a downward plunge into evil. In that situation, is there not an ethical imperative that you should attempt to convert others—anyone who will listen to you? Consider, secondly, a situation in which you are convinced that a friend has been misled in his conversion to a new faith; indeed, he is so strongly converted that he attempts to engage you in a discussion of the merits of that new religion. Does not your regard for your friend imply an ethical obligation to hear him out and to test his new faith by all the argumentative means at your disposal? Third, consider the situation in which you recently have acquired a job as a door-to-door salesperson of cleaning supplies, and you know that an elderly lady of limited means who lives next door probably will purchase something from you—just to help you work your way through school. Realizing your own need for money and her probable willingness to help you, does her financial situation dictate that you forget about stopping at her house? Finally, consider a situation in which a friend is running for campus office and is extremely involved in the election. The friend buttonholes you and asks what you think of the election and his stand on some controversial campus issues, most of which you evaluate differently. Realizing his sensitivity in what is predicted to be a tight race and realizing the minimal returns to be gained by your confronting him, do you feel compelled to refrain from engaging in argumentation?

I constructed those situations so that most of you would opt for one or the other of the choices. I may have been wrong, however, and you may have found the choices difficult precisely because the either-or choices were all I presented to you. You may have decided that either alternative was defensible. Yet, that is the point of most ethical questions: if they were always clear-cut, one-dimensional, and simplistic, the whole study of ethics would not be so difficult. Anyone who argued, for example, that you should sell the brushes to the elderly friend could easily have built a case to defend that act:

she might be embarrassed if you ignored her; she might desire strongly to help you, and a fifty-cent brush might make her feel that indeed she was helping you. The same sort of defense could have been created for any of the other situations. The fact remains, however, that whichever choice you make as an arguer or receiver, it has the potential for eliciting an ethical judgment from an observer.

The Choice of the Arguer's Purpose

A second argumentative choice that may pose a potentially ethical problem is the ancient concern over the arguer's stated or implied purpose. The traditional method of describing the issue is to discuss the arguer's goal and to ask the extent to which it is a noble goal, a base goal, or something between those extremes. The assumption when such a point is raised is that there are some activities, behaviors, and events that are inherently immoral, unethical, or at least questionable. If you were to engage in argumentation advocating something like that—say the extermination of all assistant professors—the assumption (I hope) is that you would be pursuing an unethical purpose, and your argumentation probably would be considered unethical. The major problem with this particular area of ethical controversy is that many of the goals that arguers pursue are not so easily discerned as being ethically or morally questionable. What of the arguer in your class who advocates that people should have the right to allow themselves to be killed to avoid the endless pain of a terminal illness? To students who see mercy killing as inherently wrong, the issue is clear: the arguer is pursuing an unethical goal. To others in the class, the judgment may not be so automatic nor so easy to decide. What of the student who advocates the withdrawal of troops from an area of the world where that withdrawal will result in a take-over of the country by a force that will set about executing the leaders of the old regime? Is that argumentative goal of withdrawal or support for withdrawal essentially unethical? What about the lives that might be lost if the troops continue to occupy the country and resume the fighting? Is it ethical to trade so many lives for the lives of a few (perhaps corrupt) officials? I am certain that in argumentation, disagreements will arise partly because of the divergent judgments of individuals, but I am also sure that some of the disagreement is that, despite how many years people have been arguing about the goals of argument, the issues are so complex as to make a comfortable and universally ethical decision difficult indeed.

The Choice of the Arguer's Methods

Related to the choice that arguers must make about the goals, ends, or purposes of their argumentation is a third choice with potential ethical implications, the selection of the methods or means by which argumentation is developed. When arguers choose from among the reasons that they give to receivers for the adoption of a claim, the arguers are potentially subject to a judgment of the ethicality of the selection. If, as an arguer, I submit that the strongest reason for the acceptance of the claim is that, somehow, the receivers will be able to gain somehow by harming or inconveniencing others, then I may be charged with unethical argumentation. If, again as an arguer, I somehow trick my receiver with false or misleading reasons or information, then I should be prepared to suffer any consequences of the act; I should expect, if discovered, to be labeled an unethical arguer. Clearly, all arguers are confronted with the necessity of selecting, from among the means of supporting a claim, those reasons that they actually shall employ; what is not so clear is that every such selection is a decision with potential ethical implications.

The most common discussion of the issue of choosing the methods of argumentation, however, is probably the relationship between argumentative methods and goals. Is it the case that when an honorable goal is being pursued, that any means or methods are appropriate and acceptable so long as they further that worthy goal? This, of course, has been repeated so often as an ethical issue that we have a shorthand phrase to describe it: Does the end justify the means? If I am convinced of the worthiness of my choice of candidates in a political election, am I justified in using whatever means are available—lying, misrepresentation, false information—to secure your vote for him? After all, he will be a good official; my goal was for the betterment of the community. I suspect that a class of students in argumentation will have differing views on the issue—obviously, most situations will require only a slight alteration of the truth, a white lie, or some other euphemism. Still, the issue exists as one of a number of questions involving argumentation and ethics.

The Choice of a Receiver's Purpose

The arguer in a communication situation, however, should not be the sole focus of the discussion of the relationship between ethics and argumentation. Though we have already discussed the ethical implications of the receiver's choice to engage in argumentation, let me suggest that a receiver's explicit or implied goals in challenging an arguer is a fourth important potential area of ethical concern. Once the receiver has decided that she will indeed engage in argumentation, she will have to decide the nature of her interaction with the arguer. She may have decided that the interaction will be an appropriate time to demonstrate her skill in argumentation; consequently, she may be prepared to simply challenge anything that is offered to see if the arguer can support the point further—even points with which she may agree. Or, she may have determined that the argumentative situation will be a good time to get to know the other person better; consequently, she will disagree with nothing that is offered. Finally, although there are numerous other options, she may have decided to engage in argumentation for purely social reasons (e.g., a discussion at a party), and so her challenges are made only half-seriously, half-jokingly. In none of these situations is there a hint that the receiver has any intention of entering into the argument with a serious desire to examine the claim.

Your reaction, I predict, to this cataloging of situations, in which the receiver's goal is something other than a serious analysis of the claim, is probably a rather neutral "So what?" Is such a situation really a potentially important ethical problem? I will admit that the issue normally is not highlighted in texts on argumentation. On the other hand, our approach has featured the receiver in the argumentative process, and, if we are to stress the judgments made by receivers and the standards for receiver judgments, then we would do well to scrutinize closely the ethical implications of the receiver's expressed or implied goals in engaging in argumentation. If the arguer is aware, for example, that the receiver is simply being humorous, testing the arguer's ability to argue, or being overly agreeable for the sake of sociability, then I see no problem: the exercise would be an interpersonal game with each participant knowing that the game was in progress. If, on the contrary, the rules of the game were obscure, and the arguer had been given no clue that the game was occurring, then it seems to me that a significant ethical issue, or at least its potential, has been created. Just as we normally would not condone an arguer who merely thrilled in the manipulation of his receiver, I feel that the receiver who pursues goals that are almost entirely irrelevant to the claim at hand probably should be subject to the same sort of judgment. Just as we probably would not overlook an arguer with obvious ulterior motives, we probably should examine the goals of receivers with similar care. Indeed, because of the centrality of the receiver to our continuing discussion of argumentation, it seems to me that we should pay close attention to the receiver's choice of goals in challenging the claim and its reasons.

The Choice of the Receiver's Methods

A fifth and related decision or series of decisions that may be subject to ethical judgments are the choices that receivers make of the methods by which they will analyze and challenge claims. Just as you as an arguer confront decisions about means of advancing arguments, you, when functioning as a receiver, face similar decisions about the methods that you will utilize in the receiving and judging process. Consider the situation in which the arguer has presented evidence that you know to be outdated and no longer accurate. Even if you know the situation will be embarrassing for the arguer, do you have an ethical obligation to challenge the outdated evidence? Consider a second situation in which the arguer has presented an excellent statement of reasons for his claim, but since you have responded with a counterclaim, you are highly involved with your own position. You realize that no one can prove something beyond all doubt, but, in order to gain a psychological advantage, do you repeatedly insist that he either prove the point or drop it? Consider, thirdly, a situation in which the arguer cites a commonly accepted presumption about the adverse influence of—let us say—inflation. When the arguer has not presented any reports of opinions with authoritative warrants, do you demand such support even for an obvious idea? Finally, consider a situation in which you demand certain kinds of support from the arguer who is presenting a claim that you do not favor. When the arguer presents the required information—and when you have no response for the new support—do you ignore the new material and continue to challenge the arguer? In all these situations, taken from the realm of everyday argumentation as well as formal debate, the implication is clear to me that potential ethical problems do arise from the receiver's selection of methods of challenging and examining the claim. Again, as I suggested with the issue of receiver goals, when we analyze the choices that receivers make about methods of argument, let us utilize the same sorts of standards that we normally reserve for the arguer.

The Decision to Accept a Claim

A final major argumentative decision, which seems to me to present itself as a potential ethical problem, is the decision of the receiver as to when or if to accept the claim as offered. You, as a receiver, have significant power in the argumentative situation since you must make choices of argumentative goals and methods of examining reasons, as well as the initial decision to take part in the argumentative process. One final power, though, is far more crucial than others: the choice of when or if the claim is acceptable to you. Contrary to the traditional image of the receiver as the "soft clay" of a powerful arguer, a skillful receiver is much more in control of the situation. He can demand good reasons, examine them, ask for others, ask for relationships between or among reasons, but more importantly, decide when the reasons are good enough. Consider the discussion in chapter 7 when both participants vowed never to accept the other's point of view on the legalization of marijuana. We discussed those positions as being irrational, simply because they admittedly were not modifiable—and probably not appropriate either; still, are these positions not also subject to an ethical judgment? Is it ethical behavior to deny the claim and to add that the position will never be acceptable? Consider a second situation in which you are at a social gathering where an acquaintance attempts to support a claim she made. To avoid an argument do you pretend acceptance of the claim and reasoning—only to criticize the reasoning later? Finally, in a situation where you do not understand the reasoning presented for the claim, do you feign acceptance of the claim in order not to appear unintelligent or ignorant? In these situations, the choice is clearly in the control of the receiver, but when you as a receiver make such a decision, you should be prepared for a possible ethical challenge.

This final major choice, indeed, may be the most important of the series of receiver and arguer choices that we have examined. My experience has been that much of argumentation ends with the decision by the receiver that "Well, I don't agree, but I don't want to argue," or "Okay, okay, you go ahead and believe that if you want—everyone is entitled to his or her opinion." Frequently, this plea for equality in thinking and passivity is, in actuality, a strategy that we learn to protect us from having to admit the strength of the other's claim. In order not to admit "We're wrong" (and the arguer is correct), we argue for freedom of thought. And, as is clear by now, such choices are especially fertile grounds for ethical challenges and the development of ethical issues: indeed, if we do not wish to risk changing a position, we should avoid argumentation altogether.

The areas of potential ethical judgment that we have isolated—and clearly some decisions made by arguers and receivers may not fit well into any of these classifications—are difficult areas in which to judge human behavior. How do we get inside someone's thinking to determine what his argumentative goal was? How do we determine with certainty the methods by which receivers are judging reasons and claims? How do we know whether a receiver is avoiding the responsibility to accept the reasoning for the claim when his demands have been met? In short, how do we make these ethical judgments about receiver and arguer choices?

I do not believe, first, that there is such a way—at this time at least—to ascertain with certainty the goals of an arguer or receiver;

to ask the goal of the arguer would be tantamount to seeking the real reason he was advancing a claim, and I place little faith in the attempt to establish absolute reasons. Similarly, any judgment of the methods used by an arguer or receiver to present or examine a claim would be a matter of interpretation of what occurred in relation to what was intended; my position is that we shall not discover once-and-for-all the intended method of the arguer or receiver. Finally, I have little confidence that an observer wishing to make an ethical judgment will be capable of finding the true motivation behind an arguer or receiver deciding to engage in argument. In essence, in answer to the question posed in the last paragraph about how we make those ethical judgments about receiver and arguer choices, it is submitted that we attempt to ascertain the intent of the participants as the key variable, and we support our perception of the intent with reasons supporting that judgment. Our judgments of the ethical quality of the argumentative communication, ironically but not surprisingly, will be argumentative claims themselves.

This idea of the purely argumentative nature of ethical judgments may be uncomfortable and unsatisfying for you; it would indeed be easier to be able to make such judgments with some sort of absolute system of evaluation. Unfortunately, however, such a system does not exist. If it did, then perhaps all we have discussed concerning argumentation would be unproductive. The reason that we have discussed argumentation as something different from the ideal of formal logic, geometric perfection, or other strict notions of logicality, is precisely because such attempts at making argumentation automatic inevitably result in misleading assumptions about the ease or certainty of argumentative communication. Just as we cannot avoid the difficulty and lack of certainty that accompany common argumentation, we cannot escape these same factors that also accompany the judgment of the ethical quality of that argumentation.

At the same time that I contend that the ethical judgment of argumentative activity cannot be determined on the basis of an automatic system, it does seem to me that the individual making the judgment can enhance the process by following certain types of procedural guidelines. A discussion of several standards of ethics, their relationships to human values, and their implications for the ethical judgment of argumentation is our final topic in this chapter.

Ethics, Values, and Standards

Perhaps the most crucial idea to note in the role of ethical judgment in argumentation is that such a judgment is a comparison between the argumentative communication and certain standards of what is good and not good in an ethical or moral sense. When a receiver

charges an arguer with unethical practices, we assume that the
receiver believes that the arguer has done certain unacceptable
things or not done certain expected things; that is, we note that the
argumentative performance has not met the standard set for argumentation by the receiver. Similarly, when an arguer advances the
claim that the receiver has acted somehow unethically in her examination or challenge of the claim, we assume that the arguer considers
the receiver's activity to be somehow short of the demands of good
ethical conduct in argumentation. Regardless, then, of which participant in the process advances the charge of unethical conduct, we
may be sure that the person submitting the judgment is charging that
some standard of conduct has been violated.

What is not so clear in such cases is what particular standard is
being violated. To charge simply that unethical conduct has occurred is to fail as a communicator in what is essentially a communication act: the meaning of the charge is altogether unclear. Just as
receivers, for instance, have the right to develop a certain potentially
ethical issue, arguers should have a corresponding right to know as
clearly as possible what the charge means in the context of what they
did. Obviously, the clarity of the situation would be enhanced by the
receiver (or the arguer, whoever has advanced the charge) carefully
explaining the specific conduct, strategy, goal, or method that is the
object of the charge. This clarification, though advisable and productive to the progress of the interaction, is only the beginning of an
understanding of the charge. Also necessary is a clarification of the
ethical standard that was perceived as violated by the arguer or
receiver.

Though we shall not dwell upon such ethical standards to the
extent that a text in ethics might, let us examine the following
argumentative situation and the several standards of ethical judgment that would imply different ethical judgments of the activity. In
essence, we shall focus upon the same situation and the same argumentative activity, but we shall arrive at varying ethical judgments of the quality of the argumentation. Note that we shall use
commonsense statements of ethical standards rather than highly
abstract, philosophical statements about the nature of the good.

Case Study: Ladies and Gentlemen, the President
of the United States

Consider the following hypothetical statement made by an American
President about the question of whether a new secretary of state was
to be appointed. For weeks, rumors had circulated around
Washington and other national capitals that the President was prepared to dismiss the current secretary from this crucial government

position. This nationally televised address has been planned to provide the President with an opportunity to state his position on a
number of issues, including the appointment. An estimated forty
million Americans listen to the President as he begins his address to
the nation.

"My fellow citizens, this message tonight is in keeping with the
policy of this administration to discuss with you the critical issues
that involve this country. A number of important developments have
occurred; a number of problems have arisen that you should be made
aware of. Some of these issues involve the degree of progress that the
Congress and this administration have made in solving the crucial
domestic problems of our great nation. Some involve events that
have occurred or are occurring internationally. And, finally, some
relate to decisions and problems that are the exclusive responsibility
of this office of the presidency. I should like to begin with a situation
involving a problem in that latter area. Speculation has been voiced
here in this country and elsewhere about the current secretary of
state. Let me say that in this difficult period of sensitive negotiations
on many fronts, that the secretary has served an indispensible role in
the conduct of our foreign policy. Although not all that this administration has set out to do has been accomplished internationally, we
have made progress toward those solutions that will affect all of
mankind for generations. The current secretary has played a crucial
role in that progress. I am not now considering the replacement of
the secretary of state in the cabinet of this administration.

Concerning developments in my nomination of Mr. Carter to the
Supreme Court. . . . "

At this point, we shall interrupt to note that the message of the
President quelled rumors of the intended replacement of the secretary in Washington and elsewhere. Then, two weeks later, the
secretary of state did in fact resign, and a different individual was
nominated for the position by the President, with the hope of
confirmation by the Senate.

Speculation about the decision, as you might expect, emerged in
local and syndicated newspaper columns of the country, and in the
electronic media, that the President had indeed misled the country
by his statement about the appointment. Surely, these critics reasoned, the President must have been in the throes of making such a
decision even at the time that he denied such consideration. The
explanations issued by the President's press secretary covered a
number of points, but two were particularly important. First, the
secretary of state had been involved in delicate negotiations concerning nuclear arms limitations, and it was felt that any erosion in
the secretary's official role at that time might have hindered the

progress of those accords which affected all of this generation and generations to come. Secondly, the presidential decision had already been made to replace the secretary at the time of the broadcast; indeed, the President reported the situation accurately: he was not then contemplating the decision, since the decision had already been made. The presidential statement, even though questioned in light of the events following, could be explained as something other than a deliberate falsehood.[2]

Standards of Argumentative Ethics

One potentially relevant ethical standard is the principle that certain conduct—including deceit—is unacceptable by definition, tradition, or written rule such as found in the Bible or some other document. The use of this standard implies that no exceptions should be made to the sanctions against activities such as the telling of falsehoods or the presenting of deceitful information. Clearly, various religions, traditions, and customs of cultures will vary as to what sorts of conduct is unacceptable, and conduct will always be subject to the interpretation of the evaluator, but it seems to me that the application of this sort of established ethical standard would place the President's message in the category of the unethical. The message was intended to mislead listeners into thinking that the replacement of the secretary of state was not forthcoming; in actuality, and contrary to the President's statement, the replacement had already been determined. By the standard of inflexible rules of conduct emerging from religion, custom, or social practice, the President's message probably would be judged unethical.

In contrast to this rigid standard of judgment, however, let us assume that we shall apply a standard which says, in effect, that a receiver must accept full responsibility for any misinterpretations that he may have placed upon the message. The ambiguity of language can allow the belief that receivers of messages as well as creators of language must share responsibility for the misinterpretation of a message. In this case, the President argued through his press secretary that no deceptive message had occurred; the President was not responsible for an audience who interpreted his statement that he was not now considering such a replacement as being equal to saying that no such consideration had *ever* been given the

---

[2]Though the example here may seem exaggerated, it is by no means unprecedented. One of the recent instances which this case study parallels is the announcement of the appointment of Mr. Henry Cabot Lodge as ambassador to the United Nations during President Lyndon B. Johnson's administration. Since the President's announcement was the subject of widely different ethical reactions, the example is used frequently in discussions of ethics.

decision. Just as we would be partially at fault for assuming there would be no problems with a car we bought from a salesperson who said, "You'll be talking a lot about this car to your friends," we are partially responsible for the unfortunate interpretation of the President's message. He did not lie; we merely assumed an interpretation that was not the case. Based upon the standard that the receivers of messages share responsibility for a misinterpretation of meaning, the President's message probably would not be considered unethical.

Yet, a third potential standard for the assessment of the ethical quality of the President's message stresses the importance of situational variables in the ethical judgment of conduct. Fitting into a general framework that we can term "situational ethics," the application of this standard implies the belief that certain situations will demand that rules and standards of conduct must at times be altered because of the factors of the situation. Killing, for example, is generally considered wrong, yet killing is condoned by most societies when the taking of life is in war, for self-defense, or in state-dictated executions. In all these situations, the argument goes, certain variables in the situation demand that traditional rules or standards of conduct must be abandoned in order to judge the behavior adequately and fairly. In relation to the President's message, a critic using this standard of situational ethics might judge the delicate and important negotiations as a unique situation justifying a normally unacceptable message. In that light, the President would not be guilty of unethical conduct.

Related to the standard that stresses the situational variables in the judgment of ethics is a common standard of judgment that can be phrased as "the end justifies the means" or "the end never justifies the means." Clearly one of the most commonplace of all ethical standards, this standard highlights the controversy that can arise over a particular issue in ethics. Persons espousing the belief that the end, in fact, justifies the means would probably view the President's allegedly deceitful message as being a necessary evil to achieve the goal of nuclear arms limitation. The end, or purpose, of the President's remarks, they would argue, was so beneficial that there was no particular problem in his use of less-than-candid remarks to the people whom he was ultimately helping. In direct contrast, the evaluators believing that the end never justifies the means would probably argue that the President's purpose—no matter how beneficial to the world or its people—did not justify his use of misleading statements. Indeed, they would argue, to make gains for mankind at the expense of falsehoods, deceit, and public cynicism of government is hardly an admirable process. Certainly, they might continue, the President's goal may have been admirable, but how much more ethical it would have been to accomplish that goal through honorable means. The varying interpretation of the ends-means standard, then, would probably result in widely different and conflicting judgments.

Another standard of ethical judgment that might be invoked to evaluate the quality of the President's remarks is highly culturally oriented and can be phrased as the standard of prevailing conduct. Persons advocating this standard seek to judge conduct and events, not by rigid rules or variances in situations, but by what sort of related conduct is currently being accepted by the relevant society. Utilizing this standard, the President's message would be judged by what behavior is currently acceptable in politicians. If your perception is that all politicians lie or some such cynical belief, then you would judge the President less severely than if your perception was that all politicians are generally forthright. If your perception, again, is that everybody is deceitful if it is to his advantage, then, again, your judgment is more charitable than if you believe in the basic decency and honesty of the people of our society. The standard of prevailing conduct, then, presents an attempt at judging ethics fairly in the context of what is currently acceptable. As we have found, however, your judgment—even when using this same standard—will vary markedly depending upon your judgments of the prevailing standards of acceptable conduct.

Though we have not exhausted the potential standards for ethical judgments, a final standard that we will discuss is based upon the notion that human activity is basically gamelike, has rules and accepted procedures, and should not be played by people unaware of the rules. This belief in gamesmanship, as it is sometimes called,[3] places primary emphasis upon the person making the ethical judgment. Certain areas of life, like buying used cars, trading horses, and perhaps politics should be viewed as primarily game behavior. You know, for example, that you can spend more than $400 for the used car, and the dealer knows that also; similarly, you know that the dealer is prepared to accept less for the car than he is asking, and he knows that you know that as well. The negotiation that ensues has an inevitable conclusion: the price of the car will be somewhere between what you can pay and what he has to get for the car. The whole transaction is, in essence, a game. What happens if you do not know the rules? You merely end up paying more for the car; besides, it would be argued, if you are not aware of the rules, you should not have begun playing. In relation to the President's remarks, we could

[3]This perspective on the issue of ethics (in persuasion) was first introduced to me in 1970 by Professor Wallace Fotheringham, now retired professor of the Department of Communication, The Ohio State University.

say that politics and statements to citizens are a highly stylized game where complete honesty should not be expected; nor, will it ever be given. To judge the President by this standard of gamesmanship, our evaluation would have to be positive. He simply was engaged in a highly developed game, where the rules should have been obvious to all. After all, as in most games, no harm was done to the participants.

The Decision about Ethical Standards

As we have briefly surveyed a number of potentially useful ethical standards, I suspect that you interpreted some as acceptable, others as possibly acceptable, and some others as completely unsatisfactory—perhaps even unethical. My goal has been simply to present you with a number of standards that can serve various individuals as standards of ethical judgments. I would not be successful if I were to attempt to persuade you to accept one or another of the standards that we have discussed. Indeed, even if I could be successful in such an attempt, I would not want to bear such a burden. Your decision about use of a particular ethical standard should be the product of your own careful analysis of your position on behavior, conduct, and argumentation.

You are free to simply ignore the ethical factors and potential judgments in argumentative discourse; that is your right. If you decide to engage in ethical judgments, however, you must make clear both what it is you judge to be unethical and by what standard the behavior is unethical. To claim a message is unethical is to say little; to say it is unethical because it presented a deceiving argument is better; but to claim that the message is unethical because it presents a deceiving argument based upon the ethical standard of situational appropriateness presents a clearer statement of what you mean to charge. You still must precisely explain how the argument fails to meet the standard of situational appropriateness, but the mere presentation of the standard is an extremely constructive input into the argumentative situation. In sum, given the diversity in the areas for ethical judgment in argument, in interpretations of language, and in ethical standards, you as a person wishing to make an ethical judgment of argumentation have the burden of communicating clearly the meaning of that judgment—and that is no small task.

Summary

We began this chapter with the assumption that a relationship existed between ethics and argumentation, and we analyzed several conceptions about that relationship, including the belief that argumentation was immoral, amoral, moral, or "omnimoral." Though I noted that arguers and receivers are free to ignore those potential ethical problems, I suggested that there are several decisions made by participants in the argumentative process which are particularly clear as points at which ethical judgments might be made. These included the decisions by both arguers and receivers to engage in argumentation, the decisions by arguers about the goals and methods of argumentation, the choices by receivers of goals and methods in examining or challenging claims and reasons, and the decision by receivers about when or if to accept the reasons for a claim. Although this treatment of ethics and argumentation is highly nontraditional in its attention to the ethical responsibility of receivers, the analysis is entirely consistent with the text's emphasis upon the receiver and receiver judgment of argumentation.

Having discussed major potential areas for ethical evaluation, we next explored various standards of judging the ethical quality of argumentative behavior. Each of these standards—including the appeal to rules or principles of behavior, the assumption that receivers have a responsibility for misinterpretation, situational appropriateness, the ends-means standard, prevailing levels of acceptable behavior, and gamesmanship—was explained in terms of the diverse sorts of judgments that could be made of a hypothetical presidential message. I stressed the need for clarity when an ethical judgment is being made: exactly *what* is unethical, *by what standard* is the behavior unethical, and *in what way* does the behavior fail to meet the standard? Since the ethical judgment will be in a communication situation and since the judgment is purely argumentative, the need for clarity in the communication of an ethical judgment is extreme.

Programmed Questions

To test your understanding of the material presented in this chapter, you may wish to answer the following questions. In the multiple-choice questions, the answers may be all correct, all incorrect, or several may be correct. The suggested answers to the questions appear on the last page of this chapter. If you fail to answer the questions correctly, you may wish to review the material to increase your understanding and/or to discuss the items in class.

1.   Argumentation, as viewed in the text:
     a.   is immoral
     b.   is amoral

    c. is moral
    d. is omnimoral
    e. is essentially a morally good process, regardless of how it is used
    f. is a process in which numerous decisions can become the focus of an ethical dispute or question
    g. is a process which is inherently incapable of being completed without resort to deceit
    h. is a process which is neither good nor bad, but can be used for either good or bad ends; it is ethically neutral

2.   Argumentative choices that receivers and arguers make that can become the focus for ethical evaluation include:
    a. the assumed or expressed purpose of the participant in engaging in argumentation
    b. the methods or means used by receivers in examining claims and reasons
    c. the methods used by arguers in advancing claims
    d. the simple decision by arguers to engage in argumentation
    e. the decision of a receiver as to when to consider a claim acceptable

3.   Ethical judgments about argumentative choices:
    a. can be made by ascertaining the real reasons behind the activity of the receiver or arguer
    b. can be made best about the methods used by a participant, since these are areas where precise and certain judgments can be made
    c. must be made without any help from ethical standards
    d. are essentially claims themselves: we can give reasons why we have made a particular ethical judgment
    e. should be avoided because they are difficult
    f. should include a statement about the standard used to arrive at the judgment

Consider the following situation and then answer questions 4 through 10:

    You receive a call from the representative of a local civic club, asking if you would mind if he comes by your house to sell you two tickets to a circus that the group is sponsoring for the benefit of needy children. Since he explains the cost is only $1.00 per ticket, you agree to an appointment as it is for a good cause. When he arrives, it is clear (to you at least) that his goal is to sell you a whole book of tickets (which you can distribute in the neighborhood as gifts to "kids") at a cost of $40.00. He even ignores your mention of the two tickets. You may have a number of responses, based upon your ethical standards. Match the label for an ethical standard on the left with a representative response on the right. (One answer per item.)

4. _____ certain conduct   a. "Well, I guess I simply should have
        is simply wrong   known that two tickets were for starters."

5. _____ a receiver has   b. "There is no excuse for bait and switch. I
        some responsibility   was simply tricked."
        for ambiguity

6. _____ a situational standard

    c. "Oh, well, I was taken for a good cause."

7. _____ the end justifies the means

    d. "The idea that it's a good cause should never be used as an excuse to deceive."

8. _____ the end never justifies the means

    e. "Well, I guess everybody cheats a little. So what?"

9. _____ standard of prevailing conduct

    f. "In general, I would object, but this is such a silly deception."

10. _____ gamesmanship

    g. "I guess I should have asked him if there would be any more pressure for more tickets."

Discussion Questions for Appendix Case Studies

To test your understanding of the material in this chapter, you may wish to answer the following questions that refer to the case studies in the Appendix of this book. You may wish to (a) work on the questions individually; (b) work on the questions in pairs or in groups in or before class; (c) develop written answers to the questions; (d) have class discussion based upon the questions; (e) prepare an extended paper on several related questions; or (f) develop a major paper about one case study (using the questions related to it that appear in various chapters).

1. Study "Satisfaction (Almost) Assured" beginning on page 258. Do you see any ethical problem in the manager's method of solving your problem and convincing you to allow him to sell your used-for-a-year vacuum to someone as a demonstrator? When you have determined your evaluation of the potential issue, state what sort of *ethical standard* you used in deciding one way or the other.

2. Study "A 2 or a 4?" beginning on page 266. We have discussed the several areas in which receivers can be the focus of an ethical evaluation. When Alice refuses to accept Stoner's claim that a 2 is justified, but refuses to argue the issues further, do you find her guilty of unethical argumentation? If so, or if not, what standard did you use to arrive at the decision?

3. Study "You Find Good Assets in Des Moines and Iowa" by John R. Fitzgibbon beginning on page 256. Assume that you do not agree with Mr. Fitzgibbon's optimistic outlook, but that you cannot deny the evidence he presents: you somehow just do not agree that the future is very bright. Would you consider your activity as a receiver to be ethically questionable? If so, or if not, what standards are you using?

4. Study "Letter-to-the-Editor" beginning on page 254. Once you find that Elbarc is a candidate for the council as well as a concerned citizen, do you question the sincerity of his concern? Why or why not? What ethical standard, if any, might be relevant here to evaluate his purpose or method?

5. Study "The Success of the Program" beginning on page 264. When you learn that the students who were so excited about the program were actually fulfilling an apparent class assignment, do you suspect that some of their enthusiasm might have been demanded by the situation? If so, do you see any ethical problem in their response to the antismoking program? That is, was their response, if insincere, unethical? What standard might you use to assess the situation?

6. Review your responses to the five preceding situations. Is there a consistency in your judgment? Do you find yourself prone to make unfavorable ethical judgments? Do you find yourself using a consistent set of standards or a particular standard in arriving at ethical decisions? Do these judgments, standards, and tendencies tell you anything about your general attitude toward the question of ethics in argumentation?

Research Project for Advanced Students

You probably are not aware of the numerous ethical decisions that are made during a day by you and the people around you. Begin a research project on ethics, argumentation, and behavior by creating a log or journal in which you record the various ethical-sounding decisions that you encounter in your social group. After a week or so, analyze the log, evaluating both the decisions that were made and the standards by which your social group judged those decisions.

SELECTED REFERENCES

Johannesen, Richard L. *Ethics in Human Communication*. Columbus, Ohio: Charles E. Merrill Publishing Co., 1975.

Perelman, Chaim. "Value Judgments, Justifications and Argumentation." *Philosophy Today* 6 (1962): 45-50.

Toulmin, Stephen. *Reason in Ethics*. Cambridge: Cambridge University Press, 1968.

Answers to Programmed Questions

1. d, f   2. a, b, c, d, e   3. d, f   4. b   5. g   6. f   7. c

8. d   9. e   10. a

9

Argumentation as Communication: A Concluding Argument for Readers

To be fair, I must conclude our textbook experience together by admitting freely that this text on argumentation is argumentative itself. I have written the book with several important issues in mind, and I have attempted to discuss those issues with you; more specifically, I have made claims about the conduct of argumentation, and I have sought to support those claims with reasons I hoped you would consider good. The procedure, of course, is not unusual: books are written, at least partially, because a writer or teacher perceives situations that need improvement, skills that should be enhanced, or ideas that should be explored in a somewhat different fashion. While all that is common, what is not so usual is a direct statement to you that the author considers the book to be argumentative. The section in chapter 1 having to do with the implications of studying argumentation as communication introduced certain major issues, and the text has been written to support and to develop those ideas. It is to those ideas and claims that I wish to turn in this concluding chapter.

I argued, first, that our concern in argumentation should be more for the function and not the form of argumentation. Since argumentation is merely a special kind of communicative activity, we must be prepared for the divergence of interpretations about the meaning of a particular form. An arguer, for example, can create what to him is an extremely clear and meaningful argument—only to have it misunderstood by a majority of people perceiving the message. Conversely, the receiver of an argumentative message can experience highly different interpretations of his response to any structured argumentative message or argumentative process. Thus, argumentation is likely to involve all sorts of judgments about what the argument says or what it looks like. The attempts at making argumentation follow the form of deductive logic or any rigorous inductive forms probably will overlook the crucial point. The idea most important is how the argumentative language functions, and function has little to do directly with what the argument looks like. We need not abandon all the strengths of formal logic, but we should acknowledge its limitations in providing an easy method of studying argumentation based upon a standardized form or procedure. I have argued that the major question in any argumentative situation is "What did the language *do* (for the receiver)?" instead of "Did it look like what it was supposed to look like?" This concern for function—something that *acts* as a warrant, something that *serves* as evidence, something that *is responded to* as a claim—has been one of the central themes.

Related to this idea is a second claim of the book that we should approach argumentation rather more descriptively than prescriptively. Clearly, although standard rules of logic are available and useful in certain situations, most individuals will either not know or not employ such rules. Moreover, the rigid attention to any set of rules will be difficult to maintain: given the diversity in interpretations that we have restated above, the rules as well as the success in following the rules will be subject to potentially great misunderstanding. Our approach, then, has been to avoid rules and to describe alternatives that an arguer or receiver might use and alternative standards that might apply to questions as to the quality or ethical nature of the argumentation. Arguers and receivers, certainly, will use many of these alternative strategies or standards in engaging in argumentation, and it has been my goal to explore, wherever possible, the diversity of how people might argue in all the situations we have discussed. In one sense, ironically, I have been highly prescriptive: I have argued that you should concentrate upon how people *do* argue, whether or not you agree with my own preferences about strategies, standards, and approaches to argumentation in general.

In my avoidance of the forms of argumentation and my reluctance to dwell upon the rules of argumentation, I have claimed that, third, argumentation is a tremendously difficult process in which to engage. Just as most of us realize the difficulty in achieving communication, we should note the corresponding difficulty in achieving success in *argumentative* communication. Just as we recognize the limits of the "how to" approach to oral or written communication, we should accept the limits of a prescriptive approach to argumentation. Just as we should be prepared for the awareness that much of our communication will be unsuccessful, we should be prepared to have much of our argumentation end in the failure to attain our goals. Argumentation, as we have approached it, is surely a communication activity and is likely to be just as difficult, challenging, and frustrating as any other communication activity.

One of the factors, however, that can help us adjust to the difficulty of argumentation is an acceptance of a fourth claim I advanced: in argumentation we must always stress the centrality of the receiver and his judgment in the argumentative process. While the commonsense inclination is to emphasize the arguer, his intended message, and his attempt at attaining his goal, I have suggested that the receiver's judgment will be most important. The arguer who completes a process of argumentation, fails to win acceptance of his idea, and is at a loss to explain the occurrence, is simply an arguer who has placed far too much value in what he intended to do. His emphasis should be upon the receiver, the standards of the receiver, and the judgments that the receiver makes: these will provide him with an understanding of the shortcomings of the process, and better prepare him next time for a similar argumentative situation. Thus, whether we are discussing judgments of warrants, standards of appropriateness, or standards of ethical behavior, it is my position that we must always orient our study to the receiver in the argumentative process.

But, of course, throughout this summary of the major issues of the text, you have noted my avoidance of the term *argument*, which, to me, connotes a prepared document. I feel certain this avoidance did not surprise you since I have argued, fifth, that most of our argumentation is informal and unstructured; consequently, we should focus more on those situations where argumentation occurs as a communication *process* rather than a communication *message*. Clearly, some argumentation occurs on the basis of an arguer presenting a speech, writing an editorial, or making a presentation before a group. Those instances, however, will be few in comparison to the situations where arguer and receiver(s) are involved in a dynamic give-and-take of claims, reasons, and the judgments of claims and reasons: we engage in such unstructured argumentation with friends, fellow workers, relatives, acquaintances, salespersons, professors, and countless others. Although we cannot ignore the instances where you will need to prepare an argumentative document, we also cannot afford to ignore those more common situations where argumentation occurs every day.

One of the implications of this concern for argumentation as a pervasive process is the subject of a final major claim in this text: we must be prepared to recognize and deal with argumentation in all sorts of communication situations. Your need to know how to argue in the debate or public-speaking situation is crucial, and the material we have discussed should be helpful to you in preparing for those situations. Yet, since most of our communication is not in those situations, we reasonably can expect that most of your argumentation will not occur in those contexts either. Instead, most argumentation occurs in what we have called the intrapersonal or interpersonal settings, the small-group situation, or in your participation (at whatever level) in the mass-communication situation. Just as our case studies have concerned a variety of these situations, your own knowledge and skill in argumentation should enhance your goals in all the various communication situations in which argumentation is likely to occur.

In sum, then, the text has been a prolonged statement of claims about a way of approaching argumentation and my reasons for those claims. In arguing that we should emphasize function in argumentation, that we should be more descriptive than prescriptive, that we should expect argumentation to be difficult, that we should recognize the centrality of the receiver, that we should focus upon argumentation as a process, and that we should expect to find our argumentation occurring in a variety of situations—in arguing all that, I have at times departed from certain traditional treatments of argumentation. To the extent that the claims are useful to you, we have advanced the state of your skills and knowledge about argumentation. To the extent that anything I have argued is unsatisfactory to you, your criticism of my claims and your reasoning about that criticism have still advanced your skills and knowledge. Although I have attempted to communicate my views about argumentation as clearly and as persuasively as I can within the confines of this book, we all realize the difficulty of argumentation and the limits of communication. May your reading of the text prompt you to think more deeply about argumentation, to reflect upon the ideas here, and to enter into discussions with others in ways that will contribute to our understanding of argumentation as communication.

Appendix

The Appendix consists of a number of case studies of argumentation in various communication settings. These studies can be used in a variety of ways to enhance the learning of material in the text and to encourage the application of that material to argumentation outside the confines of the text. You may wish to:

1. use the questions that appear at the end of each chapter (except chapters 1 and 9) to study further the material in each chapter. The questions refer to several of the cases, so that you can apply your understanding of the chapter to several instances of argumentation.

2. use the questions that appear at the end of each chapter as an end-of-the-term review: that is, you can consolidate all the questions (from the several chapters) that refer to any one case study. The result is that you can examine a particular case study from the perspective of four or five chapters.

3. use the cases independently of the chapter-end questions as a method of having a diverse collection of argumentative situations for any further analysis that may be desired.

4. use the cases to initiate role-playing situations in a classroom setting. Most of the cases end at a point where further argumentation is possible, so you can apply your skills in argumentation to continue the cases beyond the situation described.

Letter-to-the-Editor

Dear Sir or Madam:

I have never written to the editor of this newspaper before, and I wouldn't now except for the anger that I feel over the conduct of the city council members who, theoretically, make the major decisions and policies for our community. I simply must say that the council members lately have demonstrated themselves to be unfit for service to the city.

First, there is no doubt in my mind that all of them view the council as a place to gain notoriety. They frequently make light of a serious issue, more content to make jokes than to grapple with the difficult issues before them. Such levity—at the city's and voters' expense—make them unfit to serve the city. . . .

Secondly, each council member acts as if he or she must "choose up" sides on particular issues. On issues that concern financial affairs, for example, you can always find them . . . taking predictable positions with predictable supporters. . . . Such lack of thorough and thoughtful analysis, such allegiance to "buddies" on the council, makes them unfit for office, in anybody's book.

Thirdly, each member of the council seems to be so concerned about the reaction his or her particular constituents might have that they seem to lose track of the greater issues and how they affect the city as a whole. Issues that affect only a part of the city are continually given preference over the larger issues. The result has been a continued lack of long-range planning and effective city administration.

In sum, therefore, the attempts at personal notoriety, the choosing of sides and the buddy system, and the lack of city-wide concern are justification for concluding that the council is unfit at present to serve this community. Take a look at the transcripts and media reports of the meetings, and you will see that all I have said is accurate. The people of this city deserve better representation. . . .

E. R. Elbarc
Candidate, Councilman-at-large

How Free Is Free Will?

Ellen was an average freshman student who had lived all her life in awesome respect for the United States, its system of government, and its protection of freedom under law. Although she had read of

B. F. Skinner in several courses in high school, her knowledge of him was limited to such ideas as the Skinner box for rats, operant conditioning, and reinforcement schedules. Never before had she ever read of Skinner's rather unusual schemes for making a better society. Never before had she contemplated the whole of society as a parallel to the Skinner box. Never before had she read the idea that many of the freedoms we enjoy in this country are more illusions of freedom than freedom itself.

Then she met Tom who seemed to have read everything that Skinner had written and was familiar with Skinner's plans for a model society based upon the conditioning model: indeed, it was possible, Tom believed, for society to structure itself so that people would do what they were supposed to because they were conditioned to respond in an appropriate manner. To Ellen's amazement, Tom defended this application of Skinner's psychology by noting that much of what we take for freedom of choice—for matters of the will—is nothing but a conditioned response. We "choose" to stop at stop signs because we have been conditioned to: we do not always think of arrest as a threat. We join armies and civilian work crews during a national emergency at least partly because we have been conditioned to respond to God and country. In essence, Tom contended, much of our exercise of free will is far from free. Freedom often is an illusion.

Once, after an evening of listening to Tom, Ellen went home filled with serious misgivings about what Tom had said. As she thought about her earlier beliefs in freedom, the democratic process, and the exercise of free will, she began to wonder if all that was pure idealism. On the other hand, she wondered if the thinking of Skinner was unsupported speculation. She tried to sort things out.

On the one side, she reasoned, I have been raised believing in the freedom and liberty of American society. What kinds of things would make me believe that? . . . My parents have always reinforced the comparison between this country and any other country. Surely, they must have had something to go on when they said this. . . . Then, also, I see everyday examples of times when people choose to do something; they exercise free will. . . . More than that, all the books I read on the origin of the country talk of the differences between this country and others. Surely, not all those books can be mistaken. With all this, how can Skinner—much less Tom—think that freedom of will usually means an unconscious conditioning to respond?

Perhaps I am mistaken about Tom's interpretation of Skinner— maybe Skinner says that freedom of will *can*, but *usually doesn't* mean a conditioned choice.... That would make a difference, I guess. Maybe I could accept it then.... I don't know, though, it sounded like he really meant that *most* of the time, freedom was only conditioning that we weren't aware of. Why would he say that? It could be that he's only trying to get some publicity--that might explain it. ... On the other hand, maybe he's got a point. Maybe *I* have been conditioned to believe in the freedom of will—just like he says. Maybe those situations that I see as free will being exercised are really only things that people have been conditioned to do. Worse yet, maybe I've been conditioned so that I am prone to reject anything that doesn't mesh with what I've been taught!

Wait a minute, though, if this is such a tremendous viewpoint on society, why haven't I heard of it before? Oh great! Maybe I've been conditioned to screen out that kind of thinking when I did hear it.

Well, I'll never get to sleep if I don't get this thing settled: How does the Skinner interpretation fit in with what I already believe? Wait—I don't have to decide.... I've just been conditioned to think I have to decide and get it settled! I'm going to get a candy bar.

You Find Good Assets in Des Moines and Iowa

by John R. Fitzgibbon

[In 1974, the Iowa-Des Moines National Bank of Des Moines, Iowa, became the first bank in Iowa history to report assets of over one-half billion dollars. When the 1974 report was made available to the public in pamphlet form, it was accompanied by a statement by Iowa-Des Moines' board chairman and chief executive officer, John R. Fitzgibbon. Fitzgibbon used the pamphlet, not only as a statement of the bank's condition, but also as a time to take an argumentative position on the current economic situation. This publicly available, four-page brochure contained the title of the message and a picture of Fitzgibbon on the first page, the statement of the bank's condition on the last page, and the following message in between.—Author.]

I would like to visit with you about two questions that we all should be asking since we hear and read about so many negative things these days.

What is good with our Metropolitan Area and the State of Iowa?

The list is almost endless. From an economic standpoint we have rising sales, increasing business, and more buying power. Our unemployment rate is less than half that stated on a national level, and with a substantially higher available working force the net result is that more people are employed in Iowa than ever before. From an environmental standpoint we have clean air, open spaces, lots of water, and the type of life for which others in the country are yearning. From an agricultural standpoint we have rising values for farm land, and while farm earnings are down, 1974 production was well ahead of the average of the past decade. From a sociological standpoint we have a work force in Iowa that consistently achieves high standards of performance. We have outstanding educational institutions and churches.

What is wrong with our Metropolitan Area and the State of Iowa?

There are some wrongs and we should not close our eyes to them. The recession is having an impact and we must acknowledge this. There are Iowans without jobs and this is distressing. We should be spending more money for education in the state, we should accelerate the revitalization of our cities, and we should continue to protect our farms and farmers. But perhaps the main thing that's wrong with Iowa is that people are not recognizing what is right. In times like these when the national picture is gloomy and the state outlook could be brighter we must not just look at what's wrong. We must look at what's right and realize that Iowa is a more prosperous place than most and we should appreciate it.

At the Iowa-Des Moines National Bank as we examine our figures for 1974, we note with pride that for the first time in Iowa banking history a bank, the Iowa-Des Moines, has exceeded a half billion dollars in assets. We think it's important to view our growth as a clear reflection of the economic health of our metropolitan area and state. We believe, too, that this growth reflects our continued efforts to anticipate the financial needs of our customers. Over the years the Iowa-Des Moines has been a leader in the banking industry—we introduced twenty-four hour banking with automated tellers—we introduced Instant Interest Savings with daily compounding—we introduced the Personal Banker concept—our Yes Account is the most innovative package of personal banking services available—we introduced Master Charge in Iowa—we have strategically located three suburban full-service offices, and soon will add a fourth, to serve our customers more conveniently—and our new main bank in downtown Des Moines exemplifies our confidence in the community and state.

Iowa . . . it's a good state. Greater Des Moines . . . an excellent place to live and work. There have always been peaks and valleys in our economy and in our lives. With a positive attitude and all of us pulling together, we can continue to enjoy economic growth and prosperity.

Satisfaction (Almost) Assured

After much shopping, John Deal purchased an expensive vacuum sweeper from a reputable firm whose products (like most) are said to be guaranteed against owner dissatisfaction. John was not dissatisfied with the sweeper until a year after he bought the product when the people he hired to professionally clean his carpet told him that the carpeting was exceptionally dirty and that his sweeper probably needed replacement. Needless to say, John was not too pleased with such an announcement.

He called the small appliances department and talked with a salesperson who contended that the sweeper had been an especially well-selling item and suggested that no one had ever complained about it before. John was unaffected by those reports and was told by the salesperson that the sales manager for the department would return a call to John as soon as possible.

MANAGER: Mr. Deal? This is Ralph Trumble, sales manager in small appliances. What seems to be the problem?

JOHN: The problem is that, after a year of using a very expensive model of your sweeper, we have discovered that it has not been cleaning the carpet adequately. It apparently has only picked up the surface material, not the dirt deeper in the carpet.

MANAGER: Well, you know that your satisfaction is guaranteed here, but the delay of a year is a bit longer than usual. Didn't you sense some sort of problem earlier? Well, of course, you see, we've had virtually no complaints about the product before. I don't know whether the frequency of sweeping is a factor or not, but I certainly want to help you . . .

JOHN: I appreciate that . . .

MANAGER: But, I'm a little unclear as to what to do about the problem.

JOHN: My wife and I do a lot of business with your company, and I have always felt that the company was fair to us—of course we've never had to return anything before.

MANAGER: I am certain that we cannot simply give you a new sweeper.

JOHN: Well, we wouldn't want one like this again, anyway.

MANAGER: I see. Of course not. There is a model that just came out a year ago—it's probably the best available anywhere. We've had no complaints about it from anyone. It's really somewhat stronger than the earlier model, and so it probably will clean deeper than the type you are currently using.

JOHN: Now wait a minute; first, I was told at the time we bought
           this sweeper that it was the strongest one available—and
           it also came out a year ago. Why is mine now not quite so
           powerful?

MANAGER: Well, yours is the most powerful of those that use the
           power-in-the-head principle, but, in comparison to the
           new uprights—well, yours, sometimes, is not so power-
           ful. If you use the head attachment, that could give you
           problems.

JOHN: When you tell me that this new sweeper has not brought
           you any complaints, that doesn't mean all that much to
           me: you've said that this one I own now has never given
           anyone else any trouble before—yet, here I am. How do I
           know this new upright won't be worthless as well?

MANAGER: Mr. Deal, trust me when I say you will not regret getting the
           new one. I'll tell you what: you can buy the new one—we'll
           just charge it to your account—and we'll take your old one,
           recondition it, and sell it as a demonstrator. Whatever
           money we get from the sale will be applied to the purchase
           of your new vacuum. This could be more profitable to you
           than prorating the value of the machine you have and
           refunding only part of your money. This should work out
           better for all concerned. We do appreciate your being such
           a good customer; and, as you see, satisfaction is assured
           when you do business with us.

Address to the Catholic Lawyers' Guild

by U.S. Senator Dick Clark

[The Saint Pius Catholic Church of Cedar Rapids, Iowa, was the
scene of a special mass offered for the legal profession and public
officials on Sunday, September 8, 1974. The event is an annual
ceremony sponsored by the Archdiocese of Dubuque, Iowa, which
includes approximately the northeast third of Iowa. Following the
mass, and in the wake of what had become known as "the Watergate
scandal," U.S. Senator Dick Clark from Iowa delivered the following
address to an audience estimated at between 100 and 150 people.—
Author.]

Bishop Dunn, Monsignor Friedl, Judge McManus, judges of the
district courts, members and guests and friends of the Catholic
Lawyers' Guild. It is both a pleasure and a privilege to be able to join
you this morning. This is an important occasion—rich in sig-

nificance and tradition—and I very much appreciate your invitation to be part of it.

These are difficult times for members of the legal profession and members of the political profession. I'm reminded of the story about a young defense attorney who was questioning a prospective juror before the start of a trial. As usual, he asked the woman on the stand if she knew him. "Yes, I certainly do," the woman snapped. "You're a crook." Well, the attorney was somewhat taken aback, and he pointed to his opposing counsel and said, "That's Steve Jackson, he represents the plaintiff in this case, do you know him?" Without a moment's pause, the woman replied, "he's a crook, too." At that point, the judge summoned the two attorneys to the bench and very firmly told them: "If either of you asks her if she knows me, I'll hold you in contempt."

Just a few minutes ago, each of us—as a public official or as an attorney—asked God's assistance and guidance in our work in the year ahead. It was a simple prayer, but one with very profound implications. By asking for that help, we are recognizing that we are not infallible, not perfect, and that there must be a higher allegiance than the loyalty owed to a client or a political cause. That higher allegiance is to what is right and just. Few would dispute that proposition, but as we have seen over the last two years, it can be easily forgotten by both attorneys and public officials.

There are countless examples of men and women who have not forgotten that principle. In the last week or so, thinking about this Mass and doing some reading for it, I ran across one of the best examples: Thomas More. He was a lawyer, a legislator, a judge—and he was a saint. It's a combination that most people would agree we need more of these days.

More's career in public service began in Parliament. He made a name for himself by opposing an extravagant subsidy for the chief executive, then Henry VII, hardly a popular position. As a result, his father was fined and imprisoned in the Tower of London and More himself found it wiser to spend a considerable amount of time in France rather than England. Fortunately for More, there was a change in Administrations, and under Henry VIII, he became successively sheriff of London, ambassador, steward of Oxford, and finally, Lord Chancellor of England. In that position, he administered the courts among other things—with a reputation for fairness and efficiency. The judges here might be interested in knowing that there were more than 4,000 cases tried in his two year term. And there was never a backlog.

As most everyone knows, More quickly fell from favor when he refused to sanction the King's divorce, remarriage, and establishment of the Church of England. He was convicted of treason on perjured testimony and executed. But just before he was killed, he told his executioner that he would die "the King's good servant—but God's first."

The most recent public examples of professional ethics and morality by public officials and attorneys have hardly matched the ethics and morality of Thomas More. At last count, 13 attorneys have been convicted or indicted in what has become the worst political scandal in this country's history. They were not disreputable characters haunting the county courthouse—they were men that held the highest positions of public service and public trust: two attorney generals, a secretary of the treasury, and the President's chief domestic policy advisor, his special counsel and his own personal attorney.

The criminal charges against these men are being resolved in the courts—there is not need to recount them—but whatever the outcome of the legal process, it is clear that they shared a fundamental mistake. They forgot the example of Thomas More. Their allegiance was to a man and a political cause when it should have been to the law. As a result, they were loyal to the President, but disloyal to the country.

Almost 50 years ago, Justice Louis Brandeis explained why that higher allegiance—the commitment to the law and what is right—is so important. "Our government is the potent, omnipresent teacher," he said. "For good or evil, it teaches the whole people by example." He wrote those words, ironically enough, in a wiretapping case before the Supreme Court. And I think he would have been terribly disappointed today, because the people have not been left with a very good example.

It is not surprising that the people of this country do not hold the legal profession in the highest esteem. The preliminary results of a public opinion survey commissioned by the American Bar Association puts it in rather stark terms: six out of every ten people questioned felt that the legal system favored the rich and powerful over anyone else. Half felt that lawyers' fees were unfair. Six out of every ten said most lawyers charged more for their services than they were worth. And more than a third of the people interviewed felt that most lawyers would engage in unethical practices to help a client in an important case.

There might be some consolation if the poeple did trust and respect their public officials. But, as you know, that's simply not the case. Even when Richard Nixon's approval ratings were lowest, they still were higher than the favorable scores given to the Congress in public opinion surveys. None of this is a popularity contest. Without public trust and confidence, public office and the legal profession both are hollow institutions: they can never offer leadership, they can never be effective. Without public trust and confidence, the very existence of democracy is called into question.

So the challenge is obvious. And it is one that public officials and the legal profession share if only because the legal profession permeates every level and branch of government. There are close to 400-thousand attorneys in this country. And one out of every ten has a job in government. The nation's laws are made by legislators, mostly lawyers. The nation's laws are enforced by the executive branch, made up of mostly lawyers. And the nation's laws are interpreted by judges, nearly all of them lawyers.

As attorneys and public officials, our conduct does more than affect our own reputations and the reputations of our professions. Our conduct affects the welfare and the well-being of the entire country. And it is not asking too much that we set our own house in order so that we can begin to restore public trust and confidence in government. There already is a good foundation to build upon.

People no doubt always will remember that John Dean once asked, "How in God's name could so many lawyers get involved in something like this?" But people will also remember that a federal grand jury, a federal judge, and 28 lawyers on the House of Representatives Judicial Committee helped get us out of this. Now, it is up to us to see that it does not happen again.

I am not a lawyer, and I will not pretend to suggest what the legal profession might do to prevent the violations of ethics and morality that occurred over the last two years. But it is clear that our response to Watergate must be more fundamental, more lasting than merely punishing the lawyers who did wrong and praising those who did right. It is clear that lawyers in government must consider themselves public servants, not hired guns loyal to their superior. It is clear that lawyers and public officials must avoid not only conflicts of interest, but even the appearance of conflict.

I will not pretend to make recommendations to the legal profession, but I can and should outline for you what I think the Congress should do to help restore trust and confidence in government. Many, many steps should be taken, but three are indispensable.

First, open committee meetings. It is difficult to believe, but in the United States Senate today, there is a presumption in favor of secrecy. Open meetings are the exception, not the rule. Two years ago, just a few days after I came to the Senate, there was a vote on an open meetings bill. It would have opened every Committee meeting of the Senate with exceptions only in the interests of national security or personnel matters. The bill failed, and we will try to pass it this January when a new Congress convenes. Until we succeed, until we conduct the business of the Senate in the sunshine, it is difficult to see how people can trust the "democratic" process.

The second indispensable step is financial disclosure for public officials. The reporting requirements in effect now are woefully inadequate—but full disclosure is essential. A public official's financial status must be open because, otherwise, the public will never know whether the official's allegiance lies with the public interest or his own private interest. It is impossible to eliminate every conflict of interest. My son attends public school, for example, and every time I vote on an education bill, I have a technical conflict of interest. But if full financial disclosure is required, the public will be able to make an informed judgment on whether their representative is serving their interests above all else.

The strongest argument advanced against full financial disclosure is the individual's right of privacy. But federal courts have made it clear that a public servant does not enjoy the same degree of privacy that a private citizen does. There is no need for anyone to know the income and net worth of a private citizen, but there is a very clear need for the public to be aware of their representative's financial status. There is legislation pending that would require full financial disclosure by members of Congress. Its chances of passage are not considered good, but until it is passed into law, I think that every member of Congress should make a full financial disclosure.

The last indispensable step in restoring the people's trust and confidence in government is the establishment of public financing of political campaigns. And with this reform effort at least, we are very close to success. The Senate has passed a strong public financing bill that covers Presidential general elections and primaries and Congressional elections as well. The house has passed a weaker version that provides public financing only for Presidential campaigns. The differences in the two versions will be resolved in a conference committee in the next month or so; and as a member of the conference committee, I will do all that I can to draft legislation that is comprehensive and effective, with a strong new independent elections commission with the authority to make it work.

Until public financing becomes a reality, public officials will continue to rely on private contributions and special interest groups. And that reliance will bring with it the possibility of corruption and the continued doubt and mistrust of the people. Private money has no place in the public's business. And for a very small cost—less than a dollar a voter—public financing will enable the people to buy their government back.

These three reforms—public financing, income disclosure, and open meetings—are not revolutionary or theoretical concepts. They're very real and very practical. They can help us restore trust and confidence in the processes of government. But in the end, whether or not ethics and morality permeate government and public service will depend on the individual men and women: the men and women that vote to elect public officials and the public officials themselves. We're members of both categories, and that makes our responsibility all the greater. To a great extent, whether or not we meet that responsibility, whether or not we teach our children to meet it, will determine the future of this country.

The Success of the Program

Probably all fund-raising, charitable organizations have some overall policy-making or policy-advising body, whether it is called a "steering committee," an "advisory group," or a "board of directors." Among the multitude of specific concerns of such a group is the question of whether the fund-raising or educational programs of the organization achieve what, in fact, the organization wants accomplished. Frequently, the administrative head or chief administrator is called upon to present to the board some indication of the success of the program. Tom Williams, who heads up the area lung association, is just turning to a consideration of the effects of some recent educational efforts of that organization.

HEAD ADMINISTRATOR: Now, as you all know, we have been engaged in an intensive effort to educate area youngsters about the dangers of cigarette smoking. One of the major vehicles for such an effort has been the multimedia presentation that presents the antismoking message in animated cartoon form. The idea of creating heroes who don't smoke and villains who do smoke and try to get others to smoke, we feel, is one of the strong points of the program. We currently reach about 30 percent of the schoolchildren in the fifth grade, and we

	hope to be able to expand the program in the future. When future funding is . . .
BOARD MEMBER #1:	Excuse me, Tom . . .
HEAD ADMINISTRATOR:	Go ahead; sorry to have rattled on that way.
BOARD MEMBER #1:	What I wanted to ask was . . . well, I guess I wanted to know how we knew the program was effective? Does your staff do follow-up work on these?
HEAD ADMINISTRATOR:	It's an excellent question. I certainly was going to get to that, so why don't we turn to that now? Yes, we do do follow-up work on the various programs. After all, we are talking about several thousands of dollars, and we must be sure that they are serving the purpose that they are intended to serve. In regard to this particular program, we have had gratifying results. You see, after the completion of the program, with its preprogram activities, the actual presentation, and some follow-up discussion, we have a survey that the children fill out, indicating how the program has affected them. The overwhelming response from the children is that they will not smoke after the presentation and when they see the effects of smoking on lungs, hearts, and health, in general. We issue membership cards in the "Clean Air" club when they take an appropriate pledge. And we have issued hundreds of the membership cards. This is probably the best-received program that we have.
BOARD MEMBER #2:	Have you done follow-up studies to see if the pledges are carried out? What I mean is, do these kids really stop smoking? Or do they merely take a pledge and get a card?
HEAD ADMINISTRATOR:	Professor Wallace, I can see why we have a member of the sociology department on our board. It's a good question. It seems to me that we have enough indication from parents, teachers, and our own workers to indicate that these children really don't smoke.
BOARD MEMBER #2:	What I mean is whether or not . . .

HEAD ADMINISTRATOR: In addition to those reactions, I could cite the letters from students who praise the program and say they were very influenced as a result of it. Once a whole class wrote letters indicating how much they enjoyed the program—the teacher even collected them into a folder and delivered them to us. That was indeed rewarding. Why, I know of one little girl who said that she had been smoking since third grade by stealing cigarettes from her parents. After seeing the program she decided to stop. So you see, Professor Wallace, there is absolutely no doubt about the effectiveness of the program.

BOARD MEMBER #2:   But what I was thinking . . .

BOARD MEMBER #3:   Wait, can I get in here a minute? I have to leave early, and I was wondering whether we might need to move on to some other areas.

HEAD ADMINISTRATOR: Yes, I guess we really should. Now, in relation to some other areas, there has also been progress. Professor Wallace, you might be able to help our staff here as well . . .

A 2 or a 4?

Modern organizations have realized the advisability of attempting to chart the progress of the company and its employees. The assessment of progress, however, seems to be most accurately accomplished by the comparison of actual performance to certain stated goals. That is, how can the company assess its progress toward objectives without knowing what those objectives are? This sort of thinking has resulted in numerous companies creating a system of evaluation based on performance as compared to stated goals. Often the approach is labeled MBO—management by objectives—and often that basic approach is modified and called something else.

Midwest Electronics, Inc. uses performance objectives and has both supervisor and subordinate rank the subordinate on the basis of certain objectives that have been set by a cooperative effort between supervisor and subordinate. Thus, for example, Alice Kooper was supposed to strive toward the goal of improving her "interpersonal relationships with coworkers." This objective was deemed as crucial to all parties concerned, so the objective was listed first on the appraisal evaluation form. The form, then, looked like this:

CODE

1 = substandard   = almost always completes task below level of most employees

2 = marginal   = most of time completes assignment at the level of most employees

3 = adequate   = almost always completes assignment at the level of most employees

4 = commendable = most often completes task at a higher level than most other employees

5 = outstanding   = almost always completes task at a higher level than almost all other employees

I. General skills, attitudes, performance objectives.
   A. I will improve my interpersonal relationships with coworkers.
      Result: 1   2   3   4   5

The problem that Alice had in approaching this first objective is partly that it is phrased in such general, nonspecific terms. Part of the problem, in addition, is that it involves a qualitative judgment rather than a quantitative evaluation: counting an increase in typed words per minute is easier than judging an improvement in interpersonal skills. The major conflicting problem, however, is that her salary increment (if any) and promotion (if any) may be determined largely by the evaluation—of all the objectives.

Alice discovers that she and her supervisor have not "seen eye to eye" on the evaluations in general. In particular, her supervisor has evaluated that first objective a "2" while Alice has judged herself a "4." As is the custom with the firm, the participants discuss the relevant issues in the evaluations rather than just compromise with a "3."

STONER: Well, Alice, it seems we have a difference of opinion about a lot of these objectives—let's look at the first one.

ALICE: Okay.

STONER: Now, you seem to have rated your progress a "4" on a 5-point scale; I rated you a "2." Now a "4" is awfully high. Maybe I have overlooked some factors in your improvement in interpersonal skills with your coworkers. What prompted you to put down a "4," Alice?

ALICE: Well, I was very surprised to see your "2" evaluation. A "2" means marginal, and I think I have made great improvement in that area. A "4" describes much more accurately how I've been doing.

STONER: Okay, now, why?

ALICE: Well, obviously . . .

STONER: I'm not attacking you, or even disagreeing with your evaluation. I'm just trying to find out about your judgment.

ALICE: I understand. . . . I really have been getting along better with Doris and Tom—we even go to lunch sometimes. Now, that has to mean something positive.

STONER: Weren't you friends with them already, though? It seems to me that Helen and Mary were the ones you had conflict with—how are you doing with them?

ALICE: I haven't had any major problems with them—not like I did before. I don't think they talk about me behind my back anymore. Just those things mean I've made a great effort to get along better with those two.

STONER: You've had no problems?

ALICE: Well, you know, nobody's perfect. There have been a couple of things—but nothing important enough to affect a six-month evaluation.

STONER: Let me tell you about my evaluation. You see, I have spent a good deal of my time—in these last six months— straightening out problems in the department. Some conflict is inevitable, but when I have someone doing things that rather continually are at the core of a problem, I tend to see that person as a "2" rather than a "4" on an objective that relates to interpersonal skills.

ALICE: But . . .

STONER: Please . . . let me finish. In addition, I have had three complaints from Mary about—well, situations related to you—and she has asked for a transfer. She has never complained to a supervisor about another employee in the seven years that she has worked here. When she does, I take that as a problem. Finally, about those "couple of things": they may be minor to you, but they have created major problems for this department. And major problems mean a "2"—or a "1"—on the kind of question we are discussing.

ALICE: Well, who are you going to believe: Mary or me? I have improved, and that's all there is to it. If you would stay in the department, maybe, you'd know that—in fact, if you were around more, maybe there wouldn't be so many problems.

STONER: I would like to discuss this calmly if we could. We're really just examining *why* each of us put what we did.

Because of my problem-solving activities, the complaints, and my observations, I cannot find myself moving from a "2." I am open, though, to anything else you might want to say.

ALICE: Well, it's obvious who has influence around here and who doesn't. Okay, call it a "2," but I will never believe that that is valid. Let's talk about my typing speed.

STONER: Why don't we break for coffee and then meet again in a few minutes?

Index